Advance Praise for *Tap, Click, Read*

"In the complex field of kids media, Lisa Guernsey and Michael Levine have written an important and digestible book filled with key insights, cutting-edge research, and suggestions that all parents should heed. As someone who's immersed in this world, I can't think of two better people to shed light on interactive technology and digital learning. *Tap, Click, Read* is a must-read for all parents, teachers, and those who care about kids."

—**James P. Steyer,** founder and CEO, Common Sense Media

"A thoughtful look beneath the hood of the 'quiet crisis' of children's reading and into a world that's at once more fascinating, more nuanced, and more promising than most of us imagined. This book will be essential reading for parents, educators, developers, and policymakers for a generation."

—**Greg Toppo,** national reporter, *USA Today*, author *The Game Believes in You*

"*Tap, Click, Read* is about connecting all children to rich interactive digital learning networks, mindful clicking and playing, and the powers of traditional literacy and new digital literacies when they are mixed and melded. It transcends the old 'Is it good or bad?' debate around digital and social media and gets to the heart of the matter: How we can make old literacy and new media work for all kids in the service of a better world? It is a crucial read for teachers, parents, policymakers, and concerned citizens."

—**James Paul Gee,** PhD, professor, Arizona State University, author, *Literacy and Education*

"Explore, inquire, reflect! Guernsey and Levine remind us that reading remains central to the learning process, moving us past fear of the techno-drug to model thoughtful, directed media use that can build receptive and expressive communication skills, enlarge children's worlds and enhance their learning. *Tap, Click, Read* is our back-to-the-future guidebook to educating a smarter, kinder generation."

—**Michael Rich,** MD, MPH, "The Mediatrician," founder and director of the Center on Media and Child Health, Boston Children's Hospital, and associate professor of pediatrics, Harvard Medical School

"Amazingly comprehensive, admirably concise, and altogether compelling, *Tap, Click, Read* is an unequalled guidebook for families and educators. Guernsey and

Levine have combined their unique skills and vantage points to mine the world of research on reading and digital technology. The result is a convincing case for the vital role of parents in scaffolding children's literacy, coupled with advice and resources that will enable parents to fulfill that responsibility."

—**Joe Blatt,** EdM, Faculty Director, Technology, Innovation, and Education,
Harvard Graduate School of Education

"*Tap, Click, Read* is a truly readable, interesting, and informative book about technology for promoting (not displacing!) literacy, language, and thought. Better still, it is complete with take-homes for parents, teachers, and policymakers. I love this book!"

—**Marilyn Jager Adams,** PhD, visiting scholar, Cognitive, Linguistic &
Psychological Sciences Department, Brown University

"If you want to know the latest about the new world of media and technology and its potential for young children's literacy development, this is the book for you. Simply the best book on the topic! Highly readable, highly informative, it is a must-read for parents, educators, and policymakers."

—**Susan B Neuman**, PhD, co-author, *Giving Our Children A Fighting Chance*,
professor and chair of the Teaching and Learning Department at the Steinhardt
School of Culture, Education, and Human Development at New York University,
former assistant secretary, US Department of Education

"This excellent book provides a clarion call and a blueprint for change: rapidly advancing technology is the difference maker for a level learning field for early learning and lifelong literacy. *Tap, Click, Read* provides the evidence, the scalable models, and a fresh national strategy to ensure that every child gets a fair shot at success in a digital age."

—**Bev Purdue**, former governor, North Carolina, and chair,
Digital Learning Institute

"For everyone who cares about helping children make the most of today's digital world, *Tap, Click, Read* is the most comprehensive review of what we know about learning in this age of screen technologies. It is smart, accessible, and compelling!"

—**Ellen Wartella**, PhD, Al-Thani Professor of Communication,
professor of psychology, and professor of human development
and social policy at Northwestern University

"In this digital wild west, Guernsey and Levine are the Lewis and Clark of our time, mapping the best trails for venturesome parents and educators. They strike the perfect tone as guides for this challenging terrain: patient, optimistic, and knowledgeable. *Tap, Click, Read* helps us see how we got here and arms us to create a better future."

—**Milton Chen,** PhD, senior fellow, George Lucas Educational Foundation

"As someone committed to preparing the next generation of leaders—and as a parent—I am delighted that this truly excellent book honors technology for the great potential it has. *Tap, Click, Read* lays out a winning game plan to meet kids where they are, using technology to help them understand the interconnected world in which they live."

—**Gary E. Knell,** president & CEO of the National Geographic Society

"We're living through the early stages of a learning revolution with lots of hope and hype—particularly in early learning. The two best sources of wisdom in this space are Sesame Workshop and New America. *Tap, Click, Read* is the best review of the new literacy landscape available. It's packed with practical advice and examples and videos for parents and educators. Cut through the hype, make sense of the app explosion: get this book!"

—**Tom Vander Ark,** CEO/partner, Getting Smart, and former executive director of education at the Bill and Melinda Gates Foundation

"Digital education is the wild west. This book changes everything. It gives us a clear and conversational road map (including great videos) to inform decisions at home with our own children, in schools and libraries, and at the national level. *Tap, Click, Read* should be required reading."

—**Kyle Zimmer,** CEO, First Book

"In *Tap, Click, Read,* literacy pioneers Lisa Guernsey and Michael Levine invite educators, parents, and media makers to join them in "Readialand"—a place where the traditional literacies of reading, writing, and speaking meet technology at the intersection of child development, early learning, and digital media. Even as they identify and describe technology-mediated, evidence-based, and developmentally informed products and practices, they remind us that what matters most for growing 21st century readers is the convergence of innovative tools and interventions with 'human-powered' interactions and relationships between young children, parents and educators."

—**Chip Donohue,** PhD, director, TEC Center at Erikson Institute

"Mil gracias—a thousand thanks for imagining the class of 2030 in this superb book. The honest, asset-based, and practical view of 'equity in a new age' breaks new ground, especially for Latino families. Times have changed but some constants are forever—parents will always aspire and work hard so that their children can have a better future. Reading is key! *Tap, Click, Read* is an excellent resource that demystifies what works, what's most important, and what's possible now."

—**Sandra Gutierrez,** executive director, Abriendo Puertas (Open Doors)

"For anyone committed to increasing social equity, this book is a provocative and inspiring guide, illuminating how the rapidly changing sea of media and technologies surrounding us both creates and dissolves hurdles for people and communities struggling with access to opportunity. Guernsey and Levine invite—and challenge—readers to embrace a new role as co-creators at its dawn of an innovative learning ecosystem that can transform our ability to create children who succeed as the readers, thinkers, and learners of tomorrow."

—**Kim Syman,** managing partner, New Profit

"Teachers, parents, and anyone interested in the potential role of interactive technology for children's learning will find that this book covers all of the important issues exceptionally well. *Tap, Click Read*'s descriptions of new creative, cutting edge efforts is especially illuminating and exciting."

—**Barry Zuckerman**, MD FAAP, professor of pediatrics, Boston University School of Medicine

"An invaluable resource for any parent, educator or policymaker interested in harnessing the potential and power of media and new technologies to support young children's learning."

—**Diana Mendley Rauner,** PhD, president, Ounce of Prevention Fund

Tap, Click, Read

Growing Readers in a World of Screens

Lisa Guernsey and Michael H. Levine

JOSSEY-BASS
A Wiley Imprint
www.josseybass.com

Published by Jossey-Bass
A Wiley Brand
One Montgomery Street, Suite 1000, San Francisco, CA 94104-4594—www.wiley.com
www.josseybass.com/highereducation

Jossey-Bass books and products are available through most bookstores. To contact Jossey-Bass directly call our Customer Care Department within the U.S. at 800-956-7739, outside the U.S. at 317-572-3986, or fax 317-572-4002.

Wiley publishes in a variety of print and electronic formats and by print-on-demand. Some material included with standard print versions of this book may not be included in e-books or in print-on-demand. If this book refers to media such as a CD or DVD that is not included in the version you purchased, you may download this material at http://booksupport.wiley.com. For more information about Wiley products, visit www.wiley.com.

Library of Congress Cataloging-in-Publication Data

Guernsey, Lisa, author.
  Tap, click, read : growing readers in a world of screens / Lisa Guernsey and Michael H. Levine.
    1 online resource.
  Includes bibliographical references and index.
  Description based on print version record and CIP data provided by publisher; resource not viewed.
  ISBN 978-1-119-09175-2 (pdf) – ISBN 978-1-119-09200-1 (epub) – ISBN 978-1-119-09189-9 (paper/dvd)
1. Computers and literacy. 2. Literacy–Study and teaching (Elementary) I. Levine, Michael H., author. II. Title.
  LC149.5
  372.60285–dc23

                                                                                    2015022714

Cover design by Wiley

Cover image: © LWA/Dan Tardif/Getty Images

Printed in the United States of America

FIRST EDITION

PB Printing 10 9 8 7 6 5 4 3

Contents

Preface

We should start by telling you what this book is not. This book is not about how children learn to read (though we do highlight some essentials on that subject). Nor is it about how to teach children to learn to read (though we hope it sparks some ideas). This is a book with technology coursing through every page, but it is not a book about how digital media and new technologies will rescue schools and save the world. Nor, however, is it a book about how those technologies are destroying any good chance of raising readers for the next generation.

So what *is* it? This book presents a third way, an approach to technology that is driven by the urgent need for *all* children and parents to have access to the same twenty-first-century literacy opportunities already at the fingertips of today's affluent families. We worry that without pushing for better quality within, and access to, learning environments that harness media, low-income households will get the short end of the stick. Our firm commitment in writing this book is to stimulate a more informed debate about equity in a new age: we cannot allow technology to exacerbate social inequality instead of opening more opportunities for everyone to succeed.

To carve this new path, we will take you—today's teachers, parents, and change-makers everywhere—on a journey into the spaces of digital-age literacy learning that are still a mystery for many: the continually evolving app stores, the little-known research labs of e-book scholars, the home-based services for first-time mothers and their babies, the classrooms of elementary schools in high-need areas, and the family literacy programs that are helping immigrant families. We want to show you the state of literacy and children's reading at this tumultuous, technologically driven moment—and what it *could* look like if we forged ahead with some new ways of thinking and teaching to help a greater number of kids. We hope this book will serve as a guide to new ideas for raising the next generation of critically thinking, accomplished readers.

Young children, ages zero to eight, are our focus. Literacy learning happens throughout the life span, of course, but we wanted to figure out what it means to teach children to become literate when they have been born into a world in which smartphones, touchscreen tablets, and on-demand video are nearly ubiquitous. Which features and habits related to these new technologies will serve them well? What should be avoided? How might the answers differ for different children in different circumstances?

We also aim to be inclusive and expansive in our use of the words *media* and *technology*. In the past decade or more, these two words have taken on narrow connotations that lead to even narrower debates about what is best for children's learning. Hear "media" and you may think primarily of mass media (CNN, Fox, and so on) or anything delivered via video. Hear "technology" and you may automatically envision smartphones, electronic whiteboards, or tablets. We see those examples as only part of the world of media and technology. Books—printed or electronically available—are also a form of media. Printers, voice recognition software, and video cameras count as technology too.

Your guides on this journey are me—Lisa, a journalist and director of the Early Education Initiative and the Learning Technologies Project at New America, a think tank in Washington, D.C.—and me—Michael, a child development and policy expert and founding director of the Joan Ganz Cooney Center at Sesame Workshop in New York City. Throughout the book you'll see us pop in once in a while to distinguish who is telling which anecdote, but the vast majority of the research and reporting that went into this book was conducted in partnership over a more than two-year span that involved many members of our teams and contract writers, reporters, and video producers.

The seeds for this book were planted in early 2012 in a series of conversations with Ralph Smith of the Annie E. Casey Foundation. Ralph had just launched the Campaign for Grade-Level Reading, an ambitious national effort to catalyze and coordinate early literacy efforts and philanthropic investments in more than 150 cities and towns around the United States. Lisa had spent more than a decade reporting on education and technology and had written the book *Screen Time: How Electronic Media—From Baby Videos to Educational Software—Affects Your Young Child*. Michael was directing a series of research studies on how interactive technologies were affecting families, students, and teachers, and advising one of the world's most successful nonprofit educational media organizations on how best to navigate a fast-changing digital marketplace while making children's interests central. Ralph wondered whether the two of us might be able to scan the landscape of literacy products and literacy interventions for young children to see where technology was playing a role. The result was our report, *Pioneering Literacy in the Digital Wild West: Empowering Parents and Educators*, which came out in December 2012. The report caught the attention of Jeff Schoenberg and J. B. Pritzker of the Pritzker Children's Initiative, which provided a generous grant to allow us to continue our research, create an advisory group that intersected with the Campaign for Grade-Level Reading, and develop a book and online space that would showcase what we were learning.

We say "create" a book, not "write" a book because from the beginning we wanted to include video and graphics as well as written narrative. We wanted to explore not only how children were learning to read in an age of new media but also how book publishing could harness new media to tell stories and increase understanding among educators and parents. As you will see in part 3, we have produced five videos that provide a window onto new initiatives that hold promise. (If you are reading the print version or non-enhanced e-book version, you will find hyperlinks that take you to these videos.) Barbara Ray and Sarah Jackson of HiredPen, a communications firm in Chicago and San Francisco, coordinated the video shoots and directed the videos with Chicago-based videographer Nat Soti and his team.

The collaborative nature of this book also opened our eyes to what is possible with shared writing-and-reading spaces online. For sure, we had our share of tech-induced mishaps, and we relied on print on paper in several cases. But we would not have been able to write this together without Google Docs' functionality that allowed many of us to be writing and commenting in the margins of one document while sitting in several different cities simultaneously. We also used tools such as Skype to conduct interviews with scholars overseas. We were almost perpetually using search-and-find functions and tapping into online archives of journal articles to pinpoint materials and discover new experts. Hours of thinking and exchanging ideas happened through e-mail and chat.

Along this journey, after becoming inspired by dozens of brilliant early educators and innovators, we started to see an alternative to simply reacting to the new media marketplace and constantly lamenting what the technology industry brings forth. The alternative is not to retreat to the twentieth century. Instead we suggest ways to proactively shape children's literacy environments and envision a future that marries the best of the old with the potential of the new. We want to act on the research about effective strategies to help children become literate, while enlisting help from innovative educators and media of all kinds, from books to video to twenty-first-century tools such as tablets and e-readers. We want to stop seeing technology and reading as in opposition to each other, and instead start building places, online and off, that put media in service of reading and, more broadly, in service of literacy and critical thinking for all kids.

Teaching, parenting, and learning in these newly envisioned places will require a new approach. Public policies and private organizations will have to shift their conceptions of education and learning downward in age, positioning the early years of children's lives—including those first few years of infancy and toddlerhood—as the foundational years for literacy. Communities will need to ensure equitable access to broadband Internet and media mentorship opportunities for low-income families. And policymakers will need to open their eyes to the assets among families of different linguistic and cultural backgrounds that, when given the right support, can help children learn to read, write, and become effective communicators in English and their home languages.

For parents and teachers in particular we argue that today's children will be best served by adopting a Tap, Click, Read mindset. Not a tap, click, *cringe*, and hope-for-the-best mindset, but one imbued with that word *read*, guiding children toward literacy and learning in multiple interactions with media throughout their early years. The pages that follow introduce you to many of the educators and leaders we met who have already embraced this mindset. It looks something like this:

Tap: Instead of just tapping open apps, let's not be afraid to tap into new networks of learning for our children and for ourselves as adults. Today's media allow for educators and families to access rich worlds of content and ideas beyond their homes and communities. We should also be mining forgotten or hidden public assets, like libraries and public media.

Click: We need to recognize that to click is to choose, to make a decision, to act. Marketers and their clickbait have made us think we have no choice. But clicking is not and should not be mindless. When a child or parent clicks inside a text, they have opted to dig further, they wonder what is beyond. Let's embrace that as an opportunity and pathway that could be filled with intention—not as a distraction.

Read: Everyone interested in the success of future generations should recognize that reading will always be a critical skill and a key barometer of progress. You cannot fully function in the twenty-first century without being able to read. You cannot achieve any kind of success without literacy. We also should recognize that the contours of literacy have evolved and expanded over time, and now even more skill and attention are required to teach it well.

Many educators and parents are already pursuing this tap, click, read approach without even realizing it. They are our future advocates for blended literacy environments that harness the potential of media in all forms. By using a research-based approach that combines skill building with knowledge building, they will help raise children who are able to read and write, not only via print on paper and screen, but also via symbols and images, all the while "reading" the motivations of the authors and creators who put this media in front of us. You'll see many of them in this book, and we anticipate meeting many more in the coming years. This journey isn't over. On our websites, on TapClickRead.org, and through social media, we will be continuing to document and write about how teaching and learning literacy are changing. And we will maintain our focus on serving children and families in households who are likely to have the least access to high-quality learning environments, online and off. At a time when social mobility seems to have stalled for so many families, the act of learning to read and becoming a literate citizen of the Digital Age remains the most powerful engine for moving up. The stories of this book are, at heart, about making a life-changing imprint on the next generation.

Tap, Click, Read

PART 1

Imagining the Class of 2030

The Quiet Crisis

*I*t's graduation day, 2030. High school students and their families are filing into stadiums and auditoriums around the United States, awaiting the chant-like announcements of hundreds of students receiving their diplomas.

It seems like only yesterday these students were babies. They arrived in the world at a time of immense change in how people communicated and learned—days that began to include smartphone apps, on-the-fly video making, instant photo sharing, text messaging, blogging, YouTube, Facebook, Twitter, Instagram, and more. Some of these students have become focused, careful readers with skills in filtering, creating, and making sense of the continual streams of information coming their way. Guided by a community of parents and educators who recognized the potential of new tools and mentors, they have become über readers, literate in a way that was almost unimaginable in the days before they were born.

Others are flailing. Some didn't make it to this graduation moment at all. Never given consistent attention and disconnected from tools and teaching strategies that could help, they have failed to master the habits of mind and the requisite skills to succeed in a global and digital age. This waste of their potential will have been, tragically, wholly preventable.

The digital age brings a paradox: as workplaces become increasingly dependent on the exchange of information, good reading skills are more important than ever. And yet children and their families are increasingly surrounded by new tools and digital distractions that affect the act of reading and communication. How will children ever learn to read?

That question is what prompted this book. For many, it is a question uttered in fear. The paradigm for instilling reading skills feels like it is crumbling away, as bedtime books morph into bedtime videos and daily routines leave no time for solitary, uninterrupted hours to read and think. The percentage of children who say they read books for fun every day or at least five days a week has dropped since 2010, according to Scholastic. The National Endowment for the Arts has spotlighted what it calls a "general decline in reading," with data showing that nearly half of young adults read no books for pleasure. Publishers are reporting declines in print book sales and slowed rates of growth in e-books. Some business leaders say it is difficult to find employees who can read and write at even a high school level.

Adding to the worry is the newfound recognition that over the course of human history, our brains have had to be trained to read. "In the evolution of our brain's capacity to learn, the act of reading is not natural," writes cognitive neuroscientist Maryanne Wolf. "We were never born to read." It's the plasticity of our brains—the ability of neurons to create new connections every time we challenge ourselves in new ways—that has enabled our species to advance from utterances to words, to symbols, to print, to the fluency that enables you to read this last sentence without even having to think about it. Once it sinks in that we really *are* what we experience, the always-humming experiences of the digital age should give us pause. In her book *Proust and the Squid: The Story and Science of the Reading Brain,* Wolf puts the fear this way: "Will the present generation become so accustomed to immediate access to on-screen information that the range of attentional, inferential, and reflective capacities in the present reading brain become less developed?"

THE SORRY STATE OF READING TODAY

For us, the question of how twenty-first-century children will learn to read is not spoken with fear as much as urgency. In essence our nation is facing a "quiet crisis": an alarming number of children in the United States never become good readers. Some never really learn to read at all. According to the National Assessment of Educational Progress (NAEP), a biannual record of children's abilities published by the US Department of Education, more than two-thirds of American fourth graders are not reading at a "proficient" level.

What does proficient mean? It is the marker of whether a student has, in the words of the authors of the NAEP, "demonstrated competency" in reading texts deemed appropriate for their grade level. There are other labels too, such as "advanced," which means being better than proficient, and "basic," which is a level below proficient and means that a student has only partially mastered the skills needed for competency. Research shows that proficient readers are on track to success in school and life. They are two-and-a-half times as likely as basic readers to be earning $850 or more a week, or $44,200 or more a year. And a study in 2011 showed that children who have not reached proficiency by the time they finish third grade are at higher risk of dropping out of high school. Third graders who are not proficient and who are also growing up in poverty are even more likely to drop out. Shockingly, the rates of nonproficient fourth graders among children of color, and children in poverty, are more than 80 percent.

Not everyone agrees with the NAEP's definition of proficiency. Some education researchers say it is too high a bar and argue that children with basic reading skills might look like proficient readers on other types of tests. Yet even on other tests of reading, large proportions of American children are not doing well. Each spring every state, for example, administers standardized tests. The test items and cut scores vary considerably (a problem that understandably irritates education reformers), but even given those variations, there is no question literacy rates are troubling. Take Massachusetts, a state that gets high marks for its education system. In that state, 43 percent of third graders are not hitting Massachusetts's proficient mark in reading. That is a high number of children who are likely to have a hard time doing simple things like completing their homework. They struggle to understand the writing prompts, they can't read the five-paragraph assignment on ecosystems, or the Civil War, or how to create a line graph, and they will, without intervention, lag further and further behind.

Reading achievement scores are even more distressing when put in context over decades. Low reading skills have characterized America's nine-year-olds since they began taking national tests in 1971. Reading scores climbed in the late 1990s, but between 2004 and today, the average score has stayed relatively flat. The average score among nine-year-olds—all nine-year-olds, not just those in poverty—hovers around 220 on a 500-point scale. They are not even getting halfway to the top score.

Educators have tried valiantly to fix this. Reading and literacy have been on the radar of experts for decades as the science on how children learn to read has become more and more settled. Years ago, it wasn't unusual to find people (sometimes grouped as "whole language" advocates) who believed children learned to read almost automatically as long as they were exposed to books in one way or another. But these days, you'd be hard-pressed to find a reading expert who thinks reading happens by osmosis. Consensus has formed around a two-pronged, skills-plus-knowledge strategy: teach letters and sounds and help children practice the "de-coding" of written words *while also* immersing them in stories and back-and-forth dialogues that introduce new vocabulary and show them the multilayered worlds of science, art, history, literature, different cultures, and more. This two-pronged strategy should be at the heart of literacy learning everywhere.

Polls show the majority of the public recognizes the importance of starting early and investing in programs to help families when children are very young. This recognition should also be working in children's favor. Society is starting to realize that learning to become literate starts earlier than kindergarten or first grade. The building blocks of literacy start with the smiles and gurgles of babies looking at their parents and caregivers while those adults return the smiles and coo in response. As babies point to what they want and utter their first words, they learn to communicate, then speak, and then, over time, build upon that experience to develop as readers and writers. That framework sets them up for reading those words years later, written on a page or etched across a screen.

Our government has tried to help. The US Department of Education put considerable attention on reading for most of the 1990s and 2000s with public engagement campaigns like America Reads and well-funded programs such as Reading First, a $6-billion grant program. The administration of President Barack Obama awarded millions to "scale up" reading programs with evidence of good results, such as the Children's Literacy Initiative, Reading Recovery, and Success for All. Officials for Head Start, the federal government's early learning program for children in poverty, have required teachers to focus on early literacy skills for more than a decade. Many governors and mayors have launched early education initiatives and passed legislation devoted to get everyone reading. And a coalition of nonprofit organizations, philanthropies, business leaders, and more than 150 communities, organized by the Campaign for Grade Level Reading in 2012, has won wider attention to the quiet crisis in recent years.

Given this momentum, why are two-thirds of American children not reading proficiently and half of children from low-income families not even able to hit the lower level of "basic" on reading tests?

WHAT'S HOLDING US BACK

Unequal access to early learning, spotty funding, and weak teacher training are obvious culprits. Take Head Start, for example. Although it has been shown to moderately improve children's literacy skills after a year of enrollment, the program has never received enough funding to serve more than half of the children in poverty. And the US child poverty rate has recently climbed to one in five children. Even if all children in poverty had access, there would be many more whose parents may be earning incomes above the poverty threshold but still unable to afford tuition for quality preschool. Momentum has been building across the United States to fill that gap by creating pre-kindergarten programs for low-income families or even, as is already the case in states like Oklahoma and Georgia, free to anyone regardless of income. But universal pre-K is far from a reality in most parts of the country.

Then there is the teaching of literacy in pre-K, kindergarten, and the first through third grades. Many school districts continue to get by with a hodgepodge of approaches, zig-zagging between fads and switching curricula from year to year. Reading experts say that they have witnessed underprepared faculty in teachers' colleges and underprepared teachers in pre-kindergarten through the third grade. And sometimes the push for literacy is accompanied by uninformed or even harmful techniques, such as when teachers of young children are pressured to drill children on the ABCs and phonics without recognizing the research on how young students can develop language and literacy skills when teachers use playful techniques, expose them to complex vocabulary, and give them opportunities to ask questions and explore.

These significant hurdles have to be removed. The United States must take a more comprehensive approach to improving teaching and learning environments for children from infancy up through elementary school. But even if we do more of what we already know, is that all it would take for all children in the United States to become strong readers? Is there some elephant in the room no one wants to talk about?

TVs, touchscreens, and smartphones are now almost ubiquitous in living rooms, bedrooms, and nurseries. Many preschoolers and elementary schoolers are watching, listening to, or interacting with two to three hours of screen media per day. E-books and videos populate library shelves and coffee tables. Parents and even grandparents are incessantly looking down at personal devices. Classrooms without computers and interactive whiteboards seem antiquated. Is the real barrier to improved reading skills that books can't possibly compete with exciting multimedia products for our attention? Let's face it: screen media is the elephant in the room. True understanding of children's literacy in the twenty-first century is impossible without turning to face this creature and take a long look.

NOTES

The percentage of children: *The Kids & Family Reading Report* 2015, 12. For more information on this report, see "4 Surprises in Scholastic's National Survey of Kids and Reading," January 12, 2015, on New America's EdCentral blog: http://www.edcentral.org/4-surprises-scholastics/. Also, *Children, Teens, and Reading,* a research brief published in 2014 by the non-profit advocacy group Common Sense Media, presents data between 2006 and 2013 that could be interpreted as a dip during those years in the amount of time parents spent reading to their young children. However, the survey methodology was different between the two studies. The 2006 data were based on a random-digit-dial telephone survey, while the 2013 data were collected using a probability-based online sample. "It is not possible to know for sure," the report's authors state on page 15, "whether the difference between the findings is an artifact of the change in methodology, or reflects a real drop in reading."

The National Endowment for the Arts: *To Read* 2007.

Publishers are reporting: Milliot 2014b, "Print, Digital."

Some business leaders say: For example, see Chastity Pratt Dawsey, 2014, "As Good Jobs Finally Arrive, Few Detroiters Have the Skills to Fill Them," *Bridge,* a publication of The Center for Michigan, December 16, at http://www.mlive.com/news/detroit/index.ssf/2014/12/as_good_jobs_finally_arrive_fe.html.

"We were never born to read.": Wolf 2007, x and 3.

In her book: Ibid., x.

It is the marker: National Assessment of Educational Programs 2014.

Research shows: According to the US Department of Education, National Center for Education Statistics, in *To Read* 2007, 17.

a study in 2011: Hernandez 2011.

the rates of nonproficient fourth graders: According to data from the 2013 Nation's Report Card, "What Proportions of Student Groups Are Reaching *Proficient*?" at http://www.nationsreportcard.gov/reading_math_2013/#/student-groups.

Not everyone agrees: See Gerald Bracey, in the June 2008 issue of *The School Administrator* at http://www.aasa.org/SchoolAdministrator Article.aspx?id=5096. Bracey writes that comparisons of the NAEP and an international test known as TIMSS have shown that high-scoring countries would not do well on the NAEP. "Sweden, the highest scoring nation, would show about one-third of its students proficient while the United States had 31 percent," he says.

Take Massachusetts: Based on the 2014 MCAS results: http://www.doe.mass.edu/mcas/2014/results/summary.pdf.

The average score: The Nation's Report Card 2012.

Polls show: See the results of a July 2014 public opinion poll by Public Opinion Strategies and Hart Research Associates for the Grow America Stronger campaign, commissioned by the First Five Years Fund, at http://growamericastronger.org/poll.

Given this momentum: Forty-seven percent of fourth graders eligible for free and reduced-price meals finished below "Basic" on the NAEP reading test in 2013. See 2013 Reading Assessment Report Card, National Center for Education Statistics, page 9.

Although it has been shown: Puma et al. 2012. Of note: "There is clear evidence that access to Head Start had an impact on children's language and literacy development while children were in Head Start," as reported on page xvi. Head Start has been criticized, however, for not being able to produce enough positive change in children's outcomes to carry through five years later, and the education policy community continues to debate why that is and what it takes to ensure that children in Head Start programs continue to show growth through kindergarten and the early grades.

the program has never received: See Christina Walker, "Head Start Participants, Programs, Families and Staff in 2013," CLASP, August 2014, at http://www.clasp.org/resources-and-publications/publication-1/HSpreschool-PIR-2013-Fact-Sheet.pdf. About four in ten eligible are served.

the US child poverty rate: DeNavas-Walt and Proctor 2014.

screen media: In fact, pediatric researchers Dimitri A. Christakis and Frederick J. Zimmerman published a book in 2006 entitled *The Elephant in the Living Room: Make Television Work for Your Kids* (New York: Rodale), which includes several chapters to help parents make smart choices about the types of content their children should watch. Some of the same studies are described in Lisa's 2012 book, *Screen Time: How Electronic Media—From Baby Videos to Electronic Software—Affects Your Young Child* (New York: Basic Books).

What to Make of Media?

The introduction of new media has always alarmed the arbiters of education and knowledge. Socrates worried about an overdependence on the alphabet. He thought that writing words down, instead of committing them to memory, would lead to less depth of understanding, preferring oral language and performed poetry instead. The religious establishment of the 1400s did not like the idea of the printing press and its potential for enabling a larger number of people to read what it deemed the wrong things. Novels and other works of fiction were once disdained as unsophisticated (those lies! corrupting fantasies!). Radio, telephones, and comic books have all had their detractors.

Over the past several decades, *screen* media has become the beast to begrudge. Although the dawn of moving pictures may have caused some consternation, it was the arrival of television that really began to worry those who tracked educational achievements and social norms. In the 1950s, well before the days of *Sesame Street* and *Mister Rogers' Neighborhood*, researchers and child development experts were concerned that watching TV was a recipe for illiteracy. By the 1970s, research on libraries showed declines in the circulation of library books and drop-offs in people's interest in fiction. "The overall impact of television seems to be a reduction in reading," wrote the researcher Gary D. Gaddy, in an oft-cited 1986 article about high schoolers from *Public Opinion Quarterly*.

Now the worries extend to baby videos, electronic games, e-books, and apps. The word *media*, and in particular digital media that appears on a screen, has taken on a negative connotation as child development experts have become alarmed at how quickly and powerfully young children are captivated by the sights and sounds they see and hear. The American Academy of Pediatrics has repeatedly discouraged parents from using any "passive" screen media with children under age two. News headlines are peppered with worrisome signs of how much "screen time" today's children consume. Defining screen time is not easy, given that picture books and chapter books are now shared on screens, and even listening to a song or audiobook requires tapping on a screen. By using categories like "digital media" or "technology," surveys have attempted to measure how much technology or media children are consuming, watching, or "exposed to." According to a recent national survey of 1,600 American families, for example, more than eight in ten children (ages two to ten) use digital media every week and two-thirds have tablets or e-readers.

Naturally, many people wonder whether children's poor reading skills are related to this electronic incursion. They ask, What if a child's interaction with an app has become a substitute for interactions with Mom and Dad? What if a child's daily life is filled with watching stories instead of reading or telling them?

EARLY LEARNING AND SCREEN MEDIA: CONTENT AND CONTEXT MATTERS

For years, researchers have tried to test these hypotheses. Results are more mixed than you might think. A few studies in the mid-2000s did show associations between TV viewing in early childhood and negative outcomes. One was a well-publicized 2004 study using parents' reports of attention problems in their children. It led to a storm of criticism of videos like *Baby Einstein*, even as other studies, such as a study on infants watching about an hour a day, showed TV having no impact at all.

The problem with these studies, and many others like them, is that researchers were missing a key piece of information: They never asked, nor did they have any way to know, what the children were actually watching. It was as if the content on the screen didn't matter.

More recent studies have attempted to fill that gap. They are zooming in on what a child might see on the screen by sorting results according to the types of shows watched or the way information is presented. One study showed that babies who are regularly put in front of *adult* programming, such as TV dramas, had low scores on tests of executive functioning when they reached age four. Another, in 2007, found associations between attention problems and TV viewing among children who watched violent programming before age three, but not for children who watched educational shows before age three. Interestingly, that study was conducted by the same people who did the 2004 study that led to headlines about toddler TV causing attention disorders. Their 2004 study got prime time coverage on broadcast TV. Their 2007 study barely registered.

More insight comes from studies on video designed to be educational for children. Evidence shows that children learn new vocabulary words and acquire skills such as problem solving and self-regulation after watching videos with an intentional pedagogical approach or curriculum. Studies tracking children over time have shown a link between *Sesame Street* and school readiness, as well as connections between watching the show as a young child and doing well in high school. A recent experiment in eighty preschools in several low-income communities examined the impact of teachers incorporating video clips and intentional literacy activities from educational shows such as *The Adventures of SuperWhy!*, *Between the Lions*, and *Sesame Street* into their lessons. The teachers had previously received very little training on how to teach emergent literacy skills, but as part of this experiment they received training on the aims of the shows and how to embed and integrate video clips and hands-on projects into daily lessons. The training-plus-media combination paid off: the children performed significantly better on tests of early literacy skills than did a similar cohort whose teachers did not have the benefit of the literacy media resources and training.

HOW YOUNG IS TOO YOUNG?

Now that research is starting to highlight the importance of the content on the screen and the potential for teaching with it, the questions have shifted from *whether* children can benefit to *how young is too young*? If two-year-olds have been able to show some signs of learning from well-designed digital content, can eighteen-month-olds do so too? This is a point of fevered debate. Age two is time for the famous word spurt, that amazing period when toddlers appear to be learning dozens of new words each month and are suddenly able to speak them aloud. Science shows that babies' interactions with people are a key stimulus for that stream of speech. In an oft-cited study of babies learning the sounds of a foreign language, researchers found no evidence that American babies could distinguish the different syllables emanating from a Chinese speaker on a prerecorded video, even if that speaker looked like she was talking directly to them. The babies needed face-to-face social interaction to be able to make those distinctions. Other studies have examined whether children younger than twenty-four months can learn words when people are shown on video explicitly teaching those words by labeling and pointing to new objects. The results are mixed. In two cases, there was no evidence that the toddlers learned anything at all from those videos. In another two cases, it appeared that they did.

These mixed results can be confusing for parents and teachers alike. Fortunately, guidance has emerged from two respected sources over the past few years. In 2012, the National Association for the Education of Young Children, in conjunction with the Fred Rogers Center for Early Learning and Children's Media, released a position statement on the potential for teaching effectively with digital media while also recognizing that teachers will need to consider limits on technology and media use depending on the context of their teaching. In 2014, Zero to Three, a research, professional development and advocacy organization, published *Screen Sense: Setting the Record Straight,* a guide for parents of infants and toddlers to help them make smart decisions based on the content on the screen, and the context in which media is used including recognition of the need for limit-setting, and the needs of individual children. (It was heartening to see the guide following the framework of the Three Cs—content, context, and child—that Lisa developed based on research cited in her book *Screen Time.*)

Meanwhile, another type of screen has started rivaling the TV as the locus of worry for child development experts: the smartphone in the hands of parents. Adults texting madly or absorbed in phone conversations while children are by their side or gazing from their strollers are a common sight.

In the summer of 2013, a group of researchers led by Jenny S. Radesky from the Boston Medical Center documented some of those instances systematically. They sat in fast food restaurants in fifteen neighborhoods around Boston and spied on—*er*—carefully observed families who arrived to eat with their kids. After the researchers had recorded the interactions of fifty-five families—taking notes on whether the caregivers used devices during mealtime, what they said, their facial expressions, and the behaviors of their children—they created codes for analyzing their observations and looked for patterns. Of the fifty-five caregivers they watched, forty of them used mobile devices during the meal. Sixteen of them, the researchers reported later, "used the device almost continuously throughout the meal, eating and talking while looking at the device or only putting it down briefly to engage in other activities." When they did talk, many barked stern orders at their children to be quiet and finish their food. Even when children were bidding for the adult's attention—such as a school-age girl stabbing her food container with a fork while looking at her mother—the caregivers rarely looked up. (Though the fork-stabbing incident did eventually result in a scolding.)

Would these caregivers have initiated nurturing and positive conversations with their children *without* the devices nearby? This study gives us no way to answer that. It's a question that bedevils so many of the debates over technology's impact throughout the decades. Without knowing the particulars of different family backgrounds, it can be easy for armchair observers to assume that people would be more likely to pick up a novel, check out more books from the library, or be more attuned to their children if they didn't have screen technology around to distract them. But would they? Literacy environments and family interactions are often more complicated than meets the eye. Child advocates have witnessed parents behaving inappropriately before the dawn of digital devices, and studies like this are bound to stir debates over differing cultural expectations of how much attention parents should be giving their children. Parents from one cultural background may blanch at instances in which adults appear to be ignoring their kids' needs, while parents of another cultural background may shake their heads at how much children are spoiled by an adult's constant attention.

TAPPING INTO DIVERSITY: AN AMERICAN OPPORTUNITY

In fact, recognizing the diversity of American families and the variety among their expectations and motivations is becoming an important dimension in the study of screen media and literacy. For decades, experiments and studies of what young children might be able to learn from a screen were based on samples of white, middle-income families. Concerns about screen time have been framed from the point of view of educators and researchers who are typically white and middle class, whose careers are proof they had little trouble succeeding in the American education system, who were raised with books full of characters who looked like them, and who live in neighborhoods with easy access to libraries and bookstores. (Admittedly, this describes us too.) For many people raised this way, screen media can often seem like an uninvited visitor to be tamed or accommodated.

But the *context* in which screen media is used and incorporated into family life cannot be forgotten. The way parents use, talk about, and learn from media can have a big impact on how children grow up to use, talk

17

about, and learn from it. And different types of families may look at the emerging array of technology and digital media very differently. They may see it as a democratizing force, a vehicle for global communication, a bridge to a better life, or any number of other things. If we are going to get serious about helping *all* children to become strong readers and literate adults, we will need to get serious about acknowledging that diversity and finding opportunities for literacy that do not sound foreign, unrealistic, or patronizing to many of today's parents.

For the past few years, Michael's team at the Joan Ganz Cooney Center has been studying Hispanic families and their perspectives of media. In a national survey of 682 Hispanic parents across the United States, we found that parents whose children used educational media (such as TV shows designed for learning) see their children gaining academic skills, particularly in reading or vocabulary, and that both parents and children may be learning English skills from watching and interacting with that media. Yet parents also pointed to problems, such as a dearth of learning-oriented media in Spanish and inadequate access to high-speed Internet. In short, these parents were not so concerned about screen media as a barrier to literacy. Instead they saw it as a gateway for helping themselves and their children succeed in America. They were also likely to report using media together as a family, talking together about information they had gathered or what they had watched.

In a report on the survey, authors June Lee and Brigid Barron concluded, "More parent resources in Spanish and greater awareness of where those resources might be available will help support parents in their efforts to use media to foment their child's learning." Parent resources in Spanish could also help inform these parents about which media support their children's academic and linguistic development—and which don't live up to those promises.

Given the mounting evidence that social interaction is a crucial ingredient for literacy learning, we could all benefit from deeper understanding of how screen media demand, distract, and direct our actions, and how family culture plays a role. It's not a foregone conclusion that TV or screen-based technology is holding children back or making them lousy readers. It is not a sure thing that watching replaces reading; as we describe later, watching a character, story, or concept can motivate a child to seek out books and magazines about that character, story, or concept. And it's also becoming clear that *how* adults use communication and media tools while they are around their children could be having an impact on language development and literacy. These are questions that have not been deeply considered before now.

MARRYING READING AND MEDIA

If we are to make sense of the Digital Age's impact on literacy, we have to take two big steps. First we have to start acknowledging all the new tools and interactions that come with it. Then we have to reckon with whether the community of adults around children is well-enough equipped to select the best tools and effectively guide children's learning. No doubt, as you will see in part 2, just taking that first step feels like venturing into the wilderness. When we started this project in 2012, hundreds of thousands of apps were appearing in the iTunes app store, popping up out of nowhere to beckon educators, parents, and children alike. The landscape was filled with hidden ravines and snake oil salesmen. But as we conducted more research—visiting classrooms and libraries, exploring home-visiting and parent support initiatives, analyzing new studies and talking with families—we started to see an alternative. The presence of the screen no longer looked like single beast to be conquered but a herd of new entities to be acknowledged, puzzled over, and in some cases, embraced. Increasingly it made less and less sense to use the singular "technology" or the general moniker of "screen time." The elephant became elephants, accompanied by all sorts of other communication creatures. And they were everywhere we turned.

The more we learned, the more we realized that today's adults have a choice to make and a cause to take up. We can stumble blindly through untamed terrain, get sucked into untested products, and waste educators' time and educational dollars on technology for the sake of technology while we hope the kids figure it out. We can accept the status quo and resign ourselves to operate in communities and educational systems not designed to help even *adults* make sense of media enough to raise a literate generation. Or we can shape this ecosystem into a place that is hospitable for raising children who read, think, learn, and grow into the überliterate of the class of 2030 and in the years beyond.

Not surprisingly, we choose the latter. There is much that media can do to assist with literacy learning—whether that media is physical (as in printed books and signs), electronic (video, audio, e-books), mass (TV, movies, radio), digital (on demand, anytime anywhere), interactive (tap, click, swipe), or social (texts, Instagram, and Facebook). Lately the conventional wisdom on media has been to place it in opposition to literacy and reading. What if, instead, media and reading got married and combined their names? What if we pushed for a blend: *readia*?

We offer this notion of readia—media in service of reading and reading that includes media—to help paint a picture of a brighter future for tomorrow's readers. But we want to be clear: It will not be enough to simply create more literacy-oriented products and make them available to more families. Instead we are envisioning the embrace of readia within a new ecosystem of support for children's learning and literacy in the Digital Age. This ecosystem we call Readialand. This is not a vision for some Disney-fied fantasy space or amusement park that families visit on vacation. Think of it as cohesive network of educators and families harnessing media to bring early learning and lifelong literacy to your neighborhood, your town, your city, your state. It is a vision for creating a place where the act of reading is celebrated and critical thinking is prized, and where media of all kinds, from printed books to what appears on mobile screens, are recognized for their power to support literacy. This is a place where parents and educators occupy a place of stature and where learning to become literate is considered as essential in a twenty-first-century child's life as learning to walk and talk.

ENVISIONING READIALAND

If we were to tour this land, what would we see? Human beings in control of technology and not the other way around. Adults and children who have new purpose, new tools, and deeper engagement with each other. Parents supporting children's language and literacy development, and yes, putting devices away when they start to distract. Learning would be made from joyful everyday moments. Imagine, for example, something like this: One afternoon, in a family's living room, a caregiver and a kindergartner watch a music video about trains and planes that has been designed to introduce new concepts and highlight words as they appear on screen. The adult and child sing along and sometimes press pause, pointing to their favorite parts. On the side of the screen, an icon encourages more exploration by inviting children to dig into books on the topic, including e-books that can be opened with a click and print books that can be automatically put on hold for pickup at the local library or delivered to one's door. With an adult's help, the child creates a book-and-video playlist to share with his siblings before dinnertime. He adds to it with his classmates in kindergarten the next day, and shares it with his grandparents over Skype. He talks excitedly about making a personalized train book to print and paint for his father's birthday.

And that is just one of an infinite number of possibilities. This ecosystem makes room for interactions that support language and learning in a multitude of ways. It offers a cacophony of voices while also reserving quiet areas of focus and contemplation, lush spaces for exploration of words and ideas among adults and children, and language-rich playgrounds where children can explore on their own. Product developers make special efforts, with guidance from educators, parents, and kids, to create materials and tools that foster opportunities for language development and literacy. And adults recognize and limit situations in which technologies are impeding children's learning.

Parents speaking a wide array of languages find themselves welcome in this land, with media available in their home languages that can enable bridges for cross-communication with their new neighbors. Technologies come in all shapes and sizes—paper, books, banners, billboards, all physical forms for transmitting ideas live in relative harmony with their digital cousins—and people use both in fluid transactions between online and offline experiences to create meaning and tell stories. Teachers, guides, and mentors are available for all who enter, especially for disadvantaged children and families. It is a world built to give children opportunities for reading and learning at every turn.

Could this dream become a reality? And if so, how? To start we need to make sure we understand how children learn to read in the first place, how their brains develop to turn scribbles and symbols into words full of meaning. We need to grapple with how educators should define reading and literacy given that books now share the landscape with dozens of other creatures for communication. We need to consider how to reform today's system to better support families and educators, especially in children's youngest years. Then we need to survey what's out there and learn from the pioneers clearing the way.

It's a daunting but exciting mission, a journey into the wilds to find a better future for all of our children. Are you ready? Let's go!

NOTES

The introduction of new media: Wartella and Jennings 2000.
The overall impact of television: Gaddy 1986.
The American Academy of Pediatrics: Strasburger and Hogan, 2013.
According to a recent national survey: Rideout 2014, 6, 26, and 27.
A few studies in the mid-2000s: Christakis et al. 2004.
TV having no impact at all: Schmidt et al. 2009.
One study showed that babies: Barr et al. 2010.
Another, in 2007, found associations: Zimmerman and Christakis 2007.
Evidence shows that children learn: Singer and Singer 1998; Krcmar, Grela, and Lin 2007; Wright et al. 2001; Linebarger and Walker 2005; Penuel et al. 2009; Linebarger et al. 2009.

Studies tracking children over time: Wright et al. 2001; Anderson et al. 2001.

the children performed significantly better: Penuel et al. 2009.

In an oft-cited study of babies: Kuhl, Tsao, and Liu 2003.

The results are mixed: Krcmar, Grela, and Lin 2007; DeLoache et al. 2010; Richert et al. 2010; and Vandewater 2011. For more on these four studies, and their similarities and differences, see Guernsey 2013.

In 2012: National Association for the Education of Young Children and the Fred Rogers Center for Early Learning and Children's Media 2012.

Zero to Three: Lerner and Barr 2014.

the framework of the Three Cs: The Three Cs were first described in Guernsey's book *Into the Minds of Babes: How Screen Time Affects Children from Birth to Age 5*, published by Basic Books in 2007. The paperback edition included a new epilogue with updated research, was retitled *Screen Time*, and was published by Basic Books in 2012.

a group of researchers: Radesky et al. 2014.

Michael's team at the Joan Ganz Cooney Center: Lee and Barron 2015.

In a report on the survey: Ibid.

How Reading Happens

It was an August day in 2007 when one of us (Lisa) had the pleasure and heartbreak of walking her first-born daughter to her first day of kindergarten. The walls of the school—Mount Vernon Community, a public school in Alexandria, Virginia—were draped in primary colors, the linoleum floor was lemony clean, and the classroom was teeming with little kids and their parents seeking out their individually labeled desks and cubbies. Pieces of furniture were marked with laminated cards of single words (*door, window, bookshelf*) in Spanish and English. After some cajoling, the parents reluctantly withdrew, and the teacher motioned the children to sit on the rug facing her. She sat in a plastic chair, held a book in her hands, and started to read it aloud.

This is the classic image of children learning to read: five-year-olds sitting at attention in a semi-circle on the floor. The ABCs affixed to an easel. A teacher pointing to words on a page. An inspection of letters, one by one. A boy raising his hand to say *C-A-T, cuh-ah-tuh, cat*. The class repeating, in unison. *Cuh-ah-tuh. Cat.*

But learning to read is so much more than sounding out *C-A-T*. Those of us who grew up in the twentieth century probably recall the simple Hop on Pop rhymes of Theodor Geisel, aka Dr. Seuss, or even, if we are stretching back even further to Michael's childhood, we might recall books about Dick,

Jane, and their dog Spot. Those books made learning to read seem as simple as recounting wonderfully silly rhymes or repeating Dick and Jane calling for their black-and-white spaniel: "Come home Spot. Come. Come home." These are certainly formative, and we hope joyful, moments in a child's reading life. But science today has shown that learning to read is a process that starts far earlier and is more complicated.

LEARNING TO READ: KNOWLEDGE + SKILLS

Let's get under the hood of the two-pronged approach—building *skills* and *knowledge*—we mentioned earlier. Nonie K. Lesaux, a professor of education at Harvard University, is one of the reading researchers who has raised awareness of those two essential ingredients. Lesaux defines skills as the competencies that allow students to "master the mechanics of reading." Those mechanics include the commonly understood and relatively basic skills of learning the alphabet, reading or "decoding" words like *C-A-T*, hearing and working with spoken sounds, and spelling. Two other lesser-known skills are the ability to understand "concepts about print," such as knowing to read a page from left to right (as is standard in English) and the role of punctuation; and "fluency," which is reading without stumbling or hesitation.

Visualize an adult teaching a child to read, and these basic skills are probably what come to mind. They are critically important. Committees of renowned experts, from the National Academy of Sciences Panel Study of 1998 and the National Reading Panel of 2000, have written volumes on how to ensure that more of America's children are taught in ways that promote these skills. For children with disabilities such as dyslexia, these skills can be exceptionally difficult to acquire. An entire profession of specialists has emerged over the past fifty years to help children with these kinds of disabilities.

The teaching required for the second ingredient, knowledge, is harder to visualize. To build knowledge means that children need to learn concepts about the world and the vocabulary that accompanies them. A child has to advance, for example, from reading "See Spot run" to understanding *Where the Red Fern Grows*, the children's classic that tells the story of a boy named Billy and his dog in Cherokee country. To read a passage about Billy's grandfather talking about hunting and "treeing a coon," a child will need to decode the words while also knowing something about raccoons and animal traps. He will need to be able to follow the narrative and remember and infer information from the grandfather's memories. He will need to know words or work to infer meaning in words like *sycamore* and *hound*. Without this knowledge, reading *Where the Red Fern Grows* would be nearly impossible, even if a child could "read" or "decode" every word.

Reading expert Daniel Willingham, a psychology professor at the University of Virginia, drives this point home in his book *Why Don't Children Like School?* and his book, *Raising Kids Who Read*. It won't work to teach reading skills in a vacuum, Willingham says. Children must learn content too. There is a refrain that Willingham repeats on his blogs and YouTube videos: "Teaching content is teaching reading." To become a strong reader, a child must comprehend the words and ideas on the page. To comprehend those words and ideas, she must be able to make inferences, fill in gaps, resolve ambiguity, and make connections between seemingly disconnected thoughts expressed in sentences. To make those inferences and connections, she needs background knowledge. To acquire that background knowledge, she needs to be exposed to and taught the thousands of intricate concepts lurking within science, geography, history, government, art, music, movement, mathematics, engineering, and, yes, everyday life.

Willingham cites a story about students who, several years ago, read a passage about baseball. Some of the kids knew nothing about baseball but had tested as good readers. Other kids were not good readers but they loved and knew lots about baseball. Guess who did better on a test of reading comprehension? The baseball knowers, that's who. They scored 27.5 out of 40 on a reading test, while the "good readers" scored 18.8. As Willingham says in a YouTube video, one way to predict a "good reader" is to find the students who know a bit about everything. They have what experts call "background knowledge." They'll be the ones who know something about whatever comes up on a reading test.

Building this background knowledge can happen through face-to-face experience as well as mediated experience: it can happen through field trips and dinnertime conversation as well as through books, educational videos, and Skyping with Grandma. What matters is the content, the context, and the child—the Three Cs—in which the content is vocabulary rich and designed to be understood by a young child of a certain age; the context enables back-and-forth conversation and opportunities for exploration; and the needs and interests of the individual child are considered.

Acquiring the knowledge needed to become a reader is not only about building a base of content knowledge and vocabulary, however. It also involves two entwined areas of knowledge building: knowing how to grasp and express complex ideas, and knowing how to use *oral* language, the act of speaking and listening. Over the past twenty years, scientists have made some key discoveries in this arena. When infants, toddlers, and preschoolers are immersed in environments where caregivers are speaking and listening to them, they are far more likely to excel in literacy and become strong readers down the road. When they are *not* immersed in those environments, the reverse is true.

A landmark study published in 1995 offered groundbreaking evidence of this speech-to-reading connection. For three years, Kansas University researchers Betty Hart and Todd Risley and their graduate students patiently and methodically tape-recorded conversations in forty-two households and then carefully examined the frequency and variation of words used in those conversations. They also collected test score data on the vocabulary growth and reading comprehension of the children in those households when they reached third grade. Their analysis showed that by age four, children in low-income families have heard 30 million fewer words than higher-income children—and that that gap was linked to reading comprehension success in third grade.

Later studies have replicated or added to this research base. In 2012, Stanford University psychologist Anne Fernald used a study of brain processing speed to detect gaps in language learning and discovered that they can be observed in children as young as eighteen months old. In Fernald's lab, toddlers from low-income families were slow to look at images that corresponded with words they had been taught. They took more time than middle-income children to process the words and signal that they understood them. This slower processing speed could hamper their ability to learn additional words because their brains were still working on the first ones.

This finding, Fernald stressed, does not mean that children from struggling families are doomed. Instead, it means that those families may need more support and encouragement to communicate with their children at very young ages. In other studies, Fernald had shown that babies who receive a high amount of "child-directed talk"—conversation with their parents or caregivers—had received enough practice to be able to process information more rapidly and learn language more quickly as a result.

Scientists are confirming in study after study that child-directed talk is a key ingredient for cognitive and social-emotional growth of all kinds. For decades, researchers have been following families around in their homes and bringing babies into laboratories, watching carefully how the children respond to different moments of exposure to new words and concepts. These researchers have recorded every movement of their heads, tracked the gaze of their eyes, recorded their facial expressions, watched where they pointed their fingers, and tested whether they learned new words—all in the hopes of figuring out what conditions lead babies and toddlers to pay attention, to remember what they are shown, and to use what they have learned. What is it exactly that enables babies to pick up meaning in the words we speak? What propels them to remember those words, eventually speak them aloud, and then use them the right way?

Some answers have emerged from the Infant Language Project at the University of Delaware and the Infant and Child Lab at Temple University, two labs run by the energetic and prolific duo Roberta Golinkoff and Kathy Hirsh-Pasek. (Don't miss their accessible and entertaining books, *How Babies Talk* and *Einstein Never Used Flashcards*.) Research led by Golinkoff and Hirsh-Pasek shows that the way adults talk with their babies has a huge bearing on how well those babies learn words. When adults talk *with* babies—not *at* babies or *around* babies—those babies learn more words.

A recent study centered on twenty-one-month-olds. The researchers wanted to find out whether children at this age learned more readily when they heard speech that was directed at them—of a higher pitch, slower, using pauses, employing questions—compared to speech that sounded like an adult talking to another adult. The experiment was relatively simple: forty-eight toddlers were split into two groups. One of them saw a video of a new made-up object and heard the voice of an adult labeling the object with a new word, talking in this child-friendly way. The other group saw a similar video, teaching the same word, but the adult was speaking as if talking to another adult. Researchers watched whether the children paid attention and then tested to see whether they learned the word.

The results? Child-directed speech made a real difference. The toddlers in that group were able to learn new words, whereas the toddlers hearing adult-directed speech had more trouble. (There is one caveat: if the children already were showing relatively advanced vocabularies, the adult-directed speech was just as effective.) The study is yet another example of how important it is to tune in and talk with children in a way that communicates with them respectfully on their level.

Early childhood experts have become convinced that the amount and quality of conversation at home is part of the reason for the enduring gap in educational achievement between high- and low-income children. The findings have even earned a buzzword, "the word gap," which has prompted numerous newspaper articles, a White House event, and, as you'll see in part 3, a growing industry segment focused on developing tools to reduce this gap.

LANGUAGE AND CULTURAL ASSETS
ARE NOT LITERACY DEFICITS

Now let's throw one more crucial factor into the mix: What if the children learning to read have grown up in households with adults who speak a language other than English? Or what if these kids live in an environment where different cultural stories and conversations (spoken in languages other than English) punctuate the everyday give and take among the members of the household? Today in the United States more than 12 million children fit that description. So do more than one in three children in Head Start, the federally funded preschool program for children in poverty. Anyone who aims to help overcome the reading deficit in our current generation of schoolchildren has to consider the implications of growing up learning both one's native language and cultural cues while learning English at the same time.

Remember the first day of kindergarten described at the beginning of this chapter? More than 65 percent of the children in the school were from households where English was a second or third language. Most of the kids spoke Spanish at home, and for many this was the first time they were hearing "classroom" or "academic" English (more than a casual "Hello" and "How are you?"). They were arriving in a school system that put enormous value on students reading in English and showing knowledge of subject matter (math, science, social studies) in English. As is the case across the United States, Virginia's standardized tests are in English, and the scores on those tests eventually determine whether the school would retain its accreditation in the coming years, not to mention whether the principal and teachers would keep their jobs.

What is often underappreciated in today's education system is that these children were actually starting school with an asset, a skill coveted by English-only speakers: they were on their way to becoming bilingual. And in fact this school recognized that strength; it had opened up several dual-language classrooms to try to ensure that children received instruction in both Spanish and English. But the system in which the school operated still adhered to English-only approaches. District-wide policies favored English textbooks; various curricula were built on lessons available in English; and diagnostic tests for tracking children's literacy and language skills were typically available only in English.

During a fall afternoon a year later, it hit Lisa just how much of a disconnect existed between the desire to encourage bilingualism and the expectations for children's day-to-day literacy learning in schools like this. During a volunteer stint in a first-grade classroom, Lisa and a Spanish-speaking boy were given a set of stiff cards with the letters *E, H, N, P, S,* and *T.* The teacher asked Lisa to encourage the boy to move the cards around and see what words could be made with those letters. The boy looked down at the cards and tentatively put a few together: *P-E-N.* "Pen," he said.

"Good!" The boy clearly understood the assignment, even though as Lisa tried to explain the game it probably became clear that she knew very little Spanish. "Any others?" The boy shrugged his shoulders and started looking out the window. "What about this?" Lisa said, putting *H-E-N* next to each other. The boy had no trouble decoding. He said the word *hen* but looked blank. Suddenly it dawned on Lisa: he had not heard the English word "hen" before. In fact, many children of all kinds of ethnicities and cultural backgrounds probably had not heard the word uttered. How would they? *Hen* is not an everyday word, even in English, unless you live on a farm. There are likely no hens—chickens, yes, but not hens—being cooked for dinner or on display at the neighborhood grocery store. Many children have not grown up with "The Little Red Hen," the English story about the industrious little bird who cannot get her lazy dog and duck friends to help her plant seeds. They would have heard plenty of other stories and fables that include words English speakers would stumble over instead.

English-centric games, English-only tests, time-strapped teachers, and clueless tutors—all of these add up to a tough introduction to language and literacy for young children whose home language is not English. In fact, even experienced teachers with adequate time in the school day may not recognize how much a child's early language exposure and early exposure to cultural stories will affect his or her literacy development. More and more children in America's public schools have received early language exposure that is very different from that of the English-speaking, white, and middle-class households for which much of today's outdated instruction appears to be designed. Reading comprehension depends on several critical factors. It does require distinct habits of mind, having a store of knowledge built up in the years *before* a child is asked to read and expanded for each year thereafter. But it also has a clear cultural and sociolinguistic dimension. For children learning two languages at the same time, the hope is to not only learn how to recognize the words on the page, but to also learn the *meaning and cultural significance* of those words. Arriving at this bilingualism, the highly desired state of children being able to not only speak but also read and write in English and their native language, will only be possible with a recognition that children's home languages, and the meanings attached to the words they learn in their homes, are assets to be tapped, not problems to be fixed.

Laying out the exhaustive body of research on reading and language development is not our aim here, but we hope these key examples make clear that both *knowledge and skills* and *new cultural competencies* are needed to raise strong readers. Yes children need to know phonics and their ABCs, but they must also be immersed in experiences that help them understand the meaning of the words made up of those sounds and letters. They need to build a rich store of knowledge about how the world works and how language works while they navigate communities that are emerging as both more diverse and more connected to all of the corners of the globe than ever before.

NOTES

Lesaux defines: Lesaux 2013.
Willingham cites a story: Recht and Leslie 1988.
Willingham says in a YouTube video: Willingham 2009.

by age four: Hart and Risley, 1995; Campaign, n.d.

In Fernald's lab: Fernald, Marchman, and Weisleder 2013.

Fernald had shown: Carey 2013.

When adults talk *with* babies: Golinkoff and Hirsh-Pasek 1999.

Child-directed speech: Ma et al. 2011.

4

From Literacy to Literacies

In the 1990s, as the use of the Internet exploded, language arts teachers in the United States sat up and took notice. Anyone anywhere with a computer connected to the Internet could tap into stores of knowledge by simply typing a few lines, such as http://www.yahoo.com. Sentences could be "reprinted" and changed on the fly. Words could represent much more than themselves as they became hyperlinks, portals to new pages with images, databases, and yet more hyperlinked words. People now had access to a clickable and continually evolving stream of text, pictures, audio, and video. What was this new medium going to mean for *reading*?

THE NEW LITERACIES

Two large organizations of educators decided they had better work together to answer that question. The two groups—the National Council of Teachers of English (NCTE), which has been around for more than a century, and the International Reading Association (IRA; renamed the International Literacy Association [ILA] in 2014), a network with global reach—called their members together and got to work. Their task: predict what kinds of skills students would need for literacy in the next century.

Years later, they published a document they called a "clarion call" to anticipate "the more sophisticated literacy skills and abilities required for full participation in a global, 21st century community." Within the document were a new set of expectations for students—"standards," in education lingo—that gave teachers a sense of breadth of the challenges. It was time to stop talking about and thinking about literacy in the singular. Being literate in the twenty-first century meant possessing multiple literacies. It would mean understanding information presented in a variety of different formats and being able to create, critique, and analyze multimedia texts. Students would need to understand information in videos, databases, and computer networks. They would also need to better understand other world regions, languages, and cultures. Such is the challenge presented by a global economy in which youth will need to learn to compete and cooperate to build a shared future.

Educators have been trying out different labels for this new set of skills. The NCTE and ILA call them "21st Century Literacies." Donald J. Leu, a professor of literacy and technology at the University of Connecticut, calls them "the new literacies." Jackie Marsh, a literacy professor at the University of Sheffield in the United Kingdom, uses "technoliteracies." Jeremy Brueck, an e-book and early childhood expert, prefers "transliteracy." The Asia Society has referred to the demands for career-ready youth to engage as "global citizens" who demonstrate critical cultural, international, and linguistic literacies. Henry Jenkins, a media scholar at the Annenberg School at University of Southern California, emphasizes the need to focus on a new form of education equity, describing a growing "participation gap" in which low-income students have "unequal access to the opportunities, experiences, skills, and knowledge that will prepare youths for full participation in the world of tomorrow."

Some educators have also opted to put new competencies for a digital age under the header of "media literacy," a concept born long before the Web but still new enough to be redefined. Until recently, media literacy was often assumed to be about teaching students how to "read" commercials, critique promotional materials, and become aware of gender or racial biases in the way information is presented. But over the years, notions of media literacy have expanded to encompass the questioning and inquiry skills that help people see and understand how and why media is created. Then there's the category of "digital literacy," which has evolved from "computer literacy." Some people associate digital literacy with online survival skills, such as knowing how to protect passwords, stay safe from predators or bullies, and use Google. But it can also encompass entire constellations of new learning, such as how to create and express oneself using new media tools and how to become an active and responsible participant in a digital world.

In short, we've got this litany of literacies. Will their definitions ever be settled? Maybe not, and that may be by design. As Leu has written, "Their most important characteristic is that they change regularly; as new technologies for information and communication continually appear, still newer literacies emerge."

But one thing is for sure: no longer is literacy only about reading print on a page. All sorts of other kinds of "reading" and other approaches to gaining knowledge have taken the stage too.

TEACHING NEW LITERACIES TO YOUNG CHILDREN: A WORK IN PROGRESS

Are kindergarten teachers or even preschool teachers ready to teach this expanded notion of literacy? Old-fashioned print is highly valued among educators in preschools and elementary schools, with good reason. The skills involved in reading print—the brain's ability to recognize letters and decode words—demand attention from teachers and parents and require practice from children. As explained earlier, those skills don't just arrive via osmosis. Add to that the limited hours in the day, the crush of parents' work schedules, and the breadcrumbs with which many early educators are paid, and it can feel like simply teaching print-reading alone is more than most can handle.

So the idea of expanding early literacy to early literacies—well, that seems like a tall order. It's one thing to teach twenty-first-century literacies to adolescents who, presumably, already have the basics and know how to read print. It's trickier to answer questions of whether literacies, plural, should be taught in the formative years of preschool and early elementary school.

In *Discovering Media Literacy*, a book focused on elementary school, authors David Cooper Moore and Renee Hobbs describe educators who are beginning to recognize that "reading comprehension cannot be confined to the medium of the printed page," but it is rare to find such teachers below second or third grade. It can be tempting to just keep multimedia and online information out of the classroom in these early years and simply wait to introduce the other stuff when students pass their third grade reading tests.

But before doing that, let's back up for a second. Literacy in the younger years is not, and never has been, solely about reading print. Walk into a children's library and what do you see everywhere? *Picture* books, some with no print at all. Nor is early literacy only about reading books. Literacy has always involved speaking, listening, and writing. A student is not literate if she hasn't developed language skills, if she cannot listen and comprehend and then speak out loud (or use sign language) to communicate her ideas and needs, if she cannot use words to ask and answer questions, explain what she understands about the world, and signal her desires and emotions without acting out. Nor is a student literate if she cannot write. Though the physical act of writing can be difficult before kindergarten because of the fine motor skills required to use a pen or pencil, preschool educators encourage children to use crayons, to paint, and to "write" stories via dictation and using processes such as inventive spelling, through which young children express themselves without having to get spelling or grammar correct. In short, this broader notion of literacy skills is—or should be—already fully embraced in children's early years.

But not all literacy skills are easy to bring down onto the rug, into story time, and throughout the classroom. In classrooms of three- and four-year-olds, especially, it should not be assumed that the adults in charge have expertise in teaching young children early literacy. Huge variation exists across child care centers, preschool programs like Head Start, and pre-K classrooms. Yes, for sure, some teachers are great. They have acquired skills that are just what you would want for children; they are well prepared and well credentialed. They have class sizes that are manageable and coaches to help them improve their teaching. Other teachers . . . well, it's not really accurate to call them teachers. Many have little more than a high school degree or did not have a good education experience themselves. Nearly all have the gift of a strong commitment to caring for children, but too few have the required foundational knowledge about science-based early learning pedagogy or child and brain development. Most are paid poorly: entry-level child care teachers earn barely above the minimum wage. And they often don't receive the training they need to handle children's inevitable behavioral problems, let alone introduce them to reading and writing using appropriate techniques for three- and four-year-olds.

Which teacher will your child get? In many states and localities, the answer depends on the flushness of your bank account. If you live in a place that expects parents to pay for preschool, you may not be able to afford to give your children the experience of a good teacher. Some options do exist for very poor families: One example is Head Start. But quality varies, and many low-income families are too "rich" to be eligible for it anyway. In 2014, a family of four had to be making less than $27,000 a year or have other extenuating circumstances to qualify.

The calls for more access to high-quality pre-K are trying to rectify this fundamental unfairness. Expanding kindergarten is also critical; there are still many states and school districts that offer kindergarten for only half of the school day, and some parents have to pay fees if they want their children to attend class after lunch. Leaders and advocates have been trying to fix these disparities by injecting public dollars into new systems comprised of schools and private organizations, and in many states and cities progress is being made. Research is showing good results with public pre-K in the Boston Public Schools and Tulsa Public Schools, and new programs in New York City, San Antonio, and Seattle, among other cities, are underway.

In other words, raising children to be "twenty-first-century literate" will require an infusion of public investment in the early years. Not only should all children have equal access to trained teachers in child care centers, preschools, pre-K, and kindergarten—not to mention the primary grades of first, second, and third—those teachers will need to be trained in teaching literacy far beyond the ABCs and the basics of decoding print. First, they have to make sure to include the rest of traditional literacy: helping children learn to speak, listen, and write well. Then they need to figure out how and when to introduce litera*cies,* plural.

And here's where we come to the depth of the challenge: there are no well-known, tried-and-true curricula for teaching young children how to use online information or think critically about visual information while they are simultaneously learning to read print, listen, and speak in full sentences. This is uncharted terrain. There are no landmark studies that establish milestones for twenty-first-century literacy, digital literacy, or media literacy at age three, four, or five. It is not even clear yet what kinds of research questions need to be asked. Leading thinkers in media literacy are still testing out the best approaches for late elementary school, let alone the years before second or third grade. We have arrived at a stage of early experimentation.

SCOUTS FOR NEW LITERACIES IN EARLY EDUCATION

Thankfully there are a few guides to this new stage. One is Faith Rogow, a media literacy consultant in Pennsylvania who is among the founders of the National Association for Media Literacy Education. Rogow has spent her career considering what young children need to become critical creators and consumers of media. She knows that teaching with technology and media can make early childhood educators nervous, so she usually starts her tour with a reassurance, such as this quote from some of her recent writing: teaching media literacy "does not mean abandoning books in favor of electronics. It's not a competition. After all, books are a media technology and a quick visit to a few websites makes it clear that one cannot be media literate without being print literate."

Another mistaken assumption is that teaching new literacies to young children is about teaching them to use a mouse, tap on an app, or log in to a website. But that is not what media literacy requires at all. The point is to build the habits of mind and the skills of critical inquiry that spur learning no matter where the text comes from, no matter whether the image is on paper or a screen. When children are introduced to an array of communication tools, they can gain the building blocks of understanding how ideas are disseminated, how books are created, how media is developed, and what kinds of decisions drive the process. These kind of literacy skills, Rogow writes, "extend well beyond equipping children to use technology; they prepare children to succeed as lifelong learners in a technology-rich world."

So where do we start and how young do we go? What might that kind of teaching look like?

Rogow pointed us to Vivian Maria Vasquez and Carol Branigan Felderman, two early childhood professors who have been collecting and dissecting examples from schools and preschools around the United States and Canada. In their book *Technology and Critical Literacy in Early Childhood*, they show what this kind of teaching entails at what ages. Let's open the door to one of the classrooms and take a look.

What's the Weather? Media Literacy as a New Lens

It's a typical morning in Kevan Miller's first-grade classroom in a public school in Northern Virginia. The bell has rung, the children are settling into the classroom, and Miller starts the day the way she always has: singing what she calls "the weather song." The lyrics ask children to describe the weather outside their windows. "What's the weather? What's the weather?," she sings. "What's the weather, everyone? Is it partly cloudy? Is it cloudy? Is there rain? Or is there sun?"

Today, though, something disrupts the routine. A child asks, "What about other kinds of weather?" Miller pauses. She has never really thought about the fact that the words do not reflect the full spectrum of what her students experience. Here they were in the mid-Atlantic, where the four seasons can cause dramatic changes in temperature and big thunderstorms roll through.

At that moment, Miller's teaching changed. She asked her students to brainstorm other kinds of weather that should be mentioned in the song. The kids came alive. "Snowy!" "Foggy!" On a board, Miller wrote those words and more: *lightning, tornado, flood.* Soon the children were dictating and rehearsing a new version of the song. They asked for access to the broadcast TV room in the school, where administrators and students created morning announcements. They videotaped a segment that started with the original song, explained why it was inadequate, and then showed the whole class singing the new version. It aired on the morning announcements later that week.

To Vasquez, a professor at American University who documents cases of what she calls "critical literacy" in early childhood, this example shows how children even at very young ages can "problematize texts," critiquing what they see as missing, recognizing that the texts are constructed from a particular point of view, and reimagining them in a way that reflects their own experiences.

Would kids be able to learn these skills on their own? Not necessarily. It took the insight of Miller, the teacher, to open up that kind of learning. Having the time in the day and the flexibility to go off script probably didn't hurt either. As Vasquez puts it, "Creating an opportunity for children to redesign the weather song sent a message that texts are socially constructed with particular intent and effects on the consumer of that text."

No one could argue the kids weren't getting a dose of early literacy; they were viewing and reading new printed words like *foggy* and *tornado,* listening to each other, speaking their ideas out loud, and writing a new version with the help of their teacher. They also got to experience video tools in action by creating, collaborating, and broadcasting to an authentic audience of their peers. But they were also getting something else: a chance to build skills for probing how and why media messages are made in the first place.

Or consider this hypothetical example from a preschool classroom, adapted from Rogow's advice for educators. It's almost time for "Family Day" at the local preschool. Like many preschool teachers, Jessica has already decorated her classroom wall with photos of the children in her class, their families, and pets. But Jessica chooses to go further. She pulls out a video camera and involves her children in making a short video about what happens in their classroom "on a typical day." It is up to the kids to decide what to shoot: Should they take video of their classmates putting their backpacks in cubbies? Should they shoot a clip from dress-up time? Should they show that time when the class gerbil escaped from his cage? (To do that, Jessica explains, they may have to do what is called a "reenactment.")

As the children talk about possibilities, Jessica lets them know that the decisions they are making are the same kinds of decisions that news reporters make when they create the nightly news. She asks her kids to consider, "Which pictures would tell the truth about what our day is usually like? Which pictures show something unusual?" Later, after the videos have been shot, children can watch their teacher describe what she is doing as she uses editing software like iMovie to put clips together.

Of course, teaching this kind of critical inquiry does not have to involve video or screen media. Rogow encourages teachers to experiment with media literacy questions during traditional read-alouds and story time. Many teachers, for example, are already trained to pause during a read-aloud to ask, "What do you think is going to happen next?" To make it a media literacy moment, they simply need to ask a follow-up: "How do you know?" or "What makes you say that?"

"For the youngest children, the answers are less important than simply establishing the expectations that their answers will be based on evidence," Rogow says. "When children know they are going to be asked for explanations, they attend to media differently."

Six Behaviors of Media Literate Five-Year-Olds

At age five, children have the ability to show emerging media literacy skills. A child who has acquired these skills will be able to:

1. Routinely ask relevant questions about ideas and information and use at least two different strategies for finding credible answers
2. Exhibit the habit of linking answers to specific evidence
3. Demonstrate knowledge that media are made by people who make choices about what to include and what to leave out (i.e., that all media messages are "constructed")
4. Choose appropriate pictures to accompany a story or report they have created and provide a basic explanation for their choice
5. Create and share original stories and reports using images, sounds, and words
6. Identify media technologies as tools that people use for learning, communication, and persuasion, and that (with permission) they can use, too

Source: Faith Rogow, "Media Literacy in Early Childhood Education," *Technology and Digital Media in the Early Years* (NAEYC/Routledge, 2014), edited by Chip Donohue.

This kind of inquiry is often embedded in the Reggio Emilia approach, a popular method of preschool teaching originally pioneered in Italy. By using different types of media, says George Forman, a leading Reggio researcher, "we are helping children to ask better questions." But it's not easy: it takes an adult who is skilled in prompting this kind of thinking without telling children what to think. This takes a talented teacher or mentor who can match prompts and questions to the children she is working with, recognizing the stages of development the children are going through and giving them just enough of a challenge to motivate them. These top-level literacy teachers are guiding young children not only to listen, talk, read, and write, but also to ask critical questions about the media they are watching, reading, and creating.

NOTES

a document they called a "clarion call": National Council of Teachers of English 2013. Note that though standards were developed in the late 1990s, the framework continues to be tweaked; this particular document was last updated in February 2013.

The Asia Society: Mansilla and Jackson 2011.

Henry Jenkin: Jenkins et al. 2009.

Their most important characteristic: Leu et al. 2004.

Discovering Media Literacy: Hobbs and Moore 2013.

they often don't receive the training they need: Whitebook, Phillips, and Howes 2014.

Research is showing good results: Yoshikawa et al. 2013.

Teaching media literacy: Rogow 2014, 91.

These kind of literacy skills: Ibid., 93.

To Vasquez: Vasquez and Felderman 2013, 37.

As Vasquez puts it: Ibid., 37.

we are helping children: Alper and Herr-Stephenson 2013.

5

Paving a Path to Readialand

In Readialand, the Kevan Millers of the world would flourish. Educators would teach children to read and write using tools of all kinds while also teaching children to think critically about media created with those tools. Families and educators alike would be able to tap into resources and networks for making good choices about what best meets their needs. In short: creating this ecosystem will not necessarily require buying crates of touch-screen tablets for Head Start Centers and schools or loading up on electronic toys for the home. Some tools make sense, and some are likely to be a complete waste of time and money. Some are worthwhile for, say, first graders but not for toddlers. As with any good advice about raising children, incorporating new media and technologies into daily life will involve setting limits and understanding what is appropriate for certain ages, and it will certainly require media-literate adults.

LESSONS FROM *SESAME STREET*

In addition to these common sense guidelines, past experiences with new media also offer useful lessons.

Consider the origins of *Sesame Street*, perhaps the world's most powerful example of the benefits of well-designed, engaging, and curriculum-based preschool educational media.

In 1966, documentary television producer Joan Ganz Cooney, with support from Carnegie Corporation of New York, started the research that led to the then-revolutionary use of television to teach basic skills and social development. The launch of *Sesame Street* took place during an era when TV had been branded "the boob tube" and referred to as a "vast wasteland" by the chairman of the Federal Communications Commission, Newton Minow.

"A word about children's programs," Cooney wrote in "The Potential Uses of Television in Preschool Education," her landmark 1966 paper. "Most of those commercially sponsored seem to be inordinately noisy and mindless affairs." She added, "Beginning at an early age, we can assume, children are conditioned to expect . . . fast action thrillers . . . highly visual, slickly, and expensively produced material." This observation led her to wonder, Would it be possible to design children's programming that would be attractive and fun and at the same time realize serious educational aims? She concluded, "I believe the answer is an emphatic yes." She said that there was clear evidence that children were learning from television, but it was *what* they were learning that was of concern.

Cooney consulted leaders across several fields about the possibility of using television to educate young children. She envisioned programming of such broad appeal that it would reach all children, especially those living in disadvantaged neighborhoods. Today, her creation, *Sesame Street*, has inspired children in more than 150 countries and has left an indelible imprint on generations who fondly recall full episodes, remember special connections with characters like Mr. Hooper, and outright adore the Muppets. The show's impact on children's academic skills and their ability to perform well in school has been documented in hundreds of research and business case studies. *Sesame Street* has inspired a whole field of media creators, and entire broadcast networks, to develop programming aimed at educating and entertaining young children.

And perhaps most relevant at a time where we are deeply concerned about the isolation of some children who are exposed to media, Cooney and her colleagues thought deeply about the engagement and involvement of the entire family in creating *Sesame Street*. The sketch comedy and music performed by noted celebrities, the blended use of new technologies like animated letters and numbers, and the cultural power of real-life, diverse families led to active "co-viewing" by multiple generations.

As the first educational television program to base its content on laboratory and formative research, *Sesame Street* was often referred to as an "experiment." Researchers both within and without the Children's Television Workshop studied, among other things, the roles that parents and others in the room can play in enhancing the viewing experiences of preschoolers. They discovered that children learn more if parents view the program alongside them and extend learning beyond the media experience. Cooney and colleagues like the puppet maestro Jim Henson literally "thought outside the box."

Today, thinking outside the box may also enable educators to see new opportunities for children from different backgrounds. African American and Hispanic children, for example, are no strangers to screen-based media such as television and video games and spend more time each day with screen media than white children. African American children under the age of eight spend four hours and twenty-seven minutes a day with screen media, while white children are spending two hours and fifty-one minutes, according to surveys of their parents. And for mobile phones as Internet access devices, a Pew report in 2010 showed a digital divide in reverse, with a higher percentage of blacks and Hispanics using their phones for online searches, e-mail, and instant messages than whites.

When we embarked on this project in 2012, we interviewed dozens of leaders around the country working in elementary schools, preschools, child care centers, and home visiting programs. They expressed high interest in harnessing the power of technology to improve communication, expose parents to new resources, and provide rich content for educators to embed in curricula. Some early childhood experts and practitioners said they were skeptical about the value of apps by themselves and were wary of investing in high-priced hardware. "We're not thrilled with our options but we don't have the time or money to create our own," said Ellen Frede, who was senior vice president at Acelero Learning at the time (and who is now with the Bill & Melinda Gates Foundation). Yet she and others simultaneously expressed hope that services such as social media, texting, and video-based resources could spark exchanges and foster better relationships among educators and parents that would, in turn, focus more attention on their children's growth and development.

Since then, the hopes for social media, texting, and video-based sources, as well as for apps and e-books, have continued to climb. Questions have shifted from *whether* to *how*: How might teachers use different technologies, and under which conditions will they have the most success? Which of the new functionalities in e-books are helpful or harmful to different stages of reading? Which kinds of media are best used with parents first, or children only, or both parents and children together? At what ages? What kinds of teacher preparation and training are now needed? At what point could educators become mentors for parents?

In this book we take you from coast to coast, classroom to classroom, and marketplace to marketplace to see how educators and tech innovators are arriving at some early answers—and sometimes, early warnings. With each interview we conducted, app marketplace we scanned, and video we shot, we were guided by four main principles:

1. Children need educators who understand that building strong readers and setting the foundation for acquiring litera*cies*, plural, takes a two-pronged approach. Children need skills (such as alphabet knowledge, word reading, and print awareness) and knowledge (such as understanding concepts, oral language development, and vocabulary growth). Teaching skills alone or knowledge alone is not enough.

2. Parents are crucial to children's success. Even parents without strong reading skills themselves can make important contributions to their children's cognitive development and later reading success through conversation and joint engagement in learning via traditional and digital media.

3. Technology can be a helpful ally in literacy development, but by itself it is not the answer. What matters most is how parents, children, and educators use technology to strengthen their interactions with each other and improve their familiarity with sounds, words, language, knowledge, and the elements of critical thinking.

4. To ignore technology, however, is to miss opportunities for delivering new ideas and better teaching to the children who need it most, inadvertently allowing digital divides to grow wider.

With these four principles as a guide, we hope you will find new insights, promise, and urgency in the pages that follow. The class of 2030 is not getting any younger.

NOTES

I believe the answer is an emphatic yes: Cooney 1966.
They discovered: e.g., Reiser, Tessmer, and Phelps 1984; Salomon 1973.
African American children: Rideout 2011, 12.
for mobile phones: Zickuhr 2010.

PART 2

Surveying the New Literacy Landscape

The Apps Explosion: What's in the Store?

To cite the old Chinese proverb, "We live in interesting times." One indicator: just pause from reading this book for a moment and reflect on the recently invented digital devices you have close at hand. Open up your smartphone or tablet and observe a cornucopia of entertainment and lifestyle apps—games, photography, music, cooking, sports—as well as social ones that link you to friends, family, and colleagues across the globe, not to mention apps for messaging anyone, anytime. Most of us have instant access to the world's information via powerful, personalized search engines that fit in our pockets. Later in the book we talk to experts who now wonder about the burdens of being always connected. But how often have you wondered, How on Earth did we live without our devices?

Hard as it is to believe, a little over five years ago, there was no such thing as an iPad or touchscreen tablet computer. Similarly, smartphones as we know them, with interactive touchscreens, advanced operating systems, and anytime, anywhere access to the Internet, did not exist until the first iPhone was introduced in January 2007. In the relatively few years since their release, mobile technologies have become ubiquitous and certainly changed most Americans' lives. Today, nearly 60 percent of American adults own a smartphone. More than 50 percent have a hand-held device such as a tablet computer or dedicated e-reader like a Kindle. And the choices of content are simply dizzying. For example, as of this writing there are some 1.3 million apps available in the iPhone store alone; there were less than a hundred thousand in late 2009. Yet for those who may want to put the genie back in the bottle: there's no app for that. There's no going back to a less connected age.

Children have high rates of access to mobile devices too. A 2013 report from Common Sense Media indicates that 75 percent of children ages eight and younger live in homes with mobile technologies, up from 52 percent of children in 2011. These devices are now found in children's education settings, from preschools to high schools. In an analysis of five national surveys of teachers, the Cooney Center recently confirmed high rates of use of interactive technologies, including digital games, apps, and electronic books across K–12 education. According to a recent RAND report, on a typical day, children ages three to five spend an average of four hours with communications technology, and use is increasing among children of all ages. These trends are likely to continue in the future. School districts continue to adopt one-to-one computing programs, and many schools encourage students to bring their own devices in the growing bring-your-own-device (BYOD) movement. US government programs have helped to finance new technology infrastructure through programs such as E-Rate, which provides funds for private companies to wire schools at a discounted rate. And both governments and private organizations are trying to find ways to bring high-speed Internet connections and low-cost devices to low-income communities.

Despite this activity, parents and educators lack guideposts and roadmaps. It is far too easy for educators and parents to get lost and feel overwhelmed.

Think for a moment about the students in the opening scene of the book: graduation day for the class of 2030. The students walking down the aisle to collect their high school diplomas are the toddlers and preschoolers of today. The way they learn and develop over the next fifteen years and the environments they operate within will shape their success in the years to come. Many of their parents—within their own media-laden and increasingly busy lives—are just beginning to make decisions, perhaps fateful ones, about how the digital revolution might help their children learn to read and communicate in this new age.

FINDING THE "GOOD STUFF"

A national parent survey (http://www.joanganzcooneycenter.org/wp-content /uploads/2014/01/jgcc_learningathome.pdf) conducted by the Joan Ganz Cooney Center last year pointed to a state of transition that is just barely underway. The survey of some 1,600 parents, including more than 900 Hispanic and African Americans, found that digital games and apps for educational activities (as defined by parents) are important. According to their parents, 35 percent of children between the ages of two and ten years use educational apps at least once a week. But the same survey indicated that we still have miles to go in fulfilling an essential principle: there simply isn't enough guidance or research evidence for parents and educators who are trying to navigate today's new trails. As the number of apps has exploded since the first apps store opened in 2007, the adults in charge of teaching young children how to read, write, and do math have struggled to understand what these new digital tools could mean for everyday learning. For instance, the survey indicated that most parents are at sea in finding educational media products. Far fewer rely on experts in education or parenting (20 percent) in finding appropriate choices for their children than they do from "just browsing" online (50 percent).

A smaller survey in 2014, conducted by the site Moms with Apps also asked parents how they find apps for their children: though 96 percent report that their kids have benefited from using apps, nearly half (49 percent) said the process of finding good apps is "moderately" to "very hard."

We have wondered whether this problem of not being able to find the good stuff is a significant barrier to the productive uses of communication technologies—especially for struggling readers. The Cooney Center's survey confirms this hunch: only 21 percent of parents whose children use mobile phones at least weekly said that their child had learned "a lot" about reading or vocabulary through educational activities on mobile devices, whereas a majority pointed to television, a static and less dynamic learning option, as a far more valuable tool.

This book is propelled by a vision of blended literacy-focused environments for children and their families—spaces that are online and offline, tech assisted but human powered. It is a vision starting to come into focus for many program pioneers, scholars, and lab inventors. But most parents and educators have not yet had an opportunity to consider such a possibility. To them, the digital world, especially the realm of apps, feels overwhelming.

It is time to tame this space, and help is starting to arrive. A group of scientists recently called on industry to start "putting education in 'educational' apps" by using lessons from the science on how children learn. Librarians and software reviewers are starting to take up the task of curation (you'll see some of them listed at the end of this chapter). And as you'll see in this chapter, we have started to survey the marketplace, marking the pitfalls, and seeking the fertile ground for learning.

PIONEERING LITERACY IN THE DIGITAL WILD WEST

In the spring of 2012, the two of us with partners Cynthia Chiong and Maggie Severns conducted a snapshot analysis of popular language and literacy-focused digital media products aimed at children ages zero to eight. The findings, published as a report titled *Pioneering Literacy in the Digital Wild West,* provided inspiration for this follow-up research and book and built on prior research undertaken by the Cooney Center in a series of apps tracking studies between 2010 and 2012. The report suggested that children's language and literacy apps comprised a substantial proportion of the most popular educational apps in 2012. Based on their descriptions, most apps targeted very basic language- and literacy-related skills, such as learning letters and phonics. Our teams noted that very few apps and e-books had information available about studies of their effectiveness or educational value. The findings from *Pioneering Literacy* provided a baseline for our own and others' work focused on children's apps for learning.

Now here we are, writing these words in 2015. In the Digital Age, 2012 can feel like ancient history. With the many realities of modern-day parenting in mind, and more questions than answers, we set out to conduct a new, updated scan of the marketplace. We wanted to take a deeper look at the kinds of apps available to families with children eight years old and younger. We also wanted to put ourselves in parents' shoes. We decided to use techniques for searching that parents or educators themselves might deploy, and then see what they might encounter.

Desperately Seeking Apps

If our scan and anecdotal observation of how parents seek apps is any indication, the process looks something like this:

> A mom with a preschooler gets a smartphone. She has heard (from other parents, from teachers, from her own children) that there are good apps out there for helping children learn to read. Some cost only 99 cents. Some are even free! She is driven by a niggling worry that her son or daughter is not learning as fast as his or her peers. She is also a little curious about what these apps are all about. And besides, she wouldn't mind finding a way to occupy her child during those long waits at the doctor's office or while cooking dinner.
>
> She touches the "app store" icon on her device and a storefront appears. Colorful promotions appear for "Best New Apps" and "Best New Games." They don't look quite right for a four-year-old, so she touches on the button that says "Explore." A list of categories appears. She chooses the education category, and *voilà*, she sees a row of icons for the most popular education apps and lists of apps in subcategories. She sees one that looks promising and downloads away.

Moments like this are happening all over the country. Maybe you even recognize yourself in this scenario. (Lisa does.) Now consider that moment when the mother saw the labels *education* and *popular*. To parents, those labels are guideposts, but there is little to no information on how "education" is defined or what it takes for an app to be "popular." Nor do many parents have time to dig around and find out. They simply want to discover an app that looks like fun and might lead to learning.

This decision-making process is pretty haphazard, and it's not entirely clear why some apps are catching a parent's eye and others are not. We wondered, How many literacy and language apps are featured prominently on lists in app stores because of their popularity, what skills do they purport to teach, and with which strategies? Are parents likely to encounter the same apps if they looked at expert review sites like Common Sense Media or Children's Technology Review to guide their choices, or would the language and literacy apps promoted by these experts in the field have different attributes? One issue that intrigued us, for example, is whether there exists a disconnect between what parents buy for their children—perhaps after browsing or talking with friends and family—and what media products experts think are good for children. In short, are there efficient ways to "pan for gold" in the new Wild West?

Scanning the Marketplace

As we built a system for scanning the marketplace, we limited our investigation to interactive apps, excluding products that consisted only of e-books. (Don't worry, much more on e-books is coming in the next chapter.) To take a deep dive, we brought in two colleagues who are experts in analyzing the app marketplace: Sarah Vaala, a communications, literacy, and health promotion scholar now based at Vanderbilt University, and Anna Ly, a tech designer and industry innovations expert based at the Cooney Center. Sarah and Anna started by collecting lists of the fifty most popular paid and free apps in the education sections of three app stores—iTunes, Google Play, and Amazon apps—over eight weeks in February and March 2014. From the full list of 1,200 titles identified through this process, we filtered those titles to zoom in on the ones that focused on early language and literacy. We created that sample by identifying those apps that were (1) intended for children birth through age eight, and (2) focused at least in part on teaching language and literacy skills. Finally, we obtained lists of apps that were highly rated or that received commendation in 2014 from three well-known sites, Children's Technology Review (http://childrenstech.com/), Common Sense Media (https://www.commonsensemedia.org/), and Parents' Choice Awards (http://www.parents-choice.org/). (In the remainder of this chapter, we refer to the apps that were highly rated or awarded by expert review sites as "award-winning" or "awarded" apps.) From these three lists, our team found additional apps that we included, yielding a total sample of 184 apps.

Next, Sarah and Anna and a team of coders got to work documenting key aspects of each app's descriptions in app stores and producer websites. This involved months of work entering information into a custom-designed database with codes for basic features, such as the target age for child users, and whether it featured popular, branded characters. They coded the descriptions written by the app developers to accompany the apps—the "packaging"—for their mention of educational elements, including the language and literacy skills the app claimed to teach, stated strategies used to teach those skills, and whether the design team included experts in education or child development. To help shed some light on the nature of language-and-literacy apps for children that parents and caregivers are most likely to encounter, our analyses focused on describing the full sample of 184 apps and comparing characteristics of the apps along various dimensions, such as their price and whether they were among the most popular in the app stores or awarded by expert raters.

We emphasize that though studies like this provide information about the kind of content available and how companies describe that content to consumers, they do not get inside nor observe the use of apps, nor can they tell us the ultimate educational value of those products for individual children. As we discuss elsewhere, many activities, including ensuring that children's daily routines follow a balanced media diet, are vital when literacy development is concerned. Individual needs vary by ages and stages of development as well as the particular skills, dispositions, and knowledge parents and educators wish to build. The findings we describe should be interpreted with these limitations in mind.

But what we have found paints a highly consistent picture. Though literacy apps are among the most popular and successful apps in the education category in the markets we scanned, their content, design, production, and distribution are too often characterized by a lack of transparency, overhyped or unsubstantiated claims, a lack of curriculum guidance or alignment with standards, a paucity of child development or learning science content knowledge among developers, and an incomplete response to children's literacy needs, especially for struggling readers. Frankly, our analysis is cause for real concern: too many parents, caregivers, and even teachers are unwitting participants in a sector that grew organically from red-hot entrepreneurship with more focus on sales than on sound approaches to child development. Our findings add to the evidence that parents and educators have little choice but to rely on marketing messages and clearly need guidance.

Language and Literacy Apps Are Popular

One of our first discoveries, mirroring what we saw in 2012, was that language- and literacy-focused apps for young children represented a sizeable portion of the education marketplace. We conducted analyses of the top fifty "educational" apps in three categories: apps that require an upfront payment, which we call "paid apps" (prices typically ranged from 99 cents to $3.99), the top "free apps" (no charge to download), and "award-winning apps." Based on app titles, we found that 34 percent of Top 50 paid apps, 29 percent of Top 50 free apps, and 21 percent of awarded apps had a language-and-literacy focus and were intended for children from birth to age eight.

And there is a good chance that those numbers are conservative, because we were not putting e-books in our "language and literacy" category.

As you will see in chapter 7, although e-books can and will certainly be an important part of children's learning in the future, in this particular app scan we targeted apps that are not driven by book-like narratives but instead are focused on delivering interactive features and games. Another small minority of apps across the three subsamples were omitted from the final sample because they were considered more of a "tool" than an app with self-contained content. For example, we came across apps that allowed users to make their own flashcards. Though these too could be used for children's language and literacy learning, that learning depends not on what the developers have created but on the content that a parent or teacher might type in.

Finding Age-Appropriate Apps

Among those language and literacy apps, are parents and educators able to find what they are looking for? What their children need? Given that birth to eight is a fairly sizeable age range, representing diverse developmental stages, we wondered how many apps were clearly intended for more narrow age ranges. So bearing this in mind, we first investigated whether apps are designed to answer a primary question for parents: Is this app right for the age of my child? A parent with a two-year-old will want to know if the app will make sense to a two-year-old. A parent of a six-year-old will want to know if the app will be interesting enough to hold the interest of a six-year-old. How well does the marketplace answer this key question? Unfortunately, not very well. We found that parents may download apps with content their children have already mastered or content that is too advanced due to a lack of age guidance in app descriptions. In fact, we found that nearly 40 percent of app descriptions and accompanying websites did not clarify the age range for the target users of the app at all (see Figures 6.1 and 6.2). They used terms like *child* or *kids* instead of an age range. App developers may be wary of narrowing their base of potential buyers. But we see the lack of information on specific age ranges as a dry gulch, one to be filled with better information and guidance.

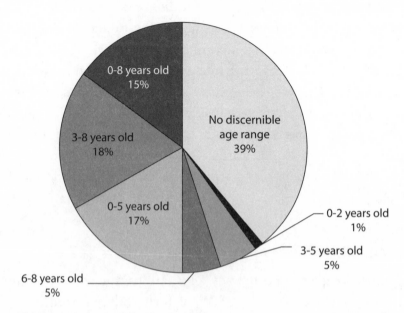

Figure 6.1 Age Ranges Mentioned in App Descriptions in Our Sample.

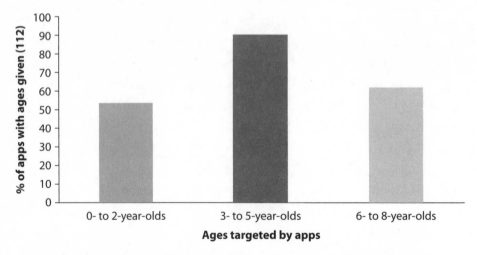

Figure 6.2 Target Age Ranges for Language/Literacy Apps in Our Sample.*

Note: Values do not sum to 100 percent as many apps' stated target audience often crossed these two-year age-ranges.

Mickey and the Muppets: Characters in the Apps Stores

Because Michael's team is based within the halls of a children's media legend—Sesame Workshop—we naturally wondered, Is there a legacy for character-driven educational media in the apps domain? The answer is yes. Nearly a fifth (19 percent) of apps in our full sample contain a familiar character, well known from outside the app or app series. Children often want to get close to, and even emulate, these characters; anyone who has seen a toddler react to spotting Elmo or Mickey Mouse on a party balloon knows this firsthand. Some studies have uncovered social and health benefits associated with these relationships; kids are more likely to try broccoli, for example, if Elmo is associated with it. And, of course, children's media producers are happy to create loyal future customers and to mobilize a parent to buy an app to respond to their child's pleadings for their favorites. The majority of the app characters in this sample came from television programs, though some were from other media like movies or book series. This is not surprising given that some of the producers of apps in our sample also create children's educational television programs, such as *Sesame Street* and *SuperWhy!* Those two shows in particular have been the subject of intense study, and we see the appearance of characters from programs backed up by peer-reviewed research as an encouraging sign. Ideally, apps labeled as "educational" should come from developers with a tradition of research and experimentation tied to children's academic and social needs.

WHERE ARE THE EXPERTS?

Other signs were not so encouraging. One aspect that seems almost invisible in today's app marketplace is the influence of expertise. As the Cooney Center survey indicated, and as suggested by our anecdotal observations of parents exploring the app store, there may not yet be symmetry between how parents operate as scouts in this Wild West and what experts think they should be discovering. To test this, we looked for matches between what shows up on the "popular" lists in the app stores and what is rated highly by three organizations we selected for their expertise in children's media. So, did those organizations and the marketplace agree on what's best or most popular? Nope. Notably, only eleven (or 17 percent) of the sixty-six award-winning apps with a focus on language and literacy were also in our sample as apps that were among the fifty most popular educational apps in the iTunes, Google Play, and/or Amazon app store during our sampling period. See Table 6.1.

In short, there appears to be a chasm between what experts like and what is showing up in the "most popular" lists in the app stores. These differences may reflect robust marketing campaigns mustered by producers of the most popular apps. Unfortunately, we cannot be sure, because the algorithms that are used by each app store to compile their Top 50

Table 6.1 Eleven Apps That Made the Cut in Our Sample in Both Categories: Popular and Award-Winning

App Name*	App Producer
Agnitus Personal Learning Program	Agnitus
Busytown Mysteries	Loud Crow Interactive, Inc.
Elmo Loves ABCs	Sesame Workshop
Endless Alphabet	Originator Inc.
Endless Reader	Originator Inc.
Letter School	Boreaal Publishers
Millie's Crazy Dinosaur Adventure—Millie Was Here	Megapops, LLC
Monkey Word School Adventure	Thup Games
Reading Rainbow	Reading Rainbow
Sago Mini Ocean Swimmer	Sago Sago
Starfall Learn to Read	Starfall Education, LLC

*Listed alphabetically; based on Feb–Mar 2014 sample of 184 apps.

lists are not publicly available. And there may be one other explanation: higher-quality and awarded apps may be more expensive to produce and therefore pricier. One striking trend from our study: the overwhelming majority—almost nine in ten of award-winning apps—were paid apps rather than freely available. This led us to wonder whether there were differences in average costs between the paid awarded apps and paid popular apps. As shown in Figure 6.3, on average, the awarded apps cost a bit more than the apps in the Top 50 educational paid apps list, although the difference was not dramatic ($1.00–$2.00 for popular apps versus $2.01–$3.00 for award-winning apps, on average).

Is it possible then that the cost of the awarded apps is creating another barrier for vulnerable parents to surmount in the new apps marketplace? Our findings appear to support this hypothesis. The reasons for this trend are not clear from our market scan, though we have a few guesses. It may be more resource intensive to produce the highest-quality apps, particularly to the extent that their creation involves the participation of education,

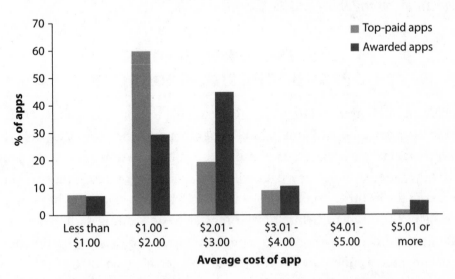

Figure 6.3 Prices of Top-Paid and Awarded Apps in Our Sample.

child development, or literacy experts. The higher cost to produce the highest-quality apps, which in turn are more likely to win accolades from ratings groups, may be reflected in their relatively higher price. It may also be that parents are drawn to lower-cost apps for their children's use, and price is one factor driving the popularity of relatively cheaper apps in app markets. Price and popularity may also have a cyclical relationship. That is, if parents are largely drawn to free apps, then the high rates of downloads may boost those apps into the Top 50 lists in app stores, putting them before the eyes of parents who mainly search for the most popular apps.

It is still unclear whether these price differences will have implications for which families download high-quality apps. But if the vast majority of award-winning apps are paid rather than free, and are more expensive than other paid apps, then it is plausible that families of means will be more likely than poor families to purchase them. In fact, a similar trend—named the "app gap" for the gap in educational app ownership between higher- and lower-income US families—has been borne out in 2013 research by Common Sense Media (https://www.commonsensemedia.org/research/zero-to-eight-childrens-media-use-in-america-2013).

MISSING OPPORTUNITIES: APPS AND THE KNOWLEDGE GAP

A central mission of Readialand will be to enable emerging and struggling readers to get a boost from school programs and the media experiences that punctuate their time out of school or at home. Apps (and books, and any other media tools they use) will need to incorporate a range of skills and content in order to effectively assist in teaching reading. These media products will need to help children master basic reading skills while also building the content knowledge and vocabulary required to comprehend texts on increasingly complex subjects. To get a sense of the skills and knowledge developers included across our sample of popular and awarded apps, we looked for twenty-three skills culled from literature and curriculum guides regarding language and literacy learning for infants through third graders. The skills included basic speech production, alphabet/letter knowledge, phonemic awareness, writing/typing individual letters, lower-versus upper-case letter identification, print concepts (the form/function of print), vocabulary, spelling, storytelling/narrative sequencing, recognizing sight words, reading comprehension, rhyming concepts, grammar, bilingual knowledge (learning a foreign language), handwriting, reading fluency, written expression, spoken expression, sign language letters, sign language words/phrases, literary forms/genres, and motivation/love of reading.

Are all of these skills represented across popular and award-winning apps, per their descriptions? Our data say no. In fact, only eight of these twenty-three skills were mentioned in the descriptions of at least ten apps in our full sample. These skills are shown in Figure 6.4. Many apps still target what we consider basic language and literacy skills, such as learning the ABCs (alphabet and letter knowledge) and learning the sounds that make up

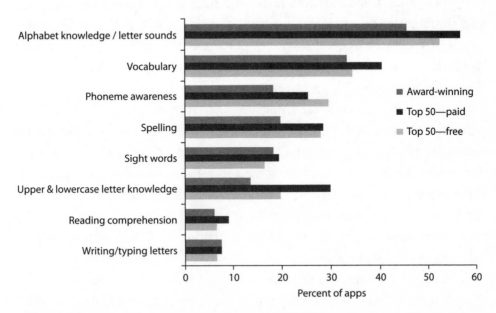

Figure 6.4 Most Common Language/Literacy Skills Targeted in Apps in Our Sample.

words (phonemic awareness). Notably, one particular skill that we consider more advanced, understanding what is read (reading comprehension), is more common than two years ago. Several of the most popular skills could be considered either basic or advanced, depending on how they are approached. Learning to spell *cat* may be a goal for kindergarten students, while third-grade students are tackling words like *calculate*. Similarly, vocabulary development is a curricular goal for toddlers through third graders, though the complexity of the targeted words varies with children's developmental stage.

We also looked for possible differences in the specific language and literacy skills that award-winning apps claim to teach, compared to the Top 50 paid and free apps. Our analysis reveals that the same few skills are among the most commonly targeted skills across all three categories. In each of the three samples, teaching basic skills like alphabet or letter–sound knowledge and vocabulary development were the most commonly encountered skills in app descriptions.

Though it's difficult to determine whether apps on the whole teach skills and content appropriate for a range of ages, it is clear that a very limited subset of skills are targeted. Sixty-five percent of the skills we searched were completely missing or rarely encountered (that is, they were found in fewer than 6 percent of apps' descriptions). It may be the case that parents are seeking out apps that teach these things, or that apps just tend to teach these particular skills well (leading to their popularity with parents and with expert media raters). A related possibility, which should be explored with a larger future sample, is that it is easier for developers to incorporate these eight skills into apps, or that perceived demand is driving their choices of the kinds of apps to design. For example, developers may perceive a greater market for apps for preschool- and kindergarten-age children compared to infants or elementary school students.

Though our analysis did not verify or test the content within the apps, it appears that developers may be focusing on just a few of the skills that children must master to learn to read. As described in chapter 3 and elsewhere, we know it takes much more than these eight skills for children to become proficient readers. We also see children using educational apps in short bursts of time—waiting for the end of a sibling's basketball practice, for example. Building skills like recognizing "sight words" (words such as *said* or *because*), mastering the alphabet, and picking up new vocabulary may be more well suited to this kind of time frame than skills such as learning another language or practicing written expression. A few of the underrepresented skills are among the tasks (such as basic speech production) that frankly may be better introduced and supported by parents and caregivers themselves. In short, apps may have a fairly narrow niche in which they are especially strong, but are not necessarily a strong foundation for the multipronged approach that children need to become proficient readers.

TEACHING STRATEGIES IN TODAY'S LITERACY APPS

Now that we have looked at the skills these apps are attempting to teach, it's time to consider *how* the apps teach these skills, according to their developers. There is a wealth of research-based knowledge regarding effective strategies for teaching children to read and communicate. For example, asking children questions and elaborating on the meaning of words are prized strategies for enhancing the benefits of shared storybook reading. Similarly, there is an evolving theory of pedagogical content knowledge that educators must consider in using apps and e-books to ensure that children benefit from their unique properties.

We coded our sample of 184 apps for twenty-one different strategies for teaching language and literacy skills and knowledge. These twenty-one strategies were culled from reviews of research and best practices for teaching young children. Of this full set of strategies, eight were mentioned in the apps' descriptions repeatedly (showing up in at least ten different apps). These eight strategies are displayed in Figure 6.5. Most of these strategies come to mind for teaching early, rote skills, such as matching letter sounds to letters, labeling objects on screen, and sounding out phonemes. Typically,

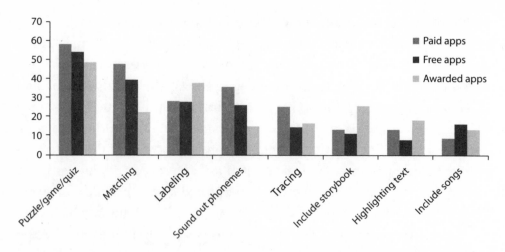

Figure 6.5 Most Common Teaching Strategies in App Descriptions in Our Sample.

these techniques do not push learners to consider meaning, relate content to their own lives, or use language to express themselves. But we note: it is difficult to know what content most apps address through puzzles, quizzes, and games; this would require a careful assessment of what is happening inside the app.

Also notable are strategies we did not find in our scan. For example, developers generally do not claim that their apps elaborate on the meanings of words, model interpersonal dialogue, ask the child open-ended questions along the way, summarize narrative or educational content, or provide opportunities for written or spoken expression. As we will see in chapters 7 and 8, the capacity to embed these deeper and more interactive literacy experiences already exists in e-books, dictionaries, and even wearable devices, but they are not yet a common feature of the apps marketplace circa 2014. Since these are more nuanced and sometimes more sophisticated strategies, they may also be more difficult or expensive to incorporate into apps' designs. Given that we coded only the descriptions of apps, we cannot be certain these strategies are entirely absent once a child gets into the app. Teaching strategies such as content quizzes, tracing letters, and highlighting text may be easier to describe, or producers may feel that these are strategies parents are looking for. What is clear is that a parent scanning the educational apps selected from app stores' Top 50 lists or expert review sites is unlikely to come away with the impression that the apps use these more nuanced, higher-order teaching and learning techniques.

CULLING THE DEVELOPERS

The reader of this book may have wondered on occasion, Are Lisa and Michael overstating their metaphor just a bit? Do parents and educators really feel like it's the digital Wild West? We will admit to some hyperbole. But we aren't making this up. One meaty finding from our scan, almost to our own disbelief, is that fewer than half of popular and award-winning language and literacy apps reveal any information about their development team. In fact, of the information we did uncover, most of it was found on the producers' websites, suggesting parents would have to do some investigating, like we did, to dig up vital information.

As shown in Figure 6.6, a slightly higher percentage of paid apps had information available about their development team, particularly in comparison to Top 50 apps available for free.

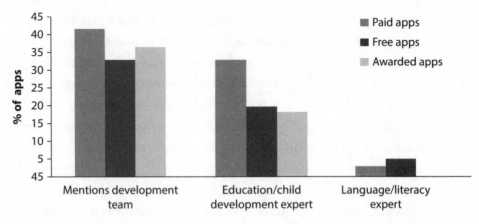

Figure 6.6 Percent of Apps in Our Sample That Provide Development Team Information.

Among the minority of app descriptions that *do* divulge any information about the developers, many say there is a child development or education expert on the team. Those kinds of experts were noted in 79 percent of paid, 60 percent of free, and 50 percent of awarded apps with available development team information. However, the inclusion of a literacy expert was quite rare; it only showed up in 11 percent of top paid and 15 percent of top free apps with available development team information. And interestingly, not one description of an award-winning app mentioned a literacy expert on the development team. Literacy experts are almost entirely MIA on the app front.

Signs of a sequenced or thoughtfully designed approach to teaching were pretty rare as well. Twenty-nine percent of the apps in our sample made any mention of having a curriculum. When a curriculum was mentioned, more than half named a specific set of standards or teaching philosophy underlying the app's development, such as the Common Core State Standards or Montessori.

Surprisingly, award-winning apps were less likely to mention a curriculum or educational approach in their descriptions. Only 18 percent named a curriculum, compared to 34 percent of top paid and 30 percent of top free apps. The reviewers making awards may be more apt to give high ratings for aesthetics or creativity than educational approach, which may be a fine approach when considering a constellation of factors parents are looking for. And, remember, our analysis coded only app *descriptions*, and could not go so far as to measure or code the experiences children have when using an app; we do not know the extent to which curricula were truly integrated into app development in those apps that claim to have followed one.

But given that these apps are sitting on a virtual store shelf labeled "Education," we wanted to probe whether there was even a fleeting reference to an underlying educational curriculum or teaching philosophy. As shown in research on educational media elsewhere, applying a scope and sequenced curriculum to guide content development can add a quality dimension. Parents with available choices in their communities would not send their children to a school that teaches concepts willy-nilly with no overarching teaching philosophy or expectation of what should be learned. Similarly, children's educational television programs like *Sesame Street* or those produced by PBS have clear, underlying curricula (as well as research evaluating curricular goals and learning outcomes), and are generally considered the gold standard among kids' educational programming. Curricula and fun, engaging, creative experiences should not be diametrically opposing concepts.

In our view, these findings are yet another sign of the unbridled nature of the media marketplace. Certainly learning is possible without a curriculum, but these findings indicate that for most apps the line separating entertainment, learning, and more structured "education" is still not clear. And this lack of clarity is confusing: as we've said, the app category—that virtual store shelf—is unabashedly called "education," which may lead some parents to assume that there is an educational structure or approach to the apps they are purchasing.

Another assumption might be as follows: an app categorized as educational implies children will learn from it. So we wondered whether there was any information provided in descriptions about efficacy, such as, What can be expected after children use their products for a period of time?, or even whether the apps were first tested with children simply to determine whether they are easy to use. We analyzed app store and producer website descriptions for any mention of research testing. Fewer than a quarter mentioned some testing of app usability or appeal. More notable is the absence of information about any testing of children's learning. Only 2 percent of apps directly mentioned that research was conducted to assess learning from the product. It is likely that more producers conduct this sort of testing but are not mentioning that research in app descriptions. In particular, we know that many of the producers who also create educational television programming test the efficacy of their apps, and they conduct research on children's learning as part of their process. Parents may not know or think to ask whether their apps have been tested, but we firmly believe that parents and educators will eventually need to demand more transparency and disclosure about whether these products were tested for their ability to help children learn.

One feature that was fairly common was endorsements. These may be direct quotations containing praise from individuals (like parents or media bloggers) or institutions (such as a media review organization), or statements indicating the app was approved, recommended, or otherwise touted by a person or institution. In our sample, 40 percent of app descriptions contained an endorsement from at least one individual or institution. Of those, more than half contained endorsements from institutions only (such as news media, prominent blogs, or media ratings sites), a quarter used statements from individuals, like parents or individual media bloggers, and slightly fewer than a quarter used both. Why does this matter? It is reasonable to expect that many parents may place greater confidence in the quality of apps that carry such statements. Decades of research have shown that celebrity endorsements are effective marketing tools, for example. A 2005 Kaiser Family Foundation report on baby media producers (think *Baby Einstein*) reported that parents find experiences of other parents to be highly informative, and thus parent endorsements often accompany these products.

FACING THE NEW FRONTIER

The parents of our 2030 high school graduates are facing a new frontier. For the many generations of parents who came before, buying something for one's child meant going to a physical store, finding a product on a shelf, and picking up that object to inspect it firsthand. Today's parents find themselves in a whole new kind of store; one where physical touch is impossible and inspection is virtual. There are also new metrics for judging quality in these markets, including producers' descriptions, user ratings, and sometimes, expert reviews. When the product in question is a mobile app, the stakes are also suddenly different. Families who are unhappy with an app they have downloaded cannot simply "take it back" to the store and return it.

So what's a parent or educator to think after a perusal of the apps stores? As our teams at the Cooney Center and New America have documented over a five-year period, apps that focus on reading and other literacy skills are very common within popular and award-winning categories. At first glance, chances look good for finding something useful. Those looking to help their children learn some basics, such as the ABCs and the sounds that letters make, will find an abundance of options. But this optimism may turn to frustration among parents searching for certain skills or teaching strategies. Parents or educators searching for apps that teach higher-order skills, like reading fluency, storytelling, or self-expression, or that use more nuanced teaching strategies, may have to dig a little deeper beyond top app lists and award-winning reviews to discover these resources. And, of course, as we see in the following chapters, there are other choices such as e-books and even newer technologies that are being designed to be responsive to children's emerging literacy needs in increasingly sophisticated ways.

Those parents in search of kids' language-and-literacy apps may also be pushed to choose between top educational apps promoted by app stores (and presumably popular among other parents) and apps with the highest accolades from expert raters. So far, very few language- and literacy-focused kids' apps seem to achieve both of these honors (see Table 6.1). Making these choices will also involve some consideration for a family's app budget, as award-winning apps tend to require a slightly higher investment than popular paid apps. Though the average difference between awarded apps and those popular in app stores tends to be fairly small ($1–$2 or so), many families may well decide to spend those few dollars on other resources. Furthermore, many parents may limit their search to apps that are available for free, narrowing their search even further. These parents will be disappointed from scans of expert review sites; the vast majority (nearly 90 percent) of kids' language- and literacy-focused apps on these sites are paid apps.

Where our hypothetical parents in search of quality language-and-literacy apps might become most frustrated is in their hunt for explicit benchmarks of apps' educational quality. In the 2014 *Learning at Home* report produced by the Cooney Center, a majority of parents surveyed said they would like more information about good digital media to support their children's learning. To the extent that these parents hope to find information about apps' underlying curricula, child development, education, or literacy experts on app development teams, or efficacy testing of apps, they are likely to be disappointed. Though parents will encounter many endorsements of apps—from other parents, self-proclaimed or legitimate experts, and organizations—endorsements ask parents to take someone's word for it. They do not convey the nuts and bolts behind quality, as does information about the people who developed the app, the educational philosophy behind its design, and evidence of its educational success. Our findings in particular illuminate key opportunities for producers to provide more information that we think parents would greatly value.

Our analysis can be summed up as follows: kids' literacy apps are abundant within the marketplace, but they have not been designed or distributed in any coherent fashion, and the vast majority are not oriented to help bridge the gulf of literacy problems faced by some families and communities, let alone broad swaths of our nation. Will educators and child development experts have any influence in the future? This is a pressing question for the education community, particularly the preschool profession, which has traditionally shied away from conversations related to educational technology. The absence of field leadership is probably not in the best interests of children and their families in the long run.

Meanwhile, however, we see hope in the growing number of curators popping up, a few of whom are trying to bring in a lens on learning in the early years. The box following, excerpted from reporting by writers Kathleen Constanza and Sarah Jackson for our blogs, gives you a glimpse of some new surveyors, guides and outposts. They offer new perspectives on what is, literally, in store.

CURATORS: SCOUTS FOR DIGITAL GOLD

Here is a list, in alphabetical order, of several sites run by reviewers who live, eat, and breathe apps and other ed tech products.

Balefire Labs

Founded by Karen Mahon, Balefire Labs was launched as a consumer report–style service to compare apps. Each app is rated on twelve criteria stemming from peer-reviewed research (http://www.balefirelabs.com/apps/?page_id=21532) on the effects of interactive features built into educational technology. The site is funded by subscriptions starting at $3.99 per month. Developers can pay a $250 fee to have their product reviewed and to receive feedback reports on how to improve. Interesting note: Mahon has found that an app's being on a Top 100 list is "pretty much meaningless" in terms of instructional quality.

Children's Technology Review

Started in 1993 by Warren Buckleitner, the Children's Technology Review includes more than 11,000 reviews, published monthly and added to its database (http://reviews.childrenstech.com/ctr/home.php) with searchable tags and filters. Subscriptions start at $8 per month. Buckleitner, who started his career as an elementary school teacher and has a PhD in educational psychology, is a well-known face and entertaining critic at ed tech conferences around the world. His aim: to sort the magic from the dust in children's technology. In addition to teams of adult reviewers, kids of all ages are consulted through the evaluation process.

Common Sense Media's Best Apps and Games

Common Sense Media, a national nonprofit, created the "Best Apps and Games" section of its site primarily for parents. It's free. Funding for the site comes from individual donors, as well as a variety of foundations and other organizations. Apps are rated according to various dimensions (https://www.commonsensemedia.org/about-us/our-mission/about-our-ratings); reviewers are staff members at Common Sense Media, led by an editor with background in education and child development. The site rates apps along a five-point learning scale, with a 5 signaling that an app is "really engaging" and has an "excellent learning approach," to a 1 meaning that the app is "not recommended for learning." Kids and parents can review apps too.

Digital Storytime

This website (http://digital-storytime.com) was founded by parents Carisa and Marc Kluver to help fellow parents and educators discover picture books for iPads and promote early literacy. Carisa, who has a background as a school counselor, health educator, and researcher in child and maternal health, reviews how well an app measures up across nine rating categories, such as, Are the e-book's interactive features well integrated into the story? Or do they interfere with reading comprehension? The site is funded by ads that are all run through third parties like Google Ads to avoid conflicts of interest.

Graphite

Launched in 2013 by Common Sense Media, Graphite uses a two-part review system. A product's first "learning review" is written by a team of educators who are coordinated by the in-house editors at Graphite. The educators, many of whom are National Board Certified in a variety of fields, are trained on a set of standards that examine a product's engagement, pedagogy, support for teachers, and feedback. Hovering right beneath the learning review is the "teacher review," a crowdsourced review that averages feedback from teachers. The lively "field note" section details teachers' firsthand experience using the product in classrooms. If the "learning review" is like a restaurant review from food critics, the "teacher review" is like Yelp. It is supported by the SCE Foundation and a personal investment from Bill Gates (https://www.graphite.org/press/press-release/06–24–13).

Moms with Apps

Founded by four mothers who were developing family-friendly apps and connected over social media in 2009, this site (https://momswithapps.com) allows developer members to provide their own descriptions and provides additional insight about what's inside the app, such as an app's privacy settings or the presence of in-app purchases. Features developer profiles so parents can learn more about the people who are creating these apps.

Parents' Choice Foundation

The longest-standing review organization in our list, Parents' Choice, started in 1978 to guide parents to books and toys that encourage a love of learning. Reviews are conducted by a core team of five, plus a number of reviewers with specialized experience and use the same guiding principles to rate educational technology products that are used to review LEGOs and building blocks. Products that receive a Parents' Choice Award (http://www.parents-choice.org/allawards.cfm) go through a multi-tiered evaluation process. Funded by processing fees from companies that submit their products for review (the fee is $250 for apps). Only about 1 in 5 products submitted to the Parents' Choice Awards receives recognition in any of the six award levels.

Teachers With Apps

Educators Jayne Clare and Anne Rachel founded Teachers With Apps in 2010 after creating their own reading app, ABC Shakedown Plus, only to see it drowned out by apps they didn't consider high quality. Today the blog is updated continually, sometimes several times a day. Its reviews cover the general experience of using an app. The site team includes a speech pathologist, an occupational therapist, primary and secondary teachers, and a few college level professors who field-test apps and write the reviews. The site is funded by ads that, Clare says, are only sold if they "respect the developer's product."

NOTES

the burdens of being always connected: Gutnick et al. 2011.

the first iPhone was introduced: "Apple Reinvents" 2007.

nearly 60 percent of American adults: Smith 2013.

More than 50 percent: Zickuhr and Rainie 2014.

as of this writing: Costello 2014.

A 2013 report: Rideout 2013.

In an analysis: Pressey 2013.

According to a recent RAND report: Daugherty et al. 2014.

many schools encourage: Goodwin 2011.

both governments and private organizations: US Department of Education 2013; EveryoneOn.

Far fewer rely: Rideout 2014.

A smaller survey in 2014: "Survey of Parents" 2014. The project was undertaken in collaboration with the Campaign for Grade-Level Reading as a first step toward mapping the previously uncharted world of new interactive technologies aimed at helping children learn to read and programs that leverage that technology.

A group of scientists: Hirsh-Pasek et al. 2015.

The findings: In the 2012 report, *Pioneering Literacy in the Digital Wild West* from Lisa and Michael with Cynthia Chiong and Maggie Stevens (New York: Joan Ganz Cooney Center) we examined the market descriptions of 137 digital media products, including apps, e-books, digital games, and websites.

a series of apps: Chiong and Shuler 2010; Shuler, Levine, and Ree 2012.

a baseline for our own and others' work: Mobile Apps 2012.

whether the design team included experts: The codebook was developed by a team of team of JGCC research staff, led by Sarah Vaala. Codes were informed by the 2012 market scan (Guernsey et al. 2012) as well as a prior content analysis of infant/toddler DVDs conducted by Vaala and colleagues (Fenstermacher et al. 2010; Vaala et al. 2010). Two members of the JGCC research staff coded the sample independently, double-coding 15 percent of apps. Inter-rater reliability for variables reported here ranged from 78 percent to 100 percent agreement. For those variables where kappa values were obtainable, values ranged from $k = .46$ to $k = .95$ (some codes were too rarely applied for kappa to be calculated).

ensuring that children's daily routines: In other writings, Michael has often referred to the need for parents to emphasize a new approach to creating a "balanced media diet" based on the needs of the child, the quality of the content, and the particular contexts in which use is occurring, and in her book *Screen Time* Lisa coined "the three Cs" (content, context, and child) as a mantra for parents making decisions about media use. A recent interpretation from Common Sense Media appears here: "3 Simple Rules for a Healthy Media Diet" by Caroline Knorr (Common Sense Media, December 29, 2012), at https://www.commonsensemedia.org/blog/3-simple-rules-for-a-healthy-media-diet.

Some studies have uncovered: Royne and Levy 2011; Kotler, Schiffman, and Hanson 2012.

only eleven (or 17 percent): Given that these apps were simultaneously top apps in the markets and highly rated by expert groups they are included in both samples in analyses comparing "Top 50" apps to "award-winning" apps.

the algorithms that are used by each app store: The "Top 50" lists were apps that were among the top apps during an eight-week period. The other awarded apps may have been in the Top 50 lists at other times. There may just be a timing mismatch between periods when apps are popular with experts and popular with parents.

twenty-three skills culled from literature and curriculum guides: Early Beginnings 2009; "Learning to Read" 1998; "Checkpoints" 1998.

there is an evolving theory: Pedagogical content knowledge addresses both basic pedagogy—the "how" of teaching, generally acquired through education coursework and personal experiences—and content knowledge, or the "what" of teaching. Pedagogical content knowledge is a form of practical knowledge that is used by teachers to guide their actions in highly contextualized classroom settings. This form of practical knowledge entails (1) knowledge of how to structure and represent academic content for direct teaching; (2) knowledge of the common conceptions, misconceptions, and difficulties that students encounter when learning particular content; and (3) knowledge of the specific teaching strategies that can be used to address students' learning needs in particular classroom circumstances. Shulman 1987.

When a curriculum was mentioned: Barron et al. 2011.

children's educational television programs: We analyzed app descriptions for any mention of an underlying curriculum or alignment with standards such as the Common Core State Standards. We applied a liberal standard here; the description did not have to use the exact word "curriculum" (for example, "educational methodology"), and we marked an app for this feature even if the name of the curriculum was not stated or was clearly developed by the app's own development team.

A 2005 Kaiser Family Foundation report: For examples see D. R. Anderson 1998, "Educational Television Is Not an Oxymoron," *Annals of the American Academy of Political and Social Science* 557: 24–38, at http://www.researchgate.net/publication/240695961_Educational_Television_is_not_an_Oxymoron; S. M. Fisch and R. T. Truglio, 2000, *G Is for Growing: 30 Years of Research on Sesame Street* (New York: Lea's Communications Series), at http://eric.ed.gov/?id=ED450939; and A. A. Wilder, 1996, *Challenging the Active Minds of Children: Blue's Clues Curriculum Guide* (New York: Nickelodeon). "New Report" 2005.

In the 2014 *Learning at Home* report: Rideout 2014.

An incomplete list of well-known sites: This is adapted from Kathleen Costanza's post, "App Reviews to Help Choose Ed Tech This Holiday Season," *New America EdCentral* blog, December 18, 2014.

7

E-books: When Print Comes Alive

Paper has some amazing properties. It is light, flexible, easy to carry, and recovers well from mishaps. Accidentally spill a glass of water on it, and the text will still be readable after just a few dabs with a paper towel. A digital device, trust us, will not fare so well.

But *digital paper*—whether it is a touchscreen tablet, smartphone, e-reader, or computer—has many enviable properties too. It can be copied at no cost and sent through the air or a tiny wire at the speed of light. It can talk. It can display video, animations, and interactive diagrams. Its text and pictures can be changed in an instant by someone sitting halfway across the world.

The new landscape of the app marketplace has emerged from the dazzling promise of these new features, and the rapid rise of e-books has even deeper roots in the wonders of digitization. Software developers have been experimenting with electronic text since spellcheck was introduced into the word processing programs of IBM and TRS personal computers in the 1980s. Now, as the ease of the touchscreen replaces the awkwardness of the computer mouse, the possibilities of digital print and illustrations are open to children at younger and younger ages. Audio narrators can be embedded in the pages, illustrations can be opened with a click, words can be pressed to be spoken aloud, hidden dictionaries can deliver word definitions the second they are requested, and animations can be activated with the touch of a finger.

Today's eagerness for apps and e-books is also stirred by recognition of the limitations of parents' and teachers' busy lives. Would it not help to have a text that reads itself aloud so children who are not yet reading can hear a story on their own? Print dictionaries are heavy, cumbersome, and rarely nearby when you need them. Wouldn't it be nice to summon, with just the touch of a finger, a disembodied voice or text balloon that tells you what a word means? When young children start paying attention to the print under the illustrations, would it not be useful to have that print highlighted as each word is pronounced?

WHAT TO WATCH FOR IN CHILDREN'S E-BOOKS

These questions are not just idle curiosities. They carry urgency for children who are growing up without the benefits of kids in positions of privilege. They usher in new possibilities for children who have developmental delays, learning difficulties, or other special needs that make reading difficult. They raise the opportunity for teachers to bring moments of practice and individualized instruction to students who would otherwise be lost and unfocused during segments of the school day when teachers' attentions are divided. They could be allies in alleviating the quiet crisis of reading problems that permeate our country.

And they can also backfire. Literacy experts who study children's e-books emphasize the many caveats and qualifiers that come with pronouncements of the promise of e-books and apps. There are right ways to create interactive media for literacy learning, and there are wrong ways. At stake is a question that permeates this book: How do we ensure that digital media improves literacy instead of impeding it? Below we call out several elements that could lead to problems and many others that could make learning to read easier.

Hotspots and Other Distractions

In the early 2000s, two literacy education professors in Holland set up an experiment with forty-eight Dutch children, ages four and five. The professors, Maria de Jong and Adriana Bus of Leiden University, were comparing the impact of print and electronic versions of *P. B. Bear's Birthday Party*, a children's book by Lee Davis. They went into four classrooms and watched what happened across six 15-minute reading sessions. Back then, e-readers and touch-screen tablets did not exist; the e-version was a CD-ROM shown on a desktop computer. And it came with two options: children could have the book read to them, or they could press the "Playtime" button to play matching games, puzzles, and mazes associated with the book.

Some of the children were instructed not to touch that button. Others received no such guidance. Reflecting on the study's results years later, Bus described what happened:

> Most children completely ignored the oral text and just played games and activated the animations. In so far as they listened to the story text, they did not listen to the pages in order. They spent more than half of the available time (about 2 hours in total) on the attractive animations and games, and the rest of the time was alternated between animations and a film about the story that was presented without (oral) text. They rarely listened to the story text and if this occurred they focused on text fragments after clicking on a sentence probably because they liked the motorial activity [namely, using their fine motor skills]. As a result, most children heard the story text in a seemingly random order that was disconnected from the visualizations.

Let's face it: this is a pretty dismal scene for those who want children to learn new vocabulary, comprehend narrative, and start to recognize the way words and letters work to build sentences and shape ideas. They discovered that children with unrestricted access to "Playtime" struggled to recall the story line. They did not learn the meaning of new words in the book.

Other experiments show similar results. A 2002 study by Ofra Korat, a literacy professor at Bar Ilan University in Ramat Gan, Israel, found that when children used commercial e-books with embedded games, they "would stop in the middle of the story and play the game." In a study of three- to five-year-olds in the United States using e-books, the youngest children were especially affected by games and items to click. While the three-year-olds could recall superficial information such as the story's characters, lead author Julia Parish-Morris wrote, "They had a harder time understanding higher level aspects of story structure and story details."

One feature to be particularly aware of is the "hotspot," an interactive element of a book that begs to be touched. In children's e-books, the stars may sparkle and the trees rustle. Those tiny movements coax children to shift their gaze. All it takes is a little touch and the star goes shooting across the page and an owl pokes out from behind the branches. Many hotspots are "surprising and amusing," Bus wrote in a recent study, but they are "irrelevant to the story."

To be fair, these extras existed before the days of e-books and tablets. Pop-up books, for example, are full of delights. They are also, according to researchers at the University of Virginia, far worse for toddlers than regular books for learning words. E-book reviewers are becoming more alert to this problem. Last year, jurors for an international e-book competition called the Bologna Ragazzi Digital Awards gave demerits for those kind of incidentals. Chris Meade, a juror for the 2014 competition, said he saw "a lot of things being trotted out that were nothing more than some illustrations for you to jab." Warren Buckleitner, a founder of the awards, urged next year's contestants to "make sure the interactivity 'does work' for the narrative."

Supporting Children's Comprehension of the Plot

Alice Wilder, an educational media expert who tests products with children, has spent much of her career making distinctions between anywhere–everywhere interactivity versus what has become known as "interactivity on the plot line." She is best known for her work on the television show *Blue's Clues*, where her research with children as testers showed that young kids can learn from media when it is designed to engage their minds and encourages them to think and respond. (In *Blue's Clues*, the character Steve pauses throughout the show to give children a chance to yell their answers back, and independent peer-reviewed research has shown that strategy to work.) Wilder has witnessed creators in the industry who are not focused on literacy goals and do not know much about child development. They assume the only way to capture children's interest is to embed games, toys, and animations. "That will make them laugh and keep them coming back," she says, "but it may not do a thing to help children become stronger readers."

Wilder is now the chief content officer for Speakaboos, a company that makes e-books designed to promote literacy. She showed us a video of three boys reading a Humpty Dumpty e-book in which the creators were very purposeful about where they placed the moment of interactivity: not within the story but *just before the end*. Once Humpty Dumpty has his great fall, the narration of the book pauses. Pieces of the broken shell are shown on the bottom of the screen. They just might fit together to make Humpty Dumpty whole again.

"Can we fix him?" one boy asks.

"Do you think we can?" Wilder asks the boys.

"No we can't," says another, shaking his head. "He's broken."

The first boy puts his finger on a puzzle piece and moves it toward another. They click together and the image comes alive.

"Ooh," says Humpty Dumpty. "That's nice!"

The skeptical boy gasps, then smiles. The third boy exclaims, "We saved the day!"

The point, Wilder says, is to help children think about the narrative. The puzzle is not there because technology now enables puzzles in the pages of a book. The puzzle is there to assist with the meaning, to empower children to write the end themselves and "be the hero of the story."

Kids in Control: Use That Power Wisely

Some of the newest research on e-books is looking at where to place interactivity and how to use that feeling of empowerment effectively. In a recent doctoral dissertation, Rutgers University student Sheila Frye interviews elementary school children about their use of e-books. Consider this conversation between Frye (denoted as R) and a second-grade girl named Adriana reading a 2013 e-book of *The Three Little Pigs* by publisher Nosy Crow:

> Adriana is describing an early scene in the book where the wolf is eavesdropping on the little pigs before they leave their parents' house. Adriana was attentive to this scene and drew a strong conclusion about how the wolf knew that the young pigs would soon be out on their own, thus, making them easy targets for lunch:
>
> R: Now, did reading an interactive eBook help you to understand the story better?
>
> ADRIANA: (Nods)
>
> R: Ok, how? Or why?
>
> ADRIANA: (Long pause) They, they said some stuff that wasn't in the story.
>
> R: Hmmm. What do you mean by that? Can you tell me a little bit more about that? ... Or give me an example?
>
> ADRIANA: Um, in the beginning, um, when they were talking to their parents about moving, the wolf was in the window and I tapped on him and he said, "Shh, don't tell them that, that I'm here." (Smiles)
>
> R: Ohhhh! What do you think, what did that tell you? How did that information add to your understanding of the story?
>
> ADRIANA: Because then I knew, um, knew that he wanted to get the pigs. (Smiles)

Frye theorized that the hotspot helped with comprehension not only because the interactivity was on the plot line. It also, she explained, gave the reader a sense of control; the wolf didn't speak until he was tapped. "These affordances triggered Adriana to think deeply about the story and predict what would happen later," Frye wrote.

Yet even if an ability to control the screen can help, is there a time in the very earliest years of a child's life when e-books are just too much for them to handle? As we noted in chapter 2, the question of "How young is too young" for exposure to TV or videos has reverberated through child development circles for years. But now that media can be designed to respond to even a toddler's touch, scholars wonder how to be responsive to their desire for engagement while recognizing how much their still-developing brains can process.

Heather Kirkorian and Koeun Choi at the University of Wisconsin have been pushing the age boundary to find out. In 2012, they examined what happened when children between the ages of twenty-four and thirty-six months were introduced to new words on a touchscreen device compared to an in-person demonstration. They also compared the difference between enabling a child to touch anywhere on the screen versus requiring a child to click on a specific image linked to the word they were learning. When the toddlers touched anywhere, they later showed no sign of learning the new words. But they did learn new words after touching on the image that represented the word.

There are still many questions about how different kinds of children may respond to different features in different contexts. Not to mention the overarching question of how many digital enhancements are too much, especially at very young ages. Researchers are starting to delve into findings from scientists untangling the mystery of how the human brain processes information. One theory, for example, is that young children's brains may be at risk of cognitive overload in certain situations where they are urged to switch between multiple tasks.

A tension is emerging between the need to guide children through the story and the urge to try new features that empower but shift children's attention in nonlinear ways. Following the sequence of a narrative is a still-developing skill in the preschool years. Developers may need help in recognizing and respecting the hard work going on in children's minds as they learn to understand the images and words on the digital page.

HIGHLIGHTING PRINT ON SCREEN

All of this talk of hotspots and games might lead you to ask, Hey, what about print? Not news*print*, but print more broadly speaking, including the letters, words, spaces, and punctuation that make sentences and paragraphs. Learning to read, spell, and write would not be possible without exposure to and practice with print. Understanding the "conventions of print" is named as a key component of early literacy standards around the world. Simply put, without print, literacy would be a shell of itself, reduced to listening and speaking. Reading and writing would not exist.

Fortunately, screen media and print are in cahoots everywhere you look, whether in e-mail, video games, or text messaging—and of course, e-books. Electronics can allow print to be viewed in large font, to be floated across a video screen, and to be highlighted in sync with the utterance of words. Electronic print can come alive and literally talk to us. Do we know whether these features might help children learn to read?

Many signs point to yes, with decades of history and research to draw from. We owe a debt of gratitude, for example, to 1970s and '80s activists in the deaf and hard of hearing communities for pushing for closed captioning on television. At one point in the 1980s, the Sears & Roebuck Company was selling a Telecaption adapter for individual households, but it cost a whopping $200. Deaf activists pushed for broadcasters to adopt technologies that would transmit and present words on screen to accompany the words being uttered. Public broadcasting stations, such as WGBH in Boston, became centers for testing various technologies, and by 1990, US law required all televisions to have a built-in decoder chip to accept the transmissions. Closed captioning, also called subtitling, is now seen as a quintessential example of Universal Design for Learning, the idea that products and spaces should be designed for *all* abilities and that doing so will lead to better outcomes for everyone, not just those with disabilities. What's more, subtitles enable immediate translation between different languages; for example, they allow English speakers to understand video recorded in Spanish, and vice versa.

In the 1980s, researchers started to design experiments to test whether the presence of captions on TV could help children learn to read. An early study experimented with classrooms full of second graders watching four- to six-minute clips of the children's TV show *Pinwheel*, (a variety show for older kids, but similar in many respects to *Sesame Street)* that aired on Nickelodeon. The results were promising. They showed that captions not only helped children recognize words and learn their meanings but also helped children transfer that learning, comprehending sentences that used the same words used in new contexts.

More robust research followed. Much of it is based on *Between the Lions*, a TV show created by the public television station WGBH and the independent production company Sirius Thinking Ltd. The episodes took place in a library modeled after the iconic lions of the New York Public Library and chronicled the adventures of a family of puppet-like lions who sang songs and read books during their daily adventures. Every song within the show featured text on screen. When Cleo Lion crooned about the beauty of *sh* at the Hush-Hush-a-Bye Club, those two letters floated near Cleo's face and merged with *ush* to make *shush*. In a musical number about homophones, *read* and *red*, *here* and *hear*, and many other pairs appeared on the screen synchronized with the moment they were sung. Every episode contained one or more short stories in the form of books read by the Lion family. According to Christopher Cerf, a cofounder of Sirius, "The stories were an essential part of the show as they tied in thematically with the rest of the episode and became an important way to present words with the featured sound in context." Like its predecessor *Reading Rainbow*, which starred LeVar Burton reading selected stories and which, by the way, has been reborn as an app, *Between the Lions* featured real books or well-known tales like "Rumpelstiltskin and "The Little Red Hen."

Deborah Linebarger, an education professor who is now at Purdue University, has conducted myriad experiments on how children learn from print on screen. With *Between the Lions*, she tested its effectiveness in kindergarten and preschool across a range of settings from Pennsylvania to Mississippi to Native American reservations in New Mexico. Preschool and kindergarten viewers performed better on early literacy and reading tests than children who did not watch the show. And an eye-tracking study of the show determined that the text highlighted during the read-alouds worked to focus children's attention on the words as they were being read. The show is now off the air, but clips are available on PBS and YouTube (http://pbskids.org/lions/videos/).

Today, the possibilities go far beyond TV shows with captions. Today, in digital form, text can appear anywhere and be manipulated in multiple ways. For example, text highlighting synched with narration—sometimes called bi-modal text—has become commonplace in reading software used in elementary schools and is a sought-after feature in children's digital picture books. Each letter, word, or sentence can be highlighted as it is spoken. In some cases, words and letters can be activated by a click or touch of the finger. Some words go bold or light up, inviting users to press or click on them. A quick touch and they open windows with definitions or audio recordings to hear pronunciations. The words themselves have become interactive gateways to more information.

The free website Starfall (Starfall.com) uses bi-modal text to teach early literacy skills and coaxes its users to start with very simple stories such as Zac the Rat, which emphasizes the short *a* sound. Hover the cursor over any word and it is highlighted in yellow. Click on the word and a writing space opens. Each letter turns red as its sound is uttered by a woman's voice: "Er. Ah. Tuh. Rat." For click-happy children, if the word *rat* is clicked yet again, Zac dances a little jig.

Starfall attracted a wide following after its launch in 2002, spurring the launch of Starfall Education, a company that produces curricular materials. By now, thirteen years later, it is by no means the only source of reading programs for children that use text highlighting. The past decade has brought a flurry of school-based software products and digital learning systems that contain similar features from companies like ABCMouse, Hatch, Footsteps2Brilliance, Pearson's SuccessMaker, TeacherMate, and more. Many e-book publishers and e-book subscription services are using the features too, including OceanHouse Media, OneMoreStory, MyOn, RazKids, Speakaboos, Storia, Tumblebooks, and new names appearing each year.

WHO (OR WHAT) IS DOING THE SCAFFOLDING?

If you are an educator, you have probably spent some time considering scaffolding, and not the plywood-and-platforms kind. Coined by psychologist Jerome Bruner in the late 1950s to describe an essential process of oral language development, "scaffolding" has become common terminology in education schools and professional development programs around the world. Teachers today are trained to scaffold students' learning. After identifying a learner's exact level of skill or conceptual understanding, teachers are supposed to provide just enough guidance and support to help them reach the next level and eventually arrive at mastery.

Scaffolding is a popular term among people who design educational technology too. The text highlighting we just described, for example, is often described as a scaffold for learning. But just as the scaffolding used to construct a building is temporary, instructional scaffolding is supposed to be temporary as well. Eventually a student has to be able to stand on his own, showing enough competency at one level *without help* to be able to reach for the next level and being to achieve enough success *with help* to reach a further level, and so on. The technological features of e-books and digital texts beg the question: What happens if the scaffolding never comes down?

Let's consider the use of audio in e-books. Audiobooks have been around for years, and many readers probably remember their own school days of sitting in the reading corner of a classroom, headphones on, listening to narrators read books while following along with the print versions in our laps. Today's e-books allow for the same scenario, but with even more personalization (enabling students to pause and replay individual words, for example) and visuals to match (such as seeing the print highlighted or watching a short animation of a character's action). These features can be incredibly helpful for beginning readers, struggling readers, students with visual impairments, students with dyslexia, and anyone else who has difficulty reading text or following storylines.

Several years ago, Lisa met Julie Hume, a reading specialist in University City, Missouri, who was experimenting with Tumblebooks, an e-book service offering children's picture books with "Read to me" features, text highlighting, and animation. Hume had been working with dozens of elementary school children who were struggling to read fluently. They seemed to know how to decode but when they read out loud they would get so stuck on certain words that by the time they finished a sentence they had forgotten what they were reading about. When Hume heard about Tumblebooks from a teacher at another school, she said to herself, "We need this."

"When students repeatedly have a strong model of the fluency, the more they hear that, the better they get it," Hume said. When children listen to narration that helps them connect to the words on the page, she said, "the hardest part of the fluency is being taken away, so they are able to focus on understanding the text, which is what you want." She raised grant money to buy a subscription and experimented with it among half of her students. The other half continued with the regular interventions. By the end of the semester, she said, the children using the e-books had progressed significantly faster than the others.

And when do they stop using the "Read to me" feature? That, Hume said, is an important question for teachers. In her case, she saw several students progress "from the picture book phase to the chapter book phase." They moved out of the intervention sessions, which used Tumblebooks, and back to their regular classrooms, which did not. It was time, she said, to "let that group loose." "We knew," she added, "that if we kept handholding them they wouldn't push themselves. I think Tumblebooks should be for intervention only."

It may be too early to know whether this kind of approach will become the norm, let alone the most effective, for today's classrooms. But Jeremy Brueck, an early education and e-book expert at the University of Akron, has witnessed many elementary school teachers making decisions about how and when students should use different kinds of e-books and e-book features. Most frequently, he said, their decisions are based on what they know about students' individual reading levels. "A good teacher," Brueck said, "would have informal assessment and evaluation going on" to alert her to situations in which she would need to redirect a student. For example, most children Brueck has observed in first- and second-grade classrooms are choosing "Read to me" instead of "Read it myself," not challenging themselves to move to more independent reading. Teachers, he said, are aware of that, and after seeing children gravitate to the e-book table repeatedly they might steer them to a physical book that can only be read by the children themselves. Good teachers, he said, know how to "make sure the kid isn't just being entertained."

Prompts, Guides, and Individualized Feedback

What about features and functions that are, in many ways, trying to simulate the behavior of teachers or parents? What about a book that pauses its narration to prompt, guide, and motivate children to think about what they have just read or heard read to them? Software can provide immediate feedback to students as they take online quizzes; online games can encourage children to take on greater and greater challenges in virtual worlds. Some game-based learning products for older students are growing increasingly sophisticated in providing immediate, personalized feedback, and many elementary school educators are using games to assess student performance on basic skills. The Cooney Center's recent national survey of teachers' uses of games in the K–8 classroom, for example, found that most teachers who used digital games valued their capacity to both engage students and provide real-time assessments of student mastery, thus making scaffolding more precise based on individual needs.

Could books become better at interactive questioning than the parents reading with their children on the couch? Research studies have quoted parents as saying that they don't need to be with kids when they use tablets because the tablets do all the interaction for them. Maybe parents have a very good reason for believing that technology is taking over their roles.

The Dutch researchers you met at the beginning of this chapter have had the same thoughts. Although evidence abounds on the distracting nature of some hotspots and games embedded in e-books, other studies have shown that children were able to learn new vocabulary more readily when using e-books rather than traditional books. Could it be that children were learning words from embedded dictionaries and embedded quizzes despite the interruptions?

In 2010, Adriana Bus teamed up with Daisy J. H. Smeets, also at Leiden University, to set up an experiment. They used five Dutch storybooks designed for kindergartners that were available in electronic format. Each book started with a "computer pal" who exclaimed, "Hi! Nice to see you! We are going to read a story together." A few of the books, however, were designed to do more than simply read the story aloud. They included moments in which the computer pal would pop up and say, "Time for a question!" Children were then prompted to answer questions about what had just been read to them. For example, in a book titled *Bear Is in Love with Butterfly*, the computer says, "Bear is shy. Where can you see that?" and then prompts children to choose from a multiple-choice array of pictures that originated from the story: bear being broken-hearted, bear being shy, and bear being angry. Some books sprinkled these questions throughout the story; other books included them only at the end.

Smeets and Bus tested which version would have the biggest impact on children's word-learning. They brought twenty kindergartners into their lab to experience the books. They randomly assigned some children to read the books with multiple-choice questions and some children to read the straight e-book versions. Then they quizzed the kids on their vocabulary knowledge.

The results showed that both groups of children learned new words, but the gains were greater for those given multiple-choice questions. Whether the questions were peppered through the story or placed at the end did not matter. The additional word learning, the researchers wrote, "is comparable to the reported additive value of adult questions during adult-child book sharing." Surprisingly, the vocabulary tests showed that children even gained the ability to pronounce the new words despite the fact that they did not practice doing so. In fact, the children were not asked to speak aloud at all while reading the book; to answer the questions they simply had to click on the right pictures.

A few years later, in 2013, Sesame Workshop, the nonprofit organization where Michael works, started to try another tech-assisted way of introducing children to new words. In this case, the company did not use a "computer pal." But it did seek to simulate what might happen if an adult was with a child pointing out and labeling the objects all around them. In Big Bird's Words, an augmented reality "Word-o-Scope"—acting as a digital eye—captures pictures of objects and words that are in the environment, such as milk and eggs, and then speaks those words aloud in Big Bird's voice using text-to-speech software. The app so far recognizes fifteen hundred words and can speak five hundred of them by name. After hearing a word, children can go deeper and click on information about what the word means and hear other words that are in the same family. Sesame Workshop conducted research on the software's impact and found that a few dozen preschoolers who were exposed to the app had a 40 percent increase in their ability to identify the target words.

SCALING UP: JUST THE BEGINNING

Is anyone examining whether these things work in the broader population with thousands of children? Actually, yes. A few studies are underway to measure the impact of comprehensive learning systems and school-based software programs that use these techniques and features. Though these systems are not yet attempting to deliver the augmented reality of Big Birds Words, most of them do take advantage of audio, text highlighting, and embedded dictionaries. The Napa County School District in California, for example, has started a five-year study to track the effects of Footsteps2Brilliance, which has been offered to every family with a preschool child in Napa County. Results from pilot programs show literacy growth for many preschool children, especially those from families where English is not the first language. In Utah, a program called UPSTART is delivering computer-based literacy instruction to more than a thousand preschool-age children in their homes. Evaluations show that the more children use UPSTART, the more they advance in tests of early literacy compared to children who do not use the program.

To give you a sense of the type of research likely to come, consider the case of the app-based learning system called Learn with Homer, which was the subject of a recent study of its impact during the downtime of summer vacation. Literacy and learning experts have long worried about the phenomenon of a "summer reading slide" for low-income students. Started by Stephanie Dua, the former chief executive officer of the New York City Fund for the Public Schools, Learn from Homer was designed to help learners who often lose ground to their more well-resourced peers. "I knew there was a lot of great research on how to teach children to read," said Dua in a recent *Forbes* interview. "But when my own daughter wanted to learn, I couldn't find any suitable materials for parents."

That's when Learn with Homer was born. It brings a mix of proven early learning techniques—story time, rich vocabulary and background knowledge content across content domains, and skills practice—together in one app. *Forbes* blogger Jordan Shapiro, a professor at Temple University who specializes in digital literacy, likes the combination: "It does some of the same things a good kindergarten or pre-school teacher would. It combines learning to read with learning to understand the world." Kids are not only learning what the letter *A* sounds like and that "alligator" starts with *A*, but also taking virtual "field trips" to the zoo, where they learn about alligators. They can also create and publish their own pictures, record their own voices, and listen to stories that emphasize the letters, sounds, and ideas. Then, Shapiro adds, "Parents can track progress, look at a Pinterest like board of drawings, and brag about their kids' genius on Facebook."

On advice from Michael, the company teamed up with literacy expert Susan B. Neuman of New York University to assess the app's impact. Neuman spent six weeks in the summer of 2014 monitoring how four- and five-year-olds in seven Brooklyn preschool classrooms were learning how to read. Half the students were given unsupervised access to Learn with Homer, while the others were given a math app as a control. At the beginning of the study, each set of students scored equally on the standardized Test of Preschool Early Literacy (TOPEL). When tested again six weeks later, the students who used Learn with Homer for approximately fifteen minutes each day saw their scores double in the area of phonological awareness, while the control group scored lower in this area. The Learn with Homer group also significantly improved in recognizing concepts of print.

Perhaps most encouraging: the children in the study came from economically disadvantaged areas, and in most cases had little or no previous exposure to iPads and other touchscreen devices. Rather than distract, Neuman said the app and touch-based interface is causing her to consider "whether this type of learning can encourage concentration for children." In a recent conversation we had with Neuman, she argued that "well-researched, well-designed media tools have huge potential, when well deployed by teachers and parents, to make a really big difference in helping struggling readers do better."

LEARNING TOGETHER: E-BOOKS PLUS

Hearing about these positive early findings, you now may be wondering more than ever: Where does this leave the teacher, let alone the parent?

Over in Israel, at Bar-Ilan University, Ofra Korat is wrestling with this question. Lisa caught up with Korat, the literacy professor we mentioned earlier in this chapter, via a pixelated conversation on Skype one late afternoon when Korat was working from home. As we talked, she alternated between Hebrew and English while chatting with her husband, who passed through the kitchen and said he liked to hear his wife talk about her obsession with e-books. Given her long experience with the good and bad of e-books, we asked her, What did you make of these studies that show positive impact with the use of the e-book or app alone? Could Adriana Bus's computer pal study, for example, be a sign that adults are no longer needed?

There are valuable insights in that study, she told us—the international e-book community is small and she's been friends with Bus for years—but Korat said we should consider media in the context of schools and families too. Letting e-books do the work that printed books typically leave to adults, "that's one way to think about it," Korat said. But she would prefer to consider whether e-books could be harnessed to engage adults at the same time. "Sometimes difficult words in e-books are difficult even for the parents," she explained. Interactive e-books could enable them to learn those words along with their kids. Besides, it is not unusual to find households in which the e-book is first read by the parent and child, and then the child rereads it independently. In scenarios like these, maybe children could learn even more with an e-book that first encourages Mom or Dad to be in the loop on the learning?

Five years ago, Korat and her Bar-Ilan University colleague Tal Or started digging into that question. They decided to test whether parents would change their behaviors with their children depending on the type of book they were reading together. Part 1 of their experiment looked at mother–child interactions with an e-book versus print book. Part 2 examined whether two different kinds of e-books—one designed by the professors to be educational and another sold as a popular commercial product—would elicit two different kinds of behaviors.

Korat and Or brought the books to the homes of forty-eight middle-class families, set up video cameras to record their interactions, and asked them to read together "as they deemed fit." Their hypothesis was that the e-books would prompt interactions because they had more sophisticated features than print books, such as interactive dictionaries and the ability to listen to an oral recording of the story with the text highlighted on the screen. Those features, they expected, would prompt the mothers to "mediate" the experience for their kids at a higher level by sparking dialogue beyond what appeared on the screen.

But when they carefully examined the videos later, they were surprised at what they saw. It turned out that the e-book–using mothers were *less* likely to expand on the content in the book than those who used print books. This reduction happened in three ways: moms were less likely to talk about the meaning of words, less likely to relate the text to personal experience ("Do you remember your father bought you a kite like this?"), and less likely to promote comprehension by elaborating on the text.

Korat said once she and her coauthor saw the interactions, the findings made perfect sense. The e-book did not leave much for the parent to do, whereas with the printed book, "the parent did provide a lot of support, extending the text, supporting the child beyond the text," she said. "There was a lot of talk between the parent and the child and more frequent utterances about the storyline—more even than in the situation of the educational ebook."

Research conducted in the United States tells a similar story. A 2012 study conducted by the Joan Ganz Cooney Center set out to determine whether the benefits of "co-viewing" and joint media engagement extended to parents reading digital books with their kids. Thirty-two pairs of parents and their three- to six-year-old children were asked to read a print book and an e-book together, with half reading a basic e-book and the other half reading an e-book "enhanced" with animation, hotspots, and other interactive experiences. The enhanced e-books led to observably different co-reading experiences than print and basic e-books. With enhanced e-books, parents spent time telling their kids what to press and click rather than talking with them about the story. Children's comprehension went down, a finding that matched the e-book study by Parish-Morris at Temple University. It was a distressing discovery.

"The role of the adult in the new era of digital storybooks," as Bus wrote last year, "seems to be a highly complicated issue." Is the science trying to tell us that print books are good for parent-child interaction, but that kids might as well read (or listen to, or watch) e-books by themselves?

Before we jump to that conclusion, remember that the study by Korat and Or had two parts. In the second half of the experiment, researchers tested what happened when parents interacted with their children around an educational book versus a commercial one. The commercial book was *Grandma and Me,* by Mercer Mayer. The educational book was *Hatractor Beargaz Hachol* (*The Tractor in the Sandbox*), which was designed to promote early literacy with an oral reading, embedded definitions of difficult words, dynamic visuals that dramatize the storyline, the highlighting of text, and words that, when clicked, are spoken aloud in an intentional way so that one can hear the syllables and sounds within. Korat and Or called these features "scaffolding mechanisms."

When they reviewed the tapes of parents' interactions around these two books, they picked up some significant differences. In this case, just as they had hypothesized, the educational book led to more expansive talk on the part of parents. The words in the tractor story were more difficult than in *Grandma and Me,* and the embedded dictionary included elaborations that "may have directed the mothers to expand the discussion about the story, including word meanings." The education book seems to have influenced the mothers, Korat suggests, to talk to their kids differently.

Consider the implications: here we have evidence that the design of a book just might be teaching parents as much (maybe even more) than it is teaching kids. Originally, "we didn't think about this, and yet we found this higher level," Korat said. "The ebook itself was an instructor to the parent." It just had to be created to truly foster learning. Another Israeli e-book study, conducted with some of the same materials but larger numbers of children, shows the promise of an e-book-plus-adult approach. The educational e-book plus "augmentation by adult instruction," wrote lead author Ora Segal-Drori, led children to gain the most.

Now Korat is conducting similar experiments with low-income families, working with scholars around the world, and talking to officials within the education agencies of the Israeli government to consider ways to use educational e-books as a way to promote parent engagement. It will be interesting to see whether the practices extend to all sorts of book-reading, in e-format or not. "We see that the e-books are a possible bridge not only to the child," she said, "but also to the parents."

NOTES

two literacy education professors in Holland: de Jong and Bus 2002.

Reflecting on the study's results: Bus, Takacs, and Kegel 2015.

They did not learn the meaning: Ibid., 12.

A 2002 study by Ofra Korat: Shamir and Korat, 2006.

In a study of three- to five-year-olds: Parish-Morris et al. 2013, 206.

Many hotspots are "surprising and amusing": Bus et al. 2015, 10.

They are also: Tare et al. 2010.

Chris Meade: Buckleitner 2013.

Warren Buckleitner: Ibid.

That will make them laugh: Phone interview with Alice Wilder on January 12, 2015.

where to place interactivity: Frye 2014, 48.

These affordances triggered Adriana: Ibid., 49.

they did learn new words: Kirkorian et al. 2014.

One theory: For more on the cognitive costs of switching tasks, see the special issue (in press) of *Developmental Review* titled "Living in the 'Net' Generation: Multitasking, Learning, and Development."

At one point in the 1980s: *Convergence of Text with Television 2010* by Gregory J. Downey from John Hopkins University Press (Baltimore) at https://jhupbooks.press.jhu.edu/content/closed-captioning.

Public broadcasting stations: Media Access Group.

by 1990, US law required: Robson 2004, 33.

Universal Design for Learning: Center for Applied Special Technology.

In the 1980s, researchers started to design experiments: "Text on Screen" 2008.

The stories were an essential part of the show: Interview with Christopher Cerf, January 31, 2015.

Preschool and kindergarten viewers performed better: Linebarger 2001; Linebarger et al. 2014.

an eye-tracking study: "Text on Screen" 2008.

children using the e-books had progressed: For more about Julie Hume and her mini- experiment with Tumblebooks, see Lisa Guernsey, "Are EBooks Any Good?" *School Library Journal*, June 7, 2011, at http://www.slj.com/2011/06/books-media/ebooks/are-ebooks-any-good/.

Jeremy Brueck: For more, see Jeremy S. Brueck and Lisa A. Lenhart, "E-Books and TPACK: What Teachers Need to Know" in *The Reading Teacher* 68, no. 5 (February 2015): 373–76.

The Cooney Center's recent national survey: Takeuchi and Vaala, 2014.

other studies have shown: Smeets and Bus 2012, 2.

The additional word learning: Ibid., 9.

Sesame Workshop conducted research: Brooks and Moon 2013.

Footsteps2Brilliance: Letter to Lisa Guernsey from Barbara Nemko, Napa County Superintendent of Schools, November 5, 2014.

Evaluations show: "Utah UPSTART," 2013.

when my own daughter wanted to learn: Shapiro 2013.

Parents can track progress: Ibid.

They significantly improved: "Study Shows" 2014.

she argued: Interview with Susan Neuman on December 18, 2014.

It turned out: Korat and Or 2010, 146–47.

There was a lot of talk: Skype Interview with Ofra Korat on December 18, 2014.

The enhanced e-books: Chiong et al. 2012.

Children's comprehension went down: Parish-Morris et al. 2013.

The role of the adult: Bus et al. 2015

The educational e-book: Segal-Drori et al. 2010, 924.

8

From Talking Toys to Watson: Dreaming Up Tech for Tomorrow's Readers

Current technologies will continue to evolve, and as research starts to show what works and what doesn't, we hope they will have a positive impact in the years ahead.

As we scanned the current landscape of apps and e-books, we also wanted to peer into laboratories of invention to see what might be around the bend. In this chapter, we offer a brief glimpse of some up-and-coming technologies that proponents see as having potential to make a significant contribution in early literacy. We asked the question that innovators often contemplate when trying to invent a solution for a vexing problem. What if? So we cast our net widely to talk with people who are undertaking bold experiments in designing and developing educational technologies and literacy applications. (And no we aren't talking about embedding a chip in your child's prefrontal cortex.) We spoke with technology experts, creators, engineers, and scientists who are thinking about media's impact and building technologies that might lead us in completely unexpected directions. We were seeking answers for young children who are struggling the most—those 2 million kids every year who are not reading well by the time they enter fourth grade.

Some of these scientists and creators are on the front lines of important debates about how our always-on culture may be changing the way we think and communicate—a key component of understanding the literacy landscape of the future. Others are introducing "far-out" technologies like the world's smartest supercomputer and toys capable of sophisticated conversations with young children. These experts' work isn't yet known by most parents or educators, but their insights might one day soon help transform literacy experiences for our kids.

Our team, led by Anna Ly, a twenty-something tech developer and design scientist, scoured the field to document these futuristic ideas, interviewing two dozen industry lab leaders and university-based innovators to examine the potential that new technologies such as artificially intelligent tutors, voice recognition software, and wearable digital devices might have for literacy learning in the next decade, or by the time our class of 2030 is in high school. As we heard their stories, we couldn't help but see practical challenges, resource and design constraints. We also recognized these pioneers' dogged patience and humility—much of the work we heard about included years of failures and close calls, and each has survived the healthy skepticism of colleagues and funders. But in a technology culture that's continually looking for the next big thing, these experts expect some of the best answers to emerge from new frontiers of science and technology, often through serendipity and unexpected breakthroughs.

AN EVOLUTIONARY SHIFT?

Technologists, neuroscientists, clinicians, and learning researchers from Cambridge, Massachusetts, to Palo Alto, California, have been propelled by national concern over mass education failure. Why are two out of three fourth graders in the wealthiest country on Earth lacking literacy proficiency? Why is the United States treading water while our international competitors are soaring ahead in math, science, and engineering? Are our school and university models designed for maximum impact or a vestige of a twentieth-century mind-set? And, of course, is our cultural immersion in mass media and ubiquitous technologies a time dump, a key barrier to future leadership in a global economy?

Gaining answers to these vexing questions in the near term may be difficult. Is it possible that we are at a historic crossroads in the social culture of learning? As media literacy experts such as Elizabeth Thoman and the Digital Age literacy critic Sven Birkerts have written, perhaps we are in an evolutionary period of change. We are fascinated by this prospect and a related debate that has embroiled scholars and pundits. Does the phenomenon of being always connected dictate that our children will likely be engaged in shallower, less satisfying academic and social interactions? Have the new millennial parents, having grown up in a media-saturated world, already changed their daily interactions in ways that are damaging to the literacy competencies of their offspring? We earnestly hope not. But the debate, and the arguments of some of its most relevant protagonists, is worth digging into. The work of the reading scholar Maryanne Wolf, whom you met at the beginning of this book, is central to the evolutionary shift. Wolf points out that reading "isn't something we're born to do—it's something we train our brains to do." She says we rewire parts of our brain and build new circuits as we learn to read. But something interesting is happening as we use new technologies for the process of reading. Because so much of it is in short-form snippets—texts, e-mails, blogs, and multimedia that demand multi-tasking and interrupted flow, Wolf argues that the circuits we're currently building in our brain are different than those we build when we read long-form books printed on paper. She wonders whether humans may eventually be less equipped to digest complex texts.

The Isolating Effects of Too Much Technology

Other experts on technological change and social behavior have complementary, albeit separate concerns—often encapsulated by the work of clinical psychologist Sherry Turkle of the Massachusetts Institute of Technology (MIT). Her book, *Alone Together*, explores how new technology is changing the way we communicate with one another. In a 2012 interview she told NPR's Terry Gross, "The pull of these devices is so strong, that we've become used to them faster than anyone would have suspected." Her research documents how devices are changing the way parents relate to their children, how friends interact, and why many people, both young and old, keep their devices in hand all the time, even as they sleep.

Turkle believes that short-form literacy experiences such as text messaging and rapid response social postings (think Facebook) are hollowing out social relationships among teens and young adults. Face-to-face interaction teaches "skills of negotiation, of reading each other's emotion, of having to face the complexity of confrontation, dealing with complex emotion," Turkle says. A related line of concern is that if parents are immersed in their own devices over dinner or during evenings with their children, won't key moments for literacy development be sacrificed? The study we described in chapter 2 that observed fifty-five caregivers at fast food restaurants in Boston found a high degree of absorption in devices. In other words, an evolution toward being "alone together" is not so conducive to the rich literacy bath of engaged, back-and-forth conversation that is essential for young children's learning. Wolf's and Turkle's related laments are cause for real concern. Are technologies causing changes that will make engaged parenting, contemplative thought, social interaction, and deeper learning harder and harder?

Perhaps, but perhaps not. Other experts have a different take. Communications and literacy scholars such as Henry Jenkins, Justine Cassell, Faith Rogow, and Marilyn Jager Adams, while sharing some concerns, welcome the potential of digital media to help transform children's literacy skills. In chapter 4 we saw children using media tools not only to watch or listen, but to participate, to narrate their own stories, to explore new interests and to become "makers." This act of participation and making meaning with new tools is what these experts hope will make literacy in a Digital Age more personally compelling and a useful basis for productive career paths.

Cassell, a scholar who has focused on kids with autism and assistive technologies who is now vice provost for Technology Strategy at Carnegie Mellon University, and Marilyn Jager Adams, an expert on children's literacy at Brown University, are pioneers in methods such as voice recognition software development and the use of artificial intelligence to design useful educational interventions. They credit the rapidly evolving technology landscape for a blossoming, not a diminution of literacy experiences. In the past decade, a slew of technologies and applications have popped up to create what Henry Jenkins of the University of Southern California calls a "participatory culture." Through YouTube and Instagram, people of all ages can upload their video and photo creations online to eager followers who comment, share, and tweet their perspectives. Social media and networking forums and thousands of websites allow for personal writing, fan fiction, and carefully curated portfolios of transmedia creations to be published. Open software products such as Scratch, created by MIT's Lifelong Kindergarten group, have led millions of users across the globe, with children as young as four or five, to design their own games and puzzles. With the explosion of mobile phones and their accommodating operating systems and app stores, children can now capture and write or record comments about what they want to share anytime, anywhere with the press of a button.

With the increasing availability of these tools, Cassell believes that kids are spending "more time with words than ever," and that they are using that time "writing more than ever before." With the refinement of new tools and the release of the iPad in 2010 with its easy-to-use interface, a more participatory culture is indeed spreading to the below-eight-year-old set. With a swipe, a three-year-old child can chop vegetables for a monster, strike a musical note in a lullaby, or paint a branch in a sunny landscape. A six-year-old can use a storytelling app such as Toontastic to narrate, videotape, and publish his own character-rich short story about pirates in his neighborhood. Production of text, art, videos, and other forms have become more common than simply consuming media online, evoking an evolutionary shift through which kids can cultivate their own new narratives and new audiences. To Cassell, reading in a digital age comes down to a new approach: learning each of the traditional foundational literacies (reading, listening, speaking, and writing), but with a new twist. The participatory tools that Jenkins and others have noted as transmedia opportunities now offer a young child a better toolkit "to explain what is in their head for someone who is not in their head." And with that, Cassell says, the "meaning of literacy has changed."

Adams sees promise in tools that can build oral language and literacy skills for students, literally enabling them to talk to texts and have their read-alouds reviewed by computers that can record and assist with words students do not know or struggle to pronounce. For more than two decades, she closely observed the promise and failures of speech recognition software development. The wide variation in young children's voice and speech patterns has made it very hard to develop anything that would have wide application in schools and at home—until now. Voice recognition has already seeped into everyday life through mobile "personal assistants" like iPhone's Siri and Google's GoogleNow. Though the use of the current generation of speech recognition tools is currently largely restricted to supporting children with special needs, beginning in upper elementary school, the sophistication and accuracy of these tools are now on the cusp of being helpful to younger children. Soon we may see these tools applied to help kids as young as four or five practice oral language and reading skills.

Adams sees the benefits of new technologies in historical terms. In a recent white paper she wrote, "Throughout history, educational aspirations and opportunities have been driven by advances in technology. Reciprocally, at least for those countries that have prospered most with each technological surge, advances in technology have quantitatively and qualitatively increased educational access or delivery in response." She adds, "With the invention of writing and then of the alphabet, with the invention of the printing press and the Renaissance it fueled, with the scientific and philosophical tools of the Enlightenment, with the productivity, infrastructure, and innovations of the Industrial Revolution—with each great technological shift, educational attainment has risen alongside." Today, Adams says, technological innovations in early reading are ripe for "breakthroughs we haven't seen in decades."

NEXT GEN LITERACY TOOLS

Knowing that much remains to be considered in the debate between those who imagine young learners with digital tools at their fingertips and those who worry they will be "alone together," we have briefly taken out our own version of a crystal ball. We asked this generation's digital world explorers to tell us about their dreams for a seamless relationship between humans and advanced media and technology. Their goal: to create an interactive, personalized, enjoyable learning experience, based on the best human-centered design projects evolving from academic labs and industry upstarts. If we are going to get the evolutionary shift right, we must recognize that the meaning of literacy has indeed changed, but we must also remain committed to a society where every child—with no exceptions—will be a capable reader, creator, and engaged curator of the world's information.

Our team identified promising work underway in many places around the United States and the world. We have chosen to highlight three cases in different stages of development, all of which might be experienced by members of our class of 2030. To add tint and texture, we provide glimpses into where these explorers are situated: one in a startup company, a second in a world-renowned academic lab, and a third in one of the world's most iconic corporate labs. So permit us to introduce three next generation ideas—from talking toys to finger wearables to the world's smartest super-computer. While the projects we describe may still seem pretty far-out, let your imagination run wild.

Creating Conversation with Toy Story Panache

For our first case, we want to be upfront: because Michael and Anna's work is closely connected to Sesame Workshop, we have a unique opportunity to see and experience (and admittedly become fascinated by) forthcoming projects that involve Sesame Street and the larger global nonprofit's divisions. One of those projects is emerging from a new partnership with ToyTalk, a startup company developing technology that endows computerized characters with enough speech recognition technology to hold a conversation with young audiences. The two organizations have agreed to produce mobile applications for preschoolers that will leverage ToyTalk's proprietary voice recognition technology. The new apps will showcase Muppet characters who can understand preschool children's speech patterns and use artificial intelligence and prerecorded dialogue to respond to the children, creating a once unimaginable, personal, tech-enabled conversation.

ToyTalk was founded in 2011 by Oren Jacob and Martin Reddy, former executives at Pixar. The company currently has its own set of apps, such as The Winston Show, SpeakaTreat, SpeakaLegend, and SpeakaZoo, in which the user can talk with the characters. These apps, which typically cost around $3, go beyond the usual linear media experience by providing a dynamic interaction in which the toy listens to a child's answers and responds in a way that allows for genuine back-and-forth conversation. These are the types of "serve and return" interactions that developmental psychologists and neuroscientists say build lasting relationships and brainpower.

When launching SpeakaZoo on the iPad, a pointy porcupine pops onto the screen with a zookeeper's voice asking the user to press the microphone when talking to the animals. The porcupine launches into a conversation, mentioning that he is sad. When a child asks why, the porcupine picks up the word *why* and responds appropriately, telling the child that he wants a hug. If the child murmurs a response that is out of sync, the animal recognizes that the words aren't relevant and cleverly steers the conversation back by saying,

"Oh, that's nice, but I still need a hug." Once in dialogue, the porcupine will continue to probe the child, asking, for example, for a description of how hugs feel. ToyTalk's Winston Show app features the same type of conversational tango, but the app's content is doled out through weekly episodes that have a storyline. A child who plays with the app can watch as her character shapes the narrative, while brandishing the oral language and listening skills that are essential for effective communication.

Though the company was not founded to develop educational apps, Jacob and his colleagues are intrigued by the potential to help educate young children with new tools that have never been used at mass scale. What's truly interesting is that the technology uses real-time play experiences to refine the voice recognition algorithms. The app will be offering Toy Story-like engagement while getting smarter and helping the ToyTalk team to provide richer conversations.

So far the early Sesame prototypes aren't tasked to tell the child whether or not they said a particular word correctly or whether they can read a word they don't know—both valuable features for oral language and literacy development. That type of interaction relies on yet-unrefined language tutoring technology that may not hit the market for another five years. Rather, Muppets will talk like the characters they represent on *Sesame Street*, but with a conversational twist. For example, Elmo might point out an orange on the screen, cleverly noting that it and several other objects are a round shape. He asks his new friend—a four-year-old who has seen his favorite character and is intrigued—to name some other objects he knows that are round. Questions are designed to elicit familiar or predictable responses to ensure that a child has a seamless experience.

Over time, the number of children who use this popular app will make the voice recognition technologies smarter. By collecting the children's voices and speech patterns in a growing database, the ToyTalk and Sesame research and engineering teams will continually iterate to improve the experience. The effort will take time.

Preschool-age children commonly have speech impediments, garbled pronunciation, different tones of voices, and varied conversational speeds. A fascinating dilemma that ToyTalk raises for educators and parents is how to fairly recognize and balance the contributions of the crowd (in this instance, the thousands of young voices that will improve the technology) with the understandable drive to make their products more popular and profitable. And privacy issues too, must be taken into account. Witness the recent media maelstrom around ToyTalk's partnership with Barbie, orchestrated by some child advocates who are concerned about who has access to the conversations the technology stimulates. Though ToyTalk's innovative thinking is building a big audience and big data, will they and partners be able to ensure that children will safely benefit from the ground up?

The FingerReader: Helping a New Generation of Readers One Finger at a Time

At the corner of Amherst Street in Cambridge, Massachusetts, stands a glass building six floors high. A large staircase brings guests to floor after floor of lab space, each one devoted to a specific research group. Peering out through the glass of the Biomechatronics lab is a runway for the team to test out prostheses prototypes. Down the hall, music gently streams out the door as a student rushes out from the Future of the Opera space. Housing all of this interdisciplinary science hustle and bustle is the Massachusetts Institute of Technology Media Lab, an iconic place devoted to exploring the convergence of design, technology, multimedia, sciences, and the arts. The group offers PhDs and master's degrees to students of varying backgrounds, including electrical engineering, philosophy, and music. Members of the news media cover the lab with great interest: its members are often featured in TED talks, and it is widely recognized for contributions to modern breakthroughs ranging from the design of the World Wide Web to robotics, face recognition, and educational technologies. One of the world's grandest and most hotly debated educational equity experiments, the One Laptop per Child effort designed by Nicholas Negroponte, grew out of the lab.

In the Fluid Interfaces space, a team gathers to discuss their projects, all of which focus on figuring out better ways for people to interact with digital information and environments through intuitive interfaces. Roy Shilkrot, a PhD student, is part of the group. Shilkrot previously worked in the Computer Graphics Lab at Tel Aviv University, where he explored advanced technologies such as augmented reality and head-mounted displays. At MIT, he is working with Maryanne Wolf and her colleague Stephanie Gottwald at the Center for Reading and Language Research to design applications for the FingerReader, an augmented user interface and communication device.

The FingerReader emerges from a relatively new field of "wearable technologies," in which users are outfitted with an assistive device. Shilkrot and his team started working on wearables back in 2011 with the EyeRing, a device that holds a microcamera to help the visually impaired capture a picture or video and send it wirelessly to a phone or computer for analysis. A user places the EyeRing onto their finger, and the device acts like an "eye" to the world. Guided by the finger, the EyeRing will then scan images and objects. Almost instantaneously, the user receives an audio message, broadcast or spoken through ear buds, that provides information about the object. The team initially decided that finger-worn devices are potentially efficient for the visually impaired because the technology is easy to use in any setting, and the user base frequently uses their hands for various tasks. By experimenting with a few EyeRing prototypes and applications, the team pinpointed a direction for their research: helping the visually impaired read printed material. After interviewing visually impaired potential users, Shilkrot and his team expanded their user base to include other groups who have difficulty reading, including people with brain trauma, those with ADHD, and children who have struggled.

The meticulous process of design iteration has led to highly functional prototypes of FingerReader. The latest version, designed for the index finger, is a thick white ring manufactured by a 3D printer. A tiny computer chip with a microcamera sticks out from the ring to follow the movements of this now augmented finger. Readers with both visual impairments and reading difficulties can scan lines of text. As they move their augmented finger over the text, the device immediately provides feedback to users through audio tones and vibration, while also reading the text out loud.

Shilkrot sees potential for the FingerReader in elementary school classrooms. As many experts know, standardized test scores in both math and reading often drop off between second and fourth grades because the test items use more complex language, such as story passages and word problems, and thereby require deeper comprehension to ease problem solving and analysis. As one possible solution to this problem in many schools in the United States, a teacher might read passages to a young girl or create mixed-ability learning groups aimed at helping struggling students by teaming them up with peers who have mastered the more complex material. This type of remediation can unintentionally add a new problem for the struggling reader. A seven- or eight-year-old student no longer faces just a "test situation" but now has to deal with a "social situation," which can make matters worse. Many will recall the pain of being ability grouped in first grade as either an adept reader (say a "blue jay") or as one who didn't quite measure up (perhaps a "sparrow"). Although this type of ability grouping is less blatant nowadays, other more subtle cues create social stigma. Many kids suffer from being labeled and lose motivation.

Shilkrot and his lab mates are seeking to remove the stigma of needing help while also giving students a tool that is personalized to their unique learning styles. With the FingerReader, the child will be able to put on at device small enough to be discreet and cool enough to become a fashion statement. After placing the ring on her finger and headphones on, the student can scan the reading passage line by line to tap into the FingerReader's audio playback feature. As a first step for their discovery process, the team is working with Wolf and Gottwald, whose research center is based at Tufts

University. Pilot studies with second and third grade children are now under-way to determine whether the device works at all, the best form it should take, and whether the children will find it appealing.

These studies are just the first step. With partners at the Lab who are testing literacy applications on tablets in more than a hundred countries around the world, innovations like the FingerReader might change literacy experiences for tens of thousands of struggling readers in the decade ahead. Wearable, personalized technologies that reduce stigma, and increase read-ing power may be coming to a school near you soon.

Learning from IBM's Watson: Will Literacy Be Elementary?

It's an hour's drive up to Yorktown Heights, the site of IBM's campus, from New York City. In the middle of a picturesque landscape on the campus lies the Thomas J. Watson Research Center, the headquarters for one of the largest and oldest industrial research organizations in the world. Since the 1940s, the group has accomplished some of the most important and notable sci-entific breakthroughs in the computing industry, such as the creation of the FORTRAN programming language, one of the earliest and most important computer-based innovations of its era. Renowned mathematicians, inven-tors, roboticists, computer scientists, and Nobel Prize winners have wandered the hallowed hallways designed by architect Eero Saarinen.

Inside the vast space, visitors can walk up to large, slightly eerie blue-lit touchscreens with menu options in the shape of atoms. Next to these screens sit colorful chairs quietly occupied by scientists and engineers, some wear-ing an employee badge signifying twenty-plus years of employment at "Big Blue." The space feels a bit too quiet. Then suddenly a small tablet breaks the silence by rolling through on top of a two-wheeled electric vehicle, stopping in front of an employee who quite naturally starts a chat with the machine.

Down the hallway, a boisterous veteran IBMer walks curious visitors through a large space that houses multiple closet-sized servers. He plants them in the middle of a family of loud, heat-emitting boxes to show off Watson, advertised as the "world's smartest supercomputer." You probably recall the huge media splash Watson made in 2011 when it soundly defeated mega-winners Ken Jennings and Brad Rutter on *Jeopardy*. Watson took the first-place prize of $1 million that night, making a statement during IBM's Centennial celebration year that Big Blue was still relevant. Watson's developers and IBM executives are investing in a future that will consist of warp-speed data mining, cognitively enhanced, personalized problem solving and practical applications to everyday life, especially in the field of education.

Satya Nitta is at the forefront in figuring out how this technology might help transform education. With the title of Master Inventor and Program Leader for Cognitive Computing for Education, Nitta works with the Watson team and other teams at IBM Research to figure out the best educational applications for artificial intelligence and cognitive computing, which is meant to simulate human thought processes like sensing, predicting, inferring, and, quite possibly, thinking itself.

Nitta and his colleagues say they plan to focus during the next two years on how to use Watson to create personalized interactions with teachers and children in classroom settings. Scientists, he tells us, will first study the needs of many different types of learners and assemble a model of what works best for each type. Then Watson's engineers will need to design programs so the computer can respond intelligently and adaptively to children's learning. For example, Watson will be tasked to assemble a playlist of suggested reading materials based on a particular student's capabilities. Right now the team is testing prototypes for a Watson-enabled teacher's aide that will help guide the way they teach, develop their skills as professionals, and figure out how to match their instruction to expectations in the Common Core State Standards.

In late 2014, IBM released a prototype of their breakthrough design for the cognitive computing space in the form of a "Watson Master Teacher." Master Teacher is designed to be a classroom assistant. It will provide precise answers, vetted concepts, and what the company calls a "non-judgmental personalization" through a cloud-based, mobile platform. Though the application is called a Teacher, Watson's form in the company's initial public demonstration was an online application that resembled a Web search engine. Teachers could ask Watson a question by typing it into a text box. Questions included "What does close reading mean?," and "For *The Adventures of Tom Sawyer*, I'm teaching the white-washing fence section. Can you give me some examples of how … ?" The scientists say they do not intend to create a robot with every answer or replace the teacher with a machine. Rather, in response to such detailed questions, they expect the software to suggest relevant answers by curating education research, curriculum outlines, videos, and online connections.

Nitta's team is in the early stage of integrating Watson into a literacy and reading companion that stems from earlier research with voice recognition technology. IBM researchers, working with struggling readers in low-income schools, have already started creating this digital companion to provide encouragement and help students read out loud. Based on how well a user reads the material aloud, the companion will provide positive reinforcement, exclaiming, "You sound great!" The experience will be adapted by the students' progress over time.

Merging Watson with the reading companion will take advantage of Watson's unique ability to rapidly parse and interpret complex, text-based content. IBM's leaders told us that they do not plan to get into the business of creating educational content. Rather, they aim to create new collaborations with expert educators to promote enhanced learning experiences. At the end of the day, Nitta says his team's goal is to "level the playing field using technology" so that "all children in the United States have access to a high-quality education."

NOTES

media literacy experts: Thoman and Jolls 2005.
Digital Age literacy critic: Birkerts 1994.
reading "isn't something we're born to do": Wolf 2007.

Sherry Turkle: *Fresh Air* 2012.

face-to-face interaction: Ibid.

a high degree of absorption: Radesky et al. 2014.

"participatory culture": Jenkins et al. 2009.

storytelling app Launchpad Toys: http://www.launchpadtoys.com/toon tastic/

transmedia opportunities: Herr-Stephenson, Alper, and Reilly 2013.

meaning of literacy has changed: Justine Cassell, Carnegie Mellon University, personal communication, December 2014.

advances in technology have quantitatively: Adams 2011.

"serve and return": Center on the Developing Child.

At MIT: "Fingerreader."

At the end of the day: Phone interview of Satya Nitta by Anna Ly, October 7, 2014.

PART 3

The Pioneers

9

Why Adults Still Matter Most

The features and functionalities of apps and e-books produce a thicket of possibilities for struggling readers, as do the tools now under development by inventors tinkering away. And with mobile anywhere–anytime access and some apps offered for free, one might think an era of equal access to learning may be at hand. But consider our past experiences with technology in education. Twenty years ago, the arrival of personal computers and laptops led many prognosticators to go gaga with pronouncements about students gaining in achievement because of new access to learning materials not previously available. That promise remains to be realized. Technology has too often been, in the words of a 2001 book by Stanford University education professor Larry Cuban, *Oversold and Underused*.

In addition to e-reading technologies not living up to the hype, here is an even more unsettling thought: What if access to all of these new tools *exacerbates* the educational divide between rich and poor? Some evidence of that already exists in a seminal study of Philadelphia's libraries in the 2000s. In an effort to ensure that income level did not become a barrier to using new learning materials, the William Penn Foundation undertook a $20 million initiative in 1996 to transform branch libraries throughout the city so that they could provide an abundance of print and technological resources to families no matter what neighborhood they came from. In a seminal ten-year study that compared literacy learning between a middle-income- and low-income area of Philadelphia after the infusion of these resources, the results were not what were predicted. The authors of the study, Susan B. Neuman and Donna C. Celano, saw that the availability of new media caused disparities to increase, "leading some students to move toward using the medium for information purposes and others for entertainment." Children from higher-income areas were surrounded by parents and other adults who guided and mentored them in ways to use media to improve their literacy skills and develop expertise. Meanwhile, the children—and adults—who came from disadvantaged areas and who needed the mentorship the most were the least likely to get it.

Breaking this cycle will take creativity and resolve. Part of the answer is to recognize that the people around children—the adults who know how to help them learn to learn—are more important than any touchscreen tablet.

But that is not always the message people hear, nor is it the image in their minds when they see what all these new tools can do. Sometimes the technology seems so sophisticated, so smart, so ubiquitous that parents and caregivers might think they are not really needed anymore. Today's swarms of apps are the latest tools to raise this possibility. When producers at PBS created a Play & Learn app to promote game-play between caregivers and their kids, they discovered that the adults did not automatically envision a role for themselves. In usability testing the adults would just give the apps to their kids. Nor did they use the parts of the app that offered parent-focused resources. In fact, in the app's early days, a comment appeared on the PBS website: "This app has too many words. My kids can't read it." Immediately under that comment, another user had responded, "You don't understand. This app is for you."

Sara Dewitt, vice president for PBS Kids Interactive, says the confusion is understandable. "If it has characters and looks like something from PBS kids," she said, "then the parents immediately think it is just for the kids." (New versions of the PBS Play & Learn app are more explicit about how parents and children can use it together.) Research from the Cooney Center shows a similar phenomenon. In a recent survey of parents with children ages two to ten, parents report that they spent about an hour each day viewing or interacting with media together, and almost all of it was via the medium of television. Only three minutes each were spent together on a mobile device, a computer, or a video game.

In a small Australian study of low-income elementary schools using iPads for the first time, parents revealed mixed feelings about how the devices changed their roles. "If children were happy and able to engage with the iPad independently," wrote Katrina McNab, a doctoral student at the University of Tasmania, "it was believed they did not require assistance from an adult." One mother said she had been "made redundant" by digital books that could read to her son. McNab probed, How do you feel about being made redundant? The mother's reply: "Well, I still get questions. The iPad can't answer questions yet so it's not quite that clever." In fact, what she may not have known is that some e-books are indeed trying to be that clever by providing dictionary definitions for unfamiliar words.

This sense of being unnecessary is no small concern. In the previous pages you saw the power of various technologies for discrete tasks, such as helping children to hear the sounds of letters and syllables or asking students multiple-choice questions to reinforce what they learned from a story. Whether in school or at home, the ease with which young children can navigate digital media by themselves means that adults do not always have to be present. And depending on how well the tools are engineered to accommodate children's fine motor skills and early cognitive development, this kind of solo experience may be possible at younger and younger ages.

The angst associated with new roles and the fear of substitution and replacement pervade many discussions of technology and literacy. Are we facing the possibility that soon a $500 device might seem to be a good-enough replacement for the living souls who work with and teach children? Could readers be made by machine?

GLOBAL EXPERIMENTS, SANS EDUCATORS

A series of experiments in India have already fueled debate over this prospect. Sugata Mitra, a professor at Newcastle University in the United Kingdom, has spoken at huge venues around the world about what happened when he embedded computers into the walls of buildings in underdeveloped villages of New Delhi where children had little access to schools and teachers, let alone exposure to computers of any kind. These "hole in the wall" experiments, which Mitra has now expanded throughout India, showed that children were naturally curious and self-propelled. They walked up to the computers, figured out how to use them, and talked among themselves to solve problems. They appeared to steer their learning with no help at all. His experiments have sparked other work in the United States and around the globe. His perspective is also often used as a reference point for reformers like Sal Khan and his Khan Academy, which makes self-directed learning possible on a mass scale.

Literacy experiments in remote areas of Uganda and the rural South in the United States are now testing the question of whether children might be able to teach themselves to read with the help of a computer tablet. The Global Literacy Project, a partnership among Georgia State, the Massachusetts Institute of Technology, and Tufts University, has already run pilot tests in Ethiopia using Motorola tablets loaded with dozens of commercially available apps and app prototypes from research labs. Initial results showed young children learning the English alphabet and, within a month, spelling simple words with no prior exposure to English. "To our surprise," said Tinsley Galyean, a specialist on the project who focuses on interactive technology for learning, "it was incredibly engaging." Video broadcast on CNN in 2012 shows dozens of children on dusty roads and in dirt-floor huts singing the English alphabet song. Galyean and literacy expert Stephanie Gottwald are now leading research to better understand how much children's own curiosity and ability to explore enables them to learn on their own after being handed the tablets. Thousands more children are part of current experiments, and the group aspires to reach more than 100 million children by the end of the decade.

Given the media attention focused on projects like these, it is no wonder that parents, and teachers too, are feeling unsure of where they fit. Somehow they are supposed to reconcile the image of "do it yourself" technology with the mounds of brain science telling them about the significance of socialization and adult relationships in a child's social and cognitive development. It can feel like there is a mismatch between engagement with a touchscreen and the increasingly prevalent studies showing that preschoolers may emerge with deficits in language development if they don't have many opportunities for authentic conversation.

But what if we broke out of this dichotomous way of thinking? We are ingrained to see battles of humans versus machines instead of seeing technologies as human-designed elements in a complex ecosystem, new entities that can advance our learning or get in the way depending on the particular circumstances of children's lives and adult's lives at a particular moment. What if the answer is not either/or, but both?

TAPPING INTO AMERICA'S PIONEERS

The line of reasoning running through this book, based on the principles laid out in chapter 5, is grounded in this "both" vision. We cannot afford to ignore the affordances of technology, especially for disadvantaged children and families of many different backgrounds and circumstances who may not otherwise have access to information and learning opportunities. And yet to leave the fate of these children to technology alone would be a big mistake. If the results of Philadelphia study tell us anything—and you'll read more about this in chapter 13—it is that children who interact with technology *while working with adults who can set good examples and guide them to new heights* are receiving tremendous advantages. If only the privileged few have the opportunity for that kind of tech-assisted but human-powered learning, divides will grow only wider.

Besides, as much as children in their elementary school years may appreciate the opportunity to learn independently, they also really like those moments when Mom or Dad (or any caring adult) takes time to be with them. In the most recent results from the publisher Scholastic's annual survey about children and reading, for example, elementary school children said they wished their parents still read to them. Across all age groups, 83 percent of kids said they loved or liked a lot those times when parents read to them aloud at home. Yet less than a quarter of six- to eight-year-olds and far fewer older children say that someone at home does so.

Instead of signaling to adults to stand back, maybe the technology of e-reading is telling us something else: our role is to do everything that a computer can't. Arthur C. Clarke, the science fiction writer and futurist, once wrote, "Any teacher that can be replaced by a machine should be." The expectations for parents and other adults engaging with children may have to reach a new level. As Digital Age educators and parents, our responsibilities are changing from being, as the saying goes, the "sage on the stage" to the "guide on the side." This requires an open mind about the potential of new technologies to assist those adults and usher in new possibilities for engagement between them and their children. Can e-reading and new modes of communication be harnessed to help those who work with children every day?

That is the challenge taken up by a cadre of innovators we have encountered around the country. They hail from home-visiting programs, preschool programs, libraries, elementary schools, university labs, for-profit startups, and nonprofit organizations. Unafraid of technology, they are experimenting with tools and outreach strategies to communicate with and ultimately empower parents and child care professionals to use interactive reading techniques and other methods for interacting with children in rich ways. We see them as pioneers, clearing the brush, creating the paths, looking outward from the hilltops toward the great unknown. Their stories, many being told here for the first time, will set the course for how and whether technologies of different kinds can be incorporated into early literacy efforts in the twenty-first century. Their quest is no less than to mold, and perhaps even rescue, the next generation, the children who will in two decades be the face of our workforce, sustaining our businesses, maintaining public safety, keeping our education and health care systems humming, voting, and running for elected office. These kids of the class of 2030 need to be reading and learning in a way that gives us confidence in the future. Can our pioneers make it happen?

NOTES

the William Penn Foundation: Neuman and Celano 2012b, 15.

the availability of new media: Neuman and Celano 2012a, 7.

This app is for you: Phone interview with Sara Dewitt, David Lowenstein, and Jean Crawford of PBS, January 27, 2014.

If it has characters: Ibid.

Only three minutes each: Rideout 2014.

If children were happy: McNab 2013, 12.

They appeared: For more, see Hole-in-the-Wall website at http://www.hole-in-the-wall.com/Beginnings.html.

"To our surprise,": Phone interview with Tinsley Galyean and Stephanie Gottwald of the Global Literacy Project, October 24, 2014.

Thousands more children: For more on the Global Literacy Project, see globallit.org.

Yet less than a quarter: *Kids & Family* 2015.

Arthur C. Clarke: "Sir Arthur's Quotations."

A Different Kind
of Screen Time

M any people know the city of Houston as home to the Astrodome and
the Johnson Space Center. But it is also the site of a different kind
of scientific innovation: the use of personalized video clips and handheld
video cameras to help parents help their babies and toddlers develop language skills.

In the early 2000s, a University of Houston pediatrics professor named
Susan Landry decided to test a new method for supporting families to be
responsive to their young children's needs. She had been studying the interactions of families with their children and knew that responsive parenting
made a significant difference in children's development of language skills as
well as other positive behaviors that promoted success in literacy and school.
With collaborator Karen Smith, also at the University of Houston, she developed a program that used the power of video.

The program, called Play and Learning Strategies, or PALS, works with
trained professionals who visit the homes of mothers with babies, toddlers,
and preschoolers in Texas and a growing number of other states. These
professionals are part of a small but growing cadre of the early childhood
workforce around the country known colloquially as "home visitors,"

specializing in providing advice and support to women who are pregnant or have recently had children. It is a field that has emerged from decades of study over the years on how to help new parents, receiving increased attention and significant federal funding under the administration of President Barack Obama.

Why do parents need home visitors? Because—let's face it—caring for babies and young children does not always look like the cuddly drawing on a Hallmark card. It is exhausting, nonstop work riddled with multiple night-time feedings, bouts of unexplainable crying, spit-up, teething, tantrums, diaper messes, anxiety-producing fevers, and oh so much more. It also can be socially isolating for first-time parents, with few opportunities to talk to other adults. The job of home visitors is to counter that. Not only do they lend a nonjudgmental ear, they are trained to provide information about health and nutrition, link mothers to social programs that help pay for food and child care, and encourage calm, nurturing interactions. This "responsive parenting," as the experts call it, is critical to brain development.

The home visitors with PALS have been given intensive training in specific methods for promoting responsive parenting. A key mission is to help parents develop their children's language and social skills and their children's abilities to gain better control over their behaviors. This is not such an easy task. No one likes to be lectured, and most professionals know it doesn't really work to tell parents what to do. Worksheets, guidebooks, and handouts may not be particularly compelling either, especially if the parents in question are not very strong readers themselves.

The PALS visitors bring parents information in a different way: they deliver it via personalized video. Video can be much easier than brochures or pamphlets to digest. And if it's a video that shows *you* on screen, well then, there's a pretty good chance that you're going to pay attention.

The PALS program works like this: a home visitor arrives. The visitor asks the mother how she is feeling and how her child is doing. Are you getting rest? Look how much she's grown! Teething, already? Then the home visitor and mom sit down to start their session. They start by watching a video together that shows moms, dads, and other caregivers interacting with their children, subtly demonstrating different techniques for being responsive to one's child. They talk about what they have seen. Then the home visitor asks the mother to try these different techniques herself. They might situate themselves in the kitchen with the child in a high chair, in the living room near the coffee table, wherever is most comfortable. The home visitor reaches for her handheld video camera and begins to record, capturing the moment on video. Minutes later, the visitor and mom watch a playback.

That playback packs a lot of power. It is an out-of-body experience, providing a perspective impossible without the technology of recorded video. Prompted by questions from the home visitor, the mother starts to take a look at herself and her baby in a new way. "They critique themselves," Landry said. "They talk about what was effective and what they want to change." The sessions occur weekly across 10–12 weeks. At the end of each session, the home visitor and mother make a plan for what Mom will focus on before her next visit.

No doubt it can feel uncomfortable to watch oneself on tape. But as one mother told the PALS staff, "A child doesn't come with instructions, so it's helpful to see videotapes and practice what I see."

Over the past fifteen years, Landry and Smith have conducted a series of experiments to evaluate PALS's impact: whether the program changed the way parents interact with their children, and even more, whether the program had a detectable impact on the children themselves. Their first study, which also included social scientist Paul Swank, looked at PALS's impact on the development of infants born prematurely compared to those born at full term. More than two hundred parents participated. They were randomly assigned to two groups: one group received ten weeks of PALS. The other group—the control group—received a home visitor for ten weeks as well, but those visitors did not have training in PALS and did not use the video playback method.

The results were definitive. Compared to the control group, the mothers who received PALS used significantly more "verbal scaffolding," meaning they explained themselves and labeled things to help their children understand the world around them. They were warmer in tone and more responsive to their babies. Their toddlers were more likely to use words and to cooperate with their mothers. They appeared generally happier. PALS had a positive effect, whether the infants were born at term or pre-term. Since then, Landry and her colleagues have rolled out PALS for parents of infants, toddlers, and preschoolers throughout the state of Texas, with more than two thousand Texas families receiving services since the early 2000s and hundreds of others served in other states. The program, which is run through the Children's Learning Institute at the University of Texas Health Science Center at Houston, continues to be a hotbed for experimentation; researchers are now experimenting with exchanging videos via touchscreen tablets and coaching mothers through online connections.

PROMOTING DIALOGIC READING

For decades, across the country and around the world, parents have been hearing a one-note message: Read to your kids. This message may resonate if you have come from a place of relative privilege. If you are one of those parents who remember your own parents reading to you each night, and if you have shelves of books at home, this probably sounds like a no-brainer. Of course we will read to our kids. We already know that.

But even middle-income parents with books at home and stability in their daily lives may not know about the power of different ways of reading to our kids. Research on literacy and reading skill shows that there is a difference between just reading the text on the page and actively engaging with children while reading a story together. The latter is the one that matters more for language development and later literacy skills. More than a decade of studies on how children learn to read point to the powerful brainwork underway in those moments of interaction around a story. This way of reading—known as interactive story time or "dialogic reading" among experts—is now promoted in parenting workshops and literacy initiatives throughout the world.

No doubt, interactive reading requires more energy, especially if you're begged to "use that funny voice, Mommy!" when you're nearly comatose from working all day. But it is also so much fun. In *Born Reading: Bringing Up Bookworms in a Digital Age,* Los Angeles writer Jason Boog brings to life the escapades of interactive reading with his daughter Olive. His book takes readers on an intimate journey into what, when, where, and how he started reading picture books with Olive from her earliest days. He paints quirky and poignant vignettes of how the two of them explored books together, from her intense concentration with Curious George, their wacky wordplay with Dr. Seuss, or his waves of nostalgia while reading the classic *Blueberries for Sal.* But what may be most interesting about Boog's book is the way it starts: he gives parents instructions and guidance on how to spur those interactive reading sessions with their kids. The Born Reading Playbook, as Boog calls it, lists fifteen actions and "conversation starters" that can apply to e-books, print books, and everything in between. "Ask lots and lots of questions" is one. Another tip is to "stop and talk about what happened," and "compare the story to personal experience."

Boog's book and his accompanying website, born-reading.com (http://www.born-reading.com/), offer a real service to parents and educators willing to pick up a 303-page paperback to read about reading. But the Born Reading Playbook cannot be, nor is it designed to be, the answer to the literacy crisis facing our country. Those who work with families across the cultural landscape are yearning for ways to reach parents and caregivers who are coming from different socioeconomic strata, for whom books may be written in a language and cultural milieu that is not their own, or who feel uncomfortable and maybe even resentful about being pushed into conversation with their babies and toddlers in a way that feels foreign and, frankly, a little silly.

One approach is to help parents see, from their very first days of parenting, how their own personal responses can lead to those joyful moments when babies smile back and stretch their arms in glee, eager for more interaction.

The PALS program was built to elicit those moments. So that got Landry thinking: What if, in addition to helping parents become more positively responsive to their children, home visiting programs could also help parents to see new ways of *reading* with their kids? Would parents, without being pushed start pausing to ask children about what they have heard so far? Could the PALS method encourage parents with infants, toddlers, and preschoolers to use books in this way with their children? Could it help turn children into readers?

Landry went back to find the parents who were part of her first study. By now their children were toddlers and preschoolers, ages two and three. She enlisted many of them to be part of another experiment, with one group receiving PALS as designed for toddlers and young preschoolers (and therefore getting the opportunity to learn from video playback) and another group getting the video-less version of home visiting. At the end of the twelve-week experiment, she and her colleagues conducted assessments of how parents acted when they read books to their kids. They passed out books like *Five Little Monkeys Jumping on the Bed* and *My Crayons Talk*, left the parents alone with their children while they recorded their interactions, and then examined every second of those recordings for evidence of different behaviors.

Again, the results provided good news. The parents who received PALS home visitors during their children's infancy and preschool years were much better at dialogic reading than their counterparts. They didn't just read the text of the books. They described story elements, explained new vocabulary words, and gave children opportunities to talk about what they saw on the page. The skills of responsive parenting had extended to those moments sharing books. "That was exciting, to see that they can make that transfer," Landry said. The corps of parents who know how to read interactively just gained some new members.

 Video Vignette: Play and Learning Strategies
bit.ly/tapclick1

A Short History on Changing Expectations for Parents

There is no specific date at which point scientists and child development experts suddenly realized the importance of helping children to build language skills. But those who know the history of developmental science have witnessed a definitive shift, almost a U-turn, in the way people think about childhood. Back at the turn of the twentieth century, some experts were warning parents not to respond to or talk affectionately with their young children, and children most certainly were not encouraged to talk back. *Infant Care*, a 1914 publication printed by the US Department of Labor Children's Bureau, warned parents not to play with infants, as it might "induce nervous disturbance." A popular book around the time of the Great Depression was *Psychological Care of Infant and Child*, published in 1928 and written by John B. Watson, the controversial psychologist known for "behaviorism," and Rosalie Rayner Watson, his wife. The Watsons discouraged adults from responding to and touching babies, and calling this "mother-love" a "dangerous instrument." Too much affection and children would become spoiled, growing into weak adults. Don't hug and kiss, they advised. "If you must, kiss them once on the forehead when they say goodnight. Shake hands with your children when you see them in the morning."

This approach changed dramatically with a big breakthrough in parenting advice and support. A practicing pediatrician who was also trained in psychoanalysis entered the parenting field with a personal, sympathetic, and psychologically attuned publication. His name: Benjamin Spock. His book, *The Common Sense Book of Baby and Child Care*, was first published in 1946 and dramatically changed the public conversation while also changing the advice given by experts about young children's well-being and parenting practices. The book, along with Dr. Spock himself, attained fame almost instantly, selling 500,000 copies in its first six months. Mothers heavily relied on Spock's advice and appreciated his friendly, reassuring tone. Spock emphasized in his book and many public appearances that, above all, parents should have confidence in their abilities and trust their instincts. The famous first line of the book reads, "Trust yourself. You know more than you think you do." His intent was to disseminate comprehensive information to all mothers, giving advice that combined the physical and psychological aspects of child care. So that any mother could afford it, the book was sold at just 25 cents.

By the early 1960s a new strategy was bubbling. Catalyzed by a disturbing view of the struggles of low-income families captured by Michael Harrington's bestselling book *The Other America* in 1962, and in the aftermath of President John F. Kennedy's assassination, President Lyndon B. Johnson launched the Great Society's War on Poverty. This program included a comprehensive set of policies intended to help reshape family supports and economic opportunities, ranging from Medicaid to the Elementary and Secondary Schools Act to the Office of Economic Opportunity and the doctrine of community engagement known as "maximum feasible participation." In 1965, President Johnson started Head Start as a summer intervention and included an explicit focus on building literacy and parenting supports. Around the same time a parent empowerment program in New York began to take shape. Called the Mother–Child Home Program, it was a precursor to today's home visiting programs.

In the early 1970s, developmental science expert Phyllis Levenstein conducted experiments on the effectiveness of the Mother–Child Home Program and wrote about attempts to expand it. The program brought professionals known as "toy demonstrators" to homes with young children to show mothers how to use toys and books to promote their kids' developing communication skills. Over time, Levenstein honed her research and created the Verbal Interaction Project, which established regular home visits that promoted substantial increases in children's vocabulary, parent-child interaction, and other literacy-learning skills. Participation in the project was found in longitudinal research to result in fewer high school dropouts for those who participated.

In 1977, a graduate student at Cornell University named David Olds started another home-visiting program that came to be called the Nurse-Family Partnership. Instead of toy demonstrators, Olds sent nurses (RNs and LPNs) into the home, and focused on infant health, including the social-emotional well-being that comes from warm, responsive interactions with caregivers. Over time, the Nurse–Family Partnership collected a few decades' worth of evidence of its impact, showing that mothers who went through the program were on a more positive life course, and their children were healthier, had fewer cognitive and behavioral problems, and were less likely than their peers to be arrested by age fifteen. These outcomes and others caught the attention of policymakers, which enabled the passage of the federal home-visiting grant program called Maternal, Infant, and Early Childhood Home Visiting (MIECHV) that started in 2010. MIECHV's programs put a premium on both health and language development, and all of the home-visiting organizations that receive funding have created systems and tools for monitoring children's language development throughout the home visits. Over the past two decades, home-visiting programs throughout the country, many of them run by independent, nonprofit organizations, have improved and expanded, though they still serve only a tiny fraction of families in need.

Meanwhile, people continue to be fascinated by the research on how children learn language. Studies on the "word gap" have become among the most captivating. In chapter 2 we described the landmark 1995 study by Betty Hart and Todd Risley showing that low-income children hear as many as 30 million words fewer than higher-income children before they enter kindergarten. And we introduced you to the research of Anne Fernald at Stanford University, whose studies showed that the brains of children who do not experience much "child-directed talk" in their first years of life are significantly slower at processing information and speech compared to children who have the benefit of that talk. These studies and many others have elevated the importance of immersing children in word-filled environments beginning in their earliest months and years of life. And they have shown that children are less likely to experience those language-rich environments if their parents are low-income and have not attained education beyond high school.

In October 2014, the White House's Office on Science and Technology Policy hosted a day-long event with researchers and educators to discuss these findings and many others. The event, which was also sponsored by the Urban Institute, Institute for Museum and Library Services, the Clinton Foundation, and Next Generation's early childhood initiative Too Small to Fail, opened with messages from former Senator Bill Frist; Cindy McCain, a prominent businesswoman and the wife of Senator John McCain; former Secretary of State Hillary Clinton; and President Obama. All urged more attention to how children learn language and literacy skills.

USING VIDEO TO HELP PARENTS RETHINK THE "ALWAYS ON" TV

And yet during all this progress—as home-visiting and parent education programs have been slowly gaining traction in communities around the country, and as language development from infancy has become more and more valued—something new has rapidly become the norm in American households. It is one of those elephants in the room again: the impact of TV.

TV has been a subject of dire concern for children's language development ever since the early 1960s when Newton Minow, the chairman of the Federal Communications Commission, gave a speech about the "vast wasteland" of commercial television. This was in the days when very little of the programming on television was design to promote learning in young children. Nor had it yet occurred to anyone—as it did in 1969 with the dawn of *Sesame Street*—to create programs for children that parents might enjoy watching with them. Many people expressed concern about what children were seeing on the screen and how their TV-watching habits would keep them from exploring the real world.

Now families are accustomed to twenty-four-hour cable television and homes have multiple TV sets. Surveys have shown that the average American child under age 8 is exposed to nearly 4 hours each day of "background TV," defined as television that is running in the background as family members go about their daily lives. According to recent research by a team of developmental scholars, this kind of "always on" TV can be detrimental to children's learning and development, diverting a child's attention from play and learning. Similarly, scientists who track children's language development and growth in social-emotional skills such as impulse control have identified negative outcomes when children are subjected to high amounts of adult-oriented television when they are infants and toddlers. Others worry about adult-directed content for a different reason: if parents are distracted by TV, they reason, they may not be spending much time with their children.

Alan Mendelsohn, a professor in the department of pediatrics at the New York University School of Medicine, is one of many health and education professionals with concerns about the impact of television on children's development. He's a national expert on how television, particularly TV that is on for hours and aimed at adults, can affect infants and toddlers. But fifteen years ago, he decided to try something different than simply telling parents to turn off their TV sets.

"We know that babies are not designed to watch TV for four hours a day," Mendelsohn said. "The question is can you work with families around media in a positive way?"

He started by recognizing the power of video. At about the same time that Susan Landry was experimenting with playback video in the Texas-based PALS program, Mendelsohn was designing a program that used video recorders to capture a family's interactions and replay them with an expert nearby. He did not have teams of home visitors, but he did work for Bellevue Hospital at the Langone Medical Center in New York City, where women were giving birth and returning frequently to visit with their babies' pediatricians. So in 1999, he started an experiment to test a new approach.

The program, called the Video Interaction Project or VIP (not to be confused with the older Verbal Interaction Project described earlier), works like this: beginning when babies were as young as two weeks old, parents and their children visit his office. A child development specialist videotapes the family while guiding them in "pretend play," reading, or other developmentally appropriate learning activities. The parents and the specialist then meet, either before or after the doctor's visit, and watch the video together, pointing out where the interaction was particularly helpful or where parents could improve.

Just as researchers discovered in the Texas-based PALS program, these video playbacks became eye-opening moments for many parents. For the first time they could see their parenting in action and get advice on how to improve. Specialists also talked about limiting TV time to ensure that children have social interactions and conversations through books and play. Parents came back nine to fifteen times over the next few years, with each session lasting thirty to forty-five minutes each. The sessions continued through age five.

Mendelsohn kept track of the children, testing them at thirty-three months and then again when they entered elementary school. The results show that the VIP program improved cognition and language development in toddlers (compared to those whose parents did not go through the program). VIP had higher IQ scores and reduced behavior problems. A second study in 2005 with more than four hundred families found that parents in VIP were more likely to talk with their children, play with them, read aloud to them, name objects, tell stories, and talk together about surroundings. According to diaries kept by the parents, their children were exposed to less adult-directed TV and exposed to more read-alouds and play time with Mom. The program had another startling effect. It lowered depressive symptoms among mothers. That's promising given that one in eleven low-income women suffer a depressive episode in a given year and 70 percent of those women experience severe effects. There is a well-documented connection between maternal depression and poorer child outcomes.

The VIP continues in New York City to this day with two specialists working with five hundred families. Jenny Arevalo is one of those specialists. With each family that visits the doctor's office, she tailors her routine. For example, she might ask the mom of a two-year-old to read *What's in Grandma's Grocery Bag?* to her son or daughter. She may also encourage the parent to help the child identify the names or colors of fruits in a picture book. In each case, Arevalo records the moment and then sits down later with the mothers to review the footage to discuss what they did well and where they could improve.

Many of Arevalo's families are recent immigrants from rural Mexico. They have never received this kind of parenting support before, she said, and may not realize that they could be their children's first teachers. "I tell them, 'you are the best person to be able to give them that experience,'" to help them build skills that will help them in school later, Arevalo said. "They get this sense of pride that they are being influential in their children's lives."

MODELING WITH READY ROSIE

Specialists in child development have a favorite verb: "modeling." They don't mean the kind of modeling that involves clicking cameras and pole-thin men and women strutting down runways. They mean "to model" as in to serve as an example, to simulate. In early learning, research shows that when adults model certain behaviors around children, those moments can be especially powerful because young children are primed to imitate the people to whom they feel connected. Do you want your children to say please and thank you, to be kind to animals, to learn to wait until a conversational pause before interrupting? Experts advise that if you behave in these very ways in front of your children—if you almost unconsciously model these actions—your kids will likely pick up the same behaviors.

Over the past few decades, the field of parenting has unearthed similar insights about adults: We need models too. It's compelling to see a parent interact with children the same age as our own, especially if we see that the parent is having some success, if the interactions are alleviating meltdowns, helping children to overcome challenges, sparking joyful moments. Now it is possible to capture key moments on video and then replay them. The video screen can be a powerful conduit for modeling.

In our search for pioneers of early literacy using new technologies, we thought video modeling could be a promising place to start. Sure enough, within months, we learned about the work of Emily Roden, a former teacher near Dallas, Texas. Roden previously was an educational consultant for the textbook company Pearson Publishing. A former teacher, her job was to visit school districts to discover how learning materials could be tweaked to respond to what educators needed. Time and again, she heard school leaders say that videos would be the best way to communicate with teachers and other employees. By the time she became a mother, she started wondering the same about communication with parents. Having a background in education, she knew well the importance of building language skills and giving children exposure to early math, science, and social studies concepts. But as a working mom with two children, Roden was starting to understand the demands on today's parents. "My time was so limited, I started to look around," she said. "I would search online for school readiness activities or early literacy activities and would either find a dissertation on oral language acquisition or an activity that involved me buying felt and Popsicle sticks. I did not have time for either and knew I needed a resource that was quick and showed me how to have conversations and play games with things I already had, like stuffed animals and fruit."

She and some colleagues who were early childhood experts started to look for prerecorded videos of simple activities that parents could do using the materials of everyday life, such as coins, bath toys, even sugar packets at restaurants. They were not easy to find. So Roden started to produce the videos herself, and incorporated her daughter's name into the company she was creating, calling it Ready Rosie. The mission was to disseminate them to parents via a daily e-mail message—she called it a "daily ding"—that contained a link to a two-minute video.

Creating the videos seemed an easy proposition: just bring in some actors, give them a script, and hit "Record." But Roden soon realized that hiring actors was a big mistake. "It was an absolute failure," Roden said. "Too scripted, too awful." Even with the very best actors she could find, "it didn't have this real feeling to it."

Within a month, Roden and her team, who had been working in several school districts in Texas, tried a different approach. They recruited real parents and made a concerted effort to bring in Spanish-speaking families. At first, the parents received scripts and were asked to memorize and replay them for the camera. That didn't work either. So Roden scrapped that idea too. The scripts had to go. For her next attempt, she created low-quality videos of reading experts demonstrating different activities with children and then sent those videos, via a YouTube link, to the parents she had recruited.

"We told the families: don't memorize the video, just take a look," Roden said. One game demonstrates that even the act of putting away groceries can be a learning and language building game, by describing and guessing items using vocabulary words, like *round*, *cylinder*, *metal*, *heavy*, and *smooth*. After watching these videos, and after being told not to attempt any rehearsal, the camera crew would arrive at the house and film the parents and their children playing the game together for the first time.

"When we compared it to when we had given them a script, they were ten times better at replicating the experience if they had *seen* it first," Roden said. "It was so exciting. And the families involved in the project said that just by having that small experience with it, they were having some of their own moments now where they use the games to just talk with their children, whether they are in the car or wherever."

After eighteen months of filming, Ready Rosie was ready for prime time. School districts in Texas were among the first customers for the subscriptions to the videos, which they made available to parents with children in preschool programs and anyone whose children attended elementary schools with high percentages of low-income children. Other customers include a migrant family literacy program in Maine called Comienza en Casa (which you will read about in chapter 12) and the Community Action Project of Tulsa, which manages Head Start and a range of other early learning programs for the city. Researchers at the University of North Texas, Penn State, and Case Western Reserve University are starting to gather data to assess the videos' impact. The Ready Rosie video library now includes 800 two-minute segments (half in Spanish, half in English). Spanish-speaking families in particular want to watch the segments in both languages.

"It was unlike anything we had seen before," said Chris Shade, director of school improvement and support in Denton Independent Unified School District, which is just north of Fort Worth. "What caught our eye was the interactive nature of the video. The resource provided was not a video that you would put in front of a child, but a video you'd put in front of a parent."

In a recent blog post for the school district, he explained why the videos have become an integral part of the community's school-readiness efforts. "It's real parents teaching real children in real places like a restaurant, the city bus, the grocery store, the doctor's office, the playground, etc.," he wrote. Thinking back on his days of raising his own children, Shade said that even as a relatively well-educated parent, he often wondered if he was doing the right thing and truly helping his children when they needed it. The videos help to reassure and build parents' confidence. "It puts me as the parent in the driver's seat," Shade wrote. "I wish I'd had Ready Rosie when my 18-year-old was three. Being stuck in traffic would have been much more fun."

LEARNING TOGETHER: VERBAL INTERACTIONS
PROMPTED BY THE SCREEN

Video playbacks during home visits, videotapes of book reading in the doctor's office, video modeling of playful activities: each of these cases highlights the power of video when used intentionally to help children learn new words and ideas. But none directly tackles an assumption made by child advocates and literacy experts alike: They assume that a parent watching TV is a parent not interacting with her child.

About five years ago, Mendelsohn and the NYU researchers behind the Video Interaction Project decided to investigate that assumption and test another theory: Maybe parents could help their babies by talking to them *while watching TV*. Mendelsohn calls this "media-specific verbal interaction" or, the shorter version, "media verbal interaction." This, he thought, could be another way to harness video and screen time to promote children's development. The researchers recruited low-income Hispanic mothers of six-month-olds to be interviewed about each hour of their previous twenty-four hours. If and when they mentioned that they had watched TV, the mothers were asked, "Did you talk to the child about the program during it or was it mostly for watching?" They could choose among these answers: "Mostly for watching," "Some talking," "A lot of talking," "Not together with child during program," "Background noise," and "Other."

The NYU team collected the diaries and started sorting the data. Then, eight months later, they saw the mothers and children again. This time they tested the children, now fourteen months old, for their nascent language skills, their ability to understand spoken words, and utter words of their own.

Their question was whether researchers would be able to detect a difference between children whose mothers talked with them while watching TV and children whose mothers did not. Would a significant difference show up in children's scores of language skills? The answer: Yes. Even more encouraging: the typically adverse effects of adult-directed TV did not show up for kids who had experienced media verbal interaction. And when the programming on the TV was educational, the talking was linked to improved language development compared to their peers. Chatting about the content on screen—even if it was chatting to a six-month-old baby—appeared to counterbalance the harm often associated with TV viewing at young ages.

In the 2010 journal article that describes these results, researchers hold out the possibility of combining the best of the study on media verbal interactions with the positive impact shown in the VIP studies. One of the outcomes from VIP is parents becoming more likely to limit adult-directed TV once they had learned about the power of their verbal interactions with their children. This suggests, the NYU researchers write, "that there is potential to address both of these issues simultaneously." It is a promising idea. Imagine taking something like VIP—or PALs, or Ready Rosie—and designing it so that parents see models of what adults talking with children *about* or *in joint attention to various kinds of media*. They could become more mindful of media and better conversationalists with their children at the same time.

NOTES

PALS had a positive effect: Landry, Smith, and Swank 2006.

interactive story time or "dialogic reading": Whitehurst and Lonigan 1998. Research on Dialogic Reading is summarized here: "Dialogic Reading." What Works Clearinghouse, US Department of Education, at http://ies.ed.gov/ncee/wwc/pdf/intervention_reports/WWC_Dialogic_Reading_020807.pdf.

The skills of responsive parenting: Landry et al. 2012.

Don't hug and kiss: Bigelow and Morris 2001.

So that any mother could afford it: Maier 2003.

Participation in the project: Levenstein et al. 1998.

the Nurse–Family Partnership: For more on the history of David Olds and NFP, see Andy Goodman, *The Story of David Olds and the Nurse Home Visiting Program* (Robert Wood Johnson Foundation, 2006) at

http://www.socialimpactexchange.org/sites/www.socialimpactexchange
.org/files/RWJ%20DavidOldsSpecialReport0606.pdf.

they still serve only a tiny fraction: In 2014, the MIECHV pro-
gram served about 15,000 families, according to page 7 of Lisa
Guernsey, Laura Bornfreund, Clare McCann, and Conor Williams,
*Subprime Learning: Early Education in America since the Great
Recession* (Washington, DC: New America, January 2014) at
http://newamerica.net/sites/newamerica.net/files/policydocs/New
America_SubprimeLearning_Release.pdf.

Surveys have shown: Lapierre, Piotroski, and Linebarger 2012.

"always on" TV can be detrimental: Lapierre, Piotroski, and Linebarger
2012; Linebarger et al. 2014.

children are subjected to high amounts of adult-oriented television: Barr
et al. 2010.

A second study in 2005: Mendelsohn et al. 2011.

It lowered depressive symptoms: Berkule et al. 2014.

well-documented connection: McDaniel and Lowenstein 2013, 1 (for stat
about 1/7) and 2 (for 70 percent stat).

They get this sense of pride: As told to Sarah Jackson, the cofounder
of HiredPen, the communications firm we hired to conduct
interviews and write blog posts related to this work. For more,
read "Pediatricians Use Video Tools to Promote Early Literacy," June 23, 2014, at New America's blog *EdCentral* at
http://www.edcentral.org/seeding-reading-pediatricians-use-video-
tools/.

I needed a resource that was quick: E-mail correspondence with Emily
Roden, December 16, 2014.

the programming on the TV was educational: Tomopoulos et al. 2010.

the NYU researchers write: Ibid., 589.

Nudged toward Conversational Duets

A few years ago, when PBS started developing apps to promote early literacy skills, it decided to make a concerted effort to help low-income families. What would work best for single mothers in poverty, for parents working the night shift or in and out of temporary jobs, for grandparents taking on the role of primary caregiver for their grandchildren? What would inspire them to talk with and read to their children? The network conducted focus groups of low-income parents and guardians, and one thing soon became clear, according to Sara Dewitt, vice president of PBS Kids Digital: "Being told, 'You should read to your children every night' was not received well." It was off-putting and disheartening for a parent to hear that she should be spending more time reading or talking with her children after, say, working back-to-back shifts and returning at night to an apartment with the heat shut off.

So PBS arrived at a different message: "Anytime is learning time." The organization developed its free Play & Learn app, supported in part by the Campaign for Grade-Level Reading, to provide ideas for parents to make up rhyming songs and try out new vocabulary words with their children while out at the store or riding the bus. Its aim, said Jean Crawford, senior content and outreach manager at PBS, was to shift from making parents feel that they have been doing something wrong "to having them feel empowered."

PBS's experience points to a two key challenges facing anyone trying out new tools and techniques to promote early literacy: first you have to figure out what message will actually spur new language interactions between parents and children. Then you have to make sure that you deliver that message without sounding clueless, patronizing, or both.

The first challenge is becoming increasingly evident as many advocates try to tackle the troubling "word gap" laid bare by Hart and Risley. In fact, Kathy Hirsh-Pasek, a developmental scientist at Temple University, dislikes the phrase "word gap." She worries that it conjures images of a space to be filled, as if educators or parents simply need to pour in a bunch of words and, *voilà*, problem solved. She worries that parents may think they should start drilling children on new vocabulary words, giving them an infant version of flash-card learning that rarely sticks.

Children's brains, she says, are not containers to be filled with words. Decades of research on babies and toddlers' language development, many of which have been conducted by Hirsh-Pasek with Roberta Golinkoff of the University of Delaware, show that babies learn words best when the person who is speaking to them *engages* with them, invites them into conversation, notices what they are noticing, and responds to their babbles and first words. This back-and-forth interaction—also described as "serve and return" by the Frontiers of Innovation initiative at Harvard University's Center for the Developing Child—is at the heart of language learning.

Instead of subjecting children to streams of words devoid of real dialogue, Hirsh-Pasek, Golinkoff, and their teams have been experimenting with more natural interventions in everyday places. In 2013, they placed signs in a few Fresh Grocer stores in Pennsylvania. In the produce section, a sign said, "Question for your child: What is your favorite kind of vegetable?" Another sign said, "Question for your child: Where does milk come from?" Over several months, the researchers observed and took notes on how much parents spoke to their children when walking through that section of the store. In middle-income neighborhoods, they detected little difference; parents were holding conversations in the supermarket with their children regardless. But "in low-income neighborhoods, we got a 33 percent increase in parent-child language when the signs were up," Hirsh-Pasek said. Other cities are also experimenting with conversation starters in everyday places: a project called Word Play uses bus stop billboards in Pittsburgh; the children's advocacy organization Too Small to Fail is doing the same in Oakland.

Researchers have various terms for this kind of back-and-forth dialogue. We've talked about the importance of dialogic reading when adults are reading books with children. David K. Dickinson, an education professor at the Peabody School at Vanderbilt University who has spent years studying and designing methods to promote early literacy, has called it "extended discourse." Too many children from low-income households, he writes, are "are not inducted into the kind of discourse that enables a smooth transition to literacy."

But terms like "discourse," "dialogic," or even "serve and return" may not be easy for most parents to relate to. Dickinson, for example, has developed a phrase he uses to help teachers and parents remember to talk to their charges: "Strive for 5," by which he means five back-and-forth turns. And at the White House in October 2014, as "word gap" experts from around the country gathered to learn of each others' research, Hirsh-Pasek pressed for different ways to talk with parents about their interactions with their kids that did not conjure images of simply filling them up with words. Instead of fixating on the word gap, she asked, could we use a different phrase?

Her suggestion: Let's encourage "conversational duets," a phrase that captures how much one speaker needs the other and vice versa, not to mention the magic of the two in combination. "If you are singing a duet, you can't do it solo," she said.

It's too early to know whether messages about conversational duets will resonate enough to help parents avoid flashcard-like learning, but either way there is still the next challenge: spreading this message without sounding, well, a little too high minded. Encouraging parents to change the way they talk with their children is not easy. Any effort to ask parents to change the way they behave with their children is like walking into an emotional minefield, and it is surely made worse when the advice-givers clearly have economic and educational advantages that parents on the receiving end don't. The pioneers you met in the last chapter—home visitors and medical specialists—know this well. They have to tread carefully, but they also need to recognize powerful assets such as linguistic diversity and cultural knowledge that are waiting to be tapped. In the same way, national programs as varied as Reach Out and Read, which enlists pediatricians in showing parents how to do interactive reading, and Every Child Ready to Read, which is run by children's librarians, are increasingly recognizing the need to be sensitive to what parents are going through. If we are going to meaningfully tackle the quiet crisis of so many children struggling with literacy, we are going to have to figure out how to reach parents in ways that empower them.

DIGITAL TAPS AND BEHAVIORAL NUDGES

Could the use of social media and peer networks help prompt that empowerment? Knowledge from the still-emerging field of behavioral economics has shown just how much human beings are apt to change their behavior based on peer pressure and encouragement from friends, as well as subtle messages in their environment. New strategies are emerging for registering to vote, complying with medical prescription regimens, creating organ donor campaigns, and donating to charities. (Were you among the Americans who donated more than $100 million to ALS research through the Ice Bucket Challenge of 2014?) These nudges—popularized in the 2009 book *Nudge*, by economists Richard Thaler and Cass Sunstein—become infinitely easier in the era of text messaging and Facebook. In the United Kingdom, the strategy has been used to expand what officials there are calling "personalised" policy compliance through the creation of a "behavioral insights team" that is part of a special agency that partners with the government.

In short, agencies can now provide a digital "tap on the shoulder" to remind citizens to pay their taxes on time or remember to apply for social services or health insurance.

It may sound like quite a stretch to expect that such a strategy would work with something as complex and context-dependent as getting parents to engage in positive parenting, responsive interactions, and more conversational duets between parents and their children. But several companies and non-profit institutions have decided to plunge ahead and see whether these digital taps could work for parents. One of them is a startup company called Parent University that uses the immediacy of text messaging to send parents information that could help them with their children. In 2013, it found a willing partner in a nationally known and highly influential early childhood organization called the Ounce of Prevention Fund, which was looking for new approaches for reaching parents. Tony Raden and Ann Hanson, leaders of research and policy at the Ounce, rolled out Parent University for three Head Start centers in Chicago, where the vast majority of parents were already using cell phones and text messages. "The idea that they would be engaging on a device they're already using all day anyway was compelling," Hanson said. She enlisted the help of Northwestern University to set up an experiment and compare two groups of parents, one receiving messages and the other not, to see if it would work.

TEXTING FOR MODERN-DAY PARENTS

Alexiss Evans, the mother of a five-year-old girl, was one of the 120 parents who participated in the Parent University experiment. One of our reporters, Maureen Kelleher, had a chance to ask her about her experiences. Evans said she mostly ignored the messages for the first few days. Like many of the parents surveyed before the program began, she didn't think the texts were going to do her any good. When polled, just over half (54 percent) of parents in the study's control group, those who did not receive the text messages, agreed that texts were a good way to receive parenting information.

But Evans became a walking example that text messages can work. For six weeks, Parent University sent Evans and other moms and dads a message between 5 p.m. and 6 p.m. each weekday. They said things such as, "While in the bathtub sing the head shoulders knees and toes song while touching each body part" and "While reading with ur child point to the words as u read"—abbreviated in "textspeak" to stay within a 140-character limit.

Then came the text she needed to hear. She was having a particularly bad day. The message pinged her during that witching hour, sometime around 5 p.m., when parents are tired and everything feels daunting. It said, "Hey mom & dad, we wanted to take a second to tell u what an awesome job ur doing!"

"That's when I started doing them every day," Evans said.

The texts prompted hands-on family activities, such as lying on the floor to form letters or cutting out pictures to create a collage. "Even if I didn't take advantage [of the advice] necessarily that day, I went back on the weekends and said, 'We can do this, this, and this,'" Evans said. "It was still there, and I could come back to it when I did have that particular fruit [that was needed for an activity] or went grocery shopping and could pull up the messages." Her daughter's dad, Brandon Jones, often joined in the fun as well.

Evans said she appreciated that the suggested activities did not feel like chores but instead led her to enjoy time with her daughter. "I felt like I was fooling her," she said. "She loved it. You would have thought I was giving her a trip to the carnival." She also liked how the activities often reinforced what her daughter was working on in school at the time.

By the end of the program, Evans was among the 91 percent of intervention group participants who said the texts were helpful. "It's not judgmental," said Joy D'Amico, family and community partnership manager at the Ounce of Prevention Fund. Parents don't have to visit a center or attend a parent-teacher conference to receive advice on helping their kids. "It's being messaged in a way that's convenient and private."

But did the program change parents' behavior? The Northwestern study, led by communications and psychology professor Ellen Wartella, was designed to help find out. Wartella and her team surveyed the parents of both groups before and after the intervention. Although the frequency of participation varied—with one-third of parents reporting doing "all" or "almost all" activities, 58 percent doing "some" or "a few," and 8 percent "hardly any" or none—parents who received the text messages said they engaged in significantly more learning activities, particularly planned ones, during the six-week program than parents who didn't receive the texts.

"What really stands out to me is how a text said to take the 'Little Red Riding Hood' story and have a real conversation with my son about stranger danger," said Camille Curry, mother of then-four-year-old Ashton. "'What did she do that you shouldn't do? And how could she have gone about not talking to strangers?' I wouldn't have thought to use that book to teach stranger danger." Curry also liked the texts' simplicity and ease. "It doesn't take much," she said. "It's a small suggestion, and it's free."

Fathers in the intervention group and parents of boys were particularly receptive to the text messages. Overall fathers reported that they engaged in more activities with their children and were more likely to play dress-up or pretend. These are encouraging findings, as research indicates that dads typically favor more rough-and-tumble play than social-based activities and that responsiveness tends to be better between parents and their daughters.

Although the findings are promising, the experiment wasn't perfect. The actions that parents reported doing may be different than the way they actually behaved. Technological hurdles sometimes got in the way. Some of the participants' prepaid mobile phones weren't able to receive automated messages. Others had phones with restrictions on how much data could be downloaded without incurring high fees. Many parents found creative ways to get around the problem—by waiting until the beginning of the month to open the Parent University texts, for example—but these technology-related barriers affected participation.

Other promising results are also emerging from San Francisco, where a similar text messaging study has been underway with a larger cohort of parents. In a program called READY4K!, experimenters sent text messages to 440 parents of four-year-olds enrolled in thirty-one preschool programs in the San Francisco Unified School District. The learning scientists who designed the program—Benjamin N. York and Susanna Loeb at Stanford University—collected data on parents' behaviors as well as children's early literacy skills to detect whether texts to parents could have an impact on their kids. To make sure that they were controlling for different possibilities, York and Loeb randomly assigned parents to one of two groups: those receiving texts about building literacy skills at home and those receiving placebo texts, which were reminders to get their children immunized. After eight months of text messages, the results showed significant differences between the two groups. Compared to those receiving placebos, the parents with literacy texts asked teachers questions more frequently about their children's learning, and their children scored higher on alphabet knowledge and letter sounds. Another positive: The intervention was very inexpensive.

"For the entire school year, we spent less than one dollar per family to send text messages," York and Loeb wrote in a working paper for the National Bureau of Economic Research.

Text Messages Plus Goal-Setting

Ariel Kalil, a developmental psychologist at the Behavioral Insights and Parenting Lab at the Harris School of Public Policy at the University of Chicago, has started experimenting with text-messaging too but with a more pointed mission: Increase the time that parents spend reading with their kids. But to gain evidence of impact, Kalil recognized that she needed to do more than just send texts. She would need to keep track of how much reading is actually happening and how many books are read. She also wondered if that act of measurement, those tallies of books read and time spent, might motivate parents to set goals and work to reach them.

The project, called Parents and Children Together (PACT), lasts for six weeks. About a hundred families in Head Start centers in Chicago have participated so far, and more than four hundred will have participated by the end of the trial run. Kalil started by randomly splitting participating families into two groups. One group was asked to commit to read to their children for a certain number of minutes each week. Parents in this group received daily text messages from the researchers reminding them of their goal and of the importance of spending time reading to their children. At the end of each week, parents received messages about the amount of time they spent reading, and they received positive recognition each week either for meeting their goals or for achieving the highest level of reading among parents in this group. The other group of parents received no such incentives, feedback, or recognition for their efforts.

In both groups parents were lent iPads with the app *A Story Before Bed*, which enables parents to record their voices reading stories to their children. (The app, developed by tech pioneer Hillel Cooperman, is popular among parents in the military or otherwise traveling for lengths of time and unable to be with their children for bedtime.) The app's audio recorder enabled Kalil and her team to measure how much time parents in either group spent using that app to read aloud with their children.

The results from the initial sample showed big gains in reading time. If continued success is achieved, Kalil said, researchers want to zoom in on which nudges were most noteworthy. Did the daily reminders do the job? Were parents influenced by having pledged their goals to the researchers and knowing that their efforts were being recorded and tracked each week? Was it because they received feedback and recognition for their efforts, thus potentially building a positive feedback loop that sustained their motivation?

"Once we find something that does work," Kalil said, "we want to make it instantly scalable, that's our goal, so that you don't need very intensive training to do these things. If text messaging works to change behavior, anyone can do it."

Such positive results and inexpensive startup costs portend many more of these programs. The Parent University partnership was a time-limited project that ended in 2013, but since then the Ounce has been working to develop a high-touch digital program for parent engagement, and the advocacy group Too Small to Fail announced a mobile parenting initiative with the organization Text4Baby that was rolled out in 2015. Parents like Evans and Curry, the mothers who were involved in Parent University, say they are ready for more. "When it stopped, I was a little disappointed," Evans said. "It was like, 'What happened to my messages?'"

■ **Video Vignette: PACT for Book Reading**
bit.ly/tapclick2

ENCOURAGEMENT VIA BROADCAST TV: UNIVISION AND TOO SMALL TO FAIL

Roberto Llamas is not your typical literacy skills pusher. An executive vice president at Univision, he is a TV guy who knows the world of telenovelas and broadcast soccer. His company has become a fast-growing network for Spanish speakers in the United States, sometimes topping FOX, NBC, and other English-speaking channels for audience share among young adults during evening hours. But in 2013 Llamas was given an unusual opportunity to launch an initiative that could have a significant impact on how Spanish-speaking parents in the United States see their role in developing children's language and literacy skills. Too Small to Fail, a national advocacy organization for early childhood launched with help from the Bill, Hillary & Chelsea Clinton Foundation, wanted to reach America's growing Spanish-speaking audience. Would Univision help?

Univision soon realized that when it came to child development, parents trusted the network's news anchors and other personalities more than they did pediatricians. Parents could relate, for example, to Barbara Bermudo, the host of the evening news program *Primer Impacto*, who is of Puerto Rican and Cuban descent and has two young children. The Univision parent audience wanted to hear what she thought about raising children to learn to read and succeed in school.

In 2014, Univision and Too Small to Fail pledged to craft a set of public service announcements (PSAs), on-air teachable moments, and community outreach projects that would take advantage of the popularity of Bermudo and other Univision personalities. They announced the initiative—*Pequeños y Valiosos* ("Young and Valuable")—at a classroom in a Head Start center in Harlem on a February day. On wooden chairs in front of a chalk board, surrounded by little kids sitting on the rug, sat three adults: Bermudo, Univision's CEO Randy Falco, and Hillary Rodham Clinton. "I believe that every child should have the same opportunity to succeed in school and in life," Clinton said. "In order for this to happen we need to start with our youngest and most valuable citizens, our smallest children. I'm happy to be part of this campaign with Univision and with you Barbara, to promote this message so that as soon as that baby is born, her parents, grandparents, aunts and uncles, everyone, start talking and singing to her, and start developing that brain for the future."

Throughout the morning, the three adults laughed, talked, and read books to the children. Recaps on the nightly news repeated Too Small to Fail's simple message: Talk, read, and sing with your baby (https://www.youtube.com/watch?v=YdVDeGkNYC4).

In a world of smartphones and text messages, examples from broadcast TV may sound a little dated. But it's the specialized and subtle cues to specific yet far-flung communities that caught our eye. For example, Univision has also broadcast PSAs that are specifically targeted. In the summer of 2014, during the network's almost nonstop coverage of the World Cup, Univision ran a PSA that showed clips of fathers playing soccer on sun-kissed fields interspersed with images of fathers talking and reading with their children. Focus groups had shown that some Latino men thought it wasn't macho to read to their kids. This PSA was trying to counteract that notion.

Given how broad an audience Univision is trying to reach, we may never know if this outreach is having any measurable impact on Spanish-speaking parents. But Stephen Massey, Too Small to Fail's senior manager of media and corporate partnerships, is optimistic. "Many parents don't understand what kind of impact they can have, and the role they play in developing their child's mind," Massey said. "Being able to dive into that through a powerful platform like TV can make a big difference."

The Too Small to Fail partnership with Univision is part of a larger strategy to infuse messages into entertainment media. Last year, during a set of briefings in Los Angeles, the organization was able to grab the attention of Hollywood producers long enough to persuade them to insert some parenting advice into the storylines of popular shows. Some producers squirmed at the idea, not wanting to sound heavy-handed, but they promised to consider some small tweaks. *Orange Is the New Black*, a drama about women in prison in New York, was one of the first to try it. In one episode, a woman talks with the father of her child, a man known for not saying much: "You have to talk to her, like, all the time," says the mother. "There's all these studies that say if you don't talk to the baby they end up f****d by the time they're five. Talk to her. Sing to her. I know you don't like to talk, but you gotta do it for her."

Video Vignette: Univision and Too Small to Fail
bit.ly/tapclick3

A FITBIT FOR WORDS AND CONVERSATIONS

Aneisha Newell, a twenty-six-year-old mother, grew up in foster care on the far south side of Chicago. It's a rough part of town, an area marked by violence and unemployment, as well as levels of poverty typically associated with failure in school. For many families like hers, having conversations with infants may not be second nature. Newell says that whenever she would talk to her baby, her friends and family gave her flak for it. "You're talking to your child like she understands you!," they would say.

But Newell said she shrugged off their criticisms, newly emboldened by a program called the Thirty Million Words Initiative, named for the 30 million word gap found in the Hart and Risley study. Like PALS and the Video Interaction Project of the previous chapter, Thirty Million Words uses home visits and video modeling to help parents see the power of simple conversations with their children to build their language skills. But this initiative takes things one step further: it counts every word that parents say to their kids.

How's that, you ask? The program uses a digital recording device called the LENA (Learning ENvironment Analysis) that tracks the number of words spoken by the parent and the child and how much back-and-forth talk is happening between them. The LENA fits easily into a pocket, typically one that is stitched into the front of a child's clothing. It was developed by Terrance Paul, an inventor who, before his death in 2014, often referred to the device as a "talk pedometer," a FitBit for conversation. When Paul discovered how much laborious counting was involved in studies of the word gap, he got an idea—why not create a device to measure how many words and conversational turns children experience at home each day? He and a team of engineers, statisticians, and linguistic experts in automatic speech recognition created a two-ounce recording device, called a digital language processor, which can capture up to sixteen hours of audio recording. It contains software created with pattern-recognition technology that analyzes three key metrics: the number of adult words spoken, the number of child vocalizations, and the number of conversational turns between adult and child.

Researchers soon became excited about the device's potential. In 2009, Paul established the nonprofit LENA Research Foundation (http://www.lenafoundation.org/)to make the tool available to the research community. Approximately two hundred groups are currently using LENA to learn more about language acquisition, child development, and supporting language development for children with autism or who have difficulty hearing.

Motivated by Weekly Tallies of Progress

The LENA device became available to Aneisha Newell and other Chicago families because of their participation in Thirty Million Words. The program asked parents to choose the day they would like to put the device on their children and do the recording. For working parents, it was usually on a weekend. After each recording each week, the home visitor gave the parent a report displaying word counts and conversational turns.

It may sound a little intrusive, if not downright Orwellian, to ask families to equip their children with recording devices. But parents have come to the Thirty Million Words Initiative voluntarily. Many were recruited to be part of a study run by Dana Suskind, a founder of the Thirty Million Words Initiative and a University of Chicago pediatric surgeon who specializes in cochlear implants for deaf and hard-of-hearing children. She became interested in children's language development after noticing that her patients from middle-class and wealthy families almost always learned to speak quickly after implant surgery, whereas her low-income patients often did not. When Suskind learned about the findings of Hart and Risley, she first created an intervention that targets low-income families who have children with hearing loss, and then she designed Thirty Million Words for typically developing children.

Newell, in fact, says she was not terribly bothered by the recording device. Our reporter Maureen Kelleher caught up with her when her daughter Alona had turned five. She says she learned so much from LENA that she is now a frequent conversationalist with her kids. She beat all previous records among study participants for adult word count. "I know what I missed out on," Newell said. "It makes it clear to me what I want to give my children."

Since her participation in Thirty Million Words, Newell has had another child, Amod, and uses what she has learned from the project on a regular basis. She said she has gone from seeing learning as something confined to certain points in the day, like story time, to seeing it as happening all the time.

For example, Newell now makes a point to talk with her children while they watch TV together and she asks questions about what they are watching. If Alona doesn't respond to a question on a video, Newell will pause it and give her time to respond. "If she didn't hear it, I'll repeat the question." When they go to visit other people's houses, Newell says that "Alona is shouting out the answers." Others complain and "say *shhh*. TV's on." But Alona isn't used to being in places where children aren't supposed to talk. "That's not how we do it in our house." Newell said.

Another parent in the program, Shurand Adams, was a little less sure of the LENA device at first. But she said she was also curious about how many words her daughter Teshiya was hearing daily. Teshiya was nineteen months old at the time, and Adams, a first-time mother who had not completed high school, was looking for guidance. "I wanted to do it right," she said. "I would go get a book in a minute about how to raise my child. All this is a learning curve."

Joining the study was a revelation. "Each week you would see how you have increased. It was really encouraging," Adams said. "I didn't know a child's most crucial time in learning is from birth until five years old. I knew you could start at home doing little things, but I thought the learning was from teachers. They're trained to do that. I didn't feel like I had the ability."

Suskind is hoping Thirty Million Words will continue to dispel that mind-set. It's designed to help parents master the Three Ts: Tune in, Talk more, and Take turns conversing with their kids. "Becoming smart is dependent on one critical factor—how and how much parents talk and interact with their children," Suskind said.

These Three Ts have stuck with Adams. "I try to use that in our everyday living," she explained. "If I sit down and talk to [Teshiya] about how many bananas we are putting in the grocery cart, we are doing math."

Evaluating Impact: Turning Parents into Long-term Conversationalists

The study she participated in showed promising initial results. Parents in the treatment group, like Adams and Newell, showed a significant

165

increase in understanding how children's language develops. During the eight weeks of the study, parents used more words and more diverse words than control group parents, and they also increased conversational turn-taking with their children. All the differences were statistically significant. Although the increase is notable, the effects had faded when the researchers retested the families four months later. The researchers note that the program was short—eight weeks—which could have limited its impact.

The researchers also stress that the study was small—only twenty-three families—which makes it hard to untangle any differences between families who signed up for the program and those who did not. There may be something unique about families who volunteer for a literacy program that makes them more amenable to the intervention, for example. A second randomized, control trial involving two hundred families with toddlers approximately fifteen months old began in January 2015 and will follow the children to kindergarten.

A separate LENA project underway in Providence, Rhode Island, should provide more evidence as well. A few years ago, the city won a $5 million grant from Bloomberg Philanthropies to roll out a LENA-assisted home visitation program called Providence Talks. In 2014 about seventy-five families participated in a pilot, and Brown University has started gathering data to see if it works. At last check, the city was aiming to enroll two thousand families by the middle of 2016.

The use of LENA is not without its critics. Just as with the worry that overplaying the word gap will lead to a boom in companies selling flashcards, some language development experts warn that comparing tallies of spoken words will oversimplify what it takes to address literacy problems. In a *PBS NewsHour* segment about the program, Brown University linguistics professor James Morgan questioned whether the emphasis on number of words was the right approach. "The device has no idea *which* words are being used; it can only estimate the total count of words," Morgan said.

But remember that LENA also counts how many times there is an exchange of words between an adult and a child. The next research question and the next challenge for our pioneers may be how to incorporate those conversational turns into campaigns for promoting early literacy. Could some combination of nudges and social media systems reward parents for engaging in conversation as well as for reading a certain amount of books or using more words? Over the next few years, we'll have to keep watching—and counting—to find out.

NOTES

You should read to your children every night: Phone interview with Sara Dewitt, David Lowenstein, and Jean Crawford of PBS, January 27, 2014.

"to having them feel empowered": Ibid.

parents may think: For an extensive and entertaining look at why how children learn language and why flashcards are not the answer, see Hirsh-Pasek and Golinkoff (with Diane Eyer), *Einstein Never Used Flashcards* (Emmaus, PA: Rodale, 2004) at http://www.amazon.com/Einstein-Never-Used-Flashcards-Learn/dp/1594860688.

"we got a 33 percent increase": Personal correspondence with Kathy Hirsh-Pasek and Roberta Golinkoff, February 12, 2015; see also Hirsh-Pasek, "Language and Literacy: Why Third Grade Reading Starts at Birth," Leading for Literacy Meeting, April 15, 2013, at http://earlysuccess.org/sites/default/files/Hirsh-Pasek%20Language%20and%20Literacy.pdf.

Too Small to Fail: With thanks to Heidi Moore and Barbara Ray for conducting interviews on Parent University and helping to write some of this section.

a smooth transition to literacy: Dickinson and McCabe 2001.

If you are singing a duet: E-mail correspondence with Kathy Hirsh-Pasek, March 30, 2015.

"behavioral insights team": Behavioural Insights.

The idea that they would be engaging: Moore 2014.

parents who received the text messages: Ray 2014.

After eight months of text messages: York and Loeb 2014.

If text messaging works to change behavior: Phone interview with Ariel Kalil, August 11, 2014.

What happened to my messages?: Maureen Kelleher, a reporter for Hired-Pen, conducted the interview with Paul in the spring of 2014. Kelleher and Barbara Ray, the cofounder of HiredPen, wrote a part of this section.

His company has become a fast-growing network: "Univision" 2014.

I'm happy to be part of this campaign with Univision: Interview with Hillary Clinton on *Primer Impacto*, a program on Univision, on February 4, 2014. See Spanish version here: https://www.youtube.com/watch?v=YdVDeGkNYC4.

Being able to dive into: See accompanying video in this book of Univision and Too Small to Fail for Barbara Ray's interview with Massey recorded in October 2014.

The researchers note: Suskind et al. Forthcoming.

Science, Social Studies, and More: The Knowledge Readers Need

One recent day in California, a six-year-old boy named Brandon was hanging out at home, watching one of Disney's *Ice Age* movies, when he saw a scene that captivated him. On the screen were the lovable animations of *Ice Age*'s prehistoric beasts, loping along the barren, icy terrain. Brandon turned to his father: "Papi, at that time, what was it like? There weren't any buses?" Smiling, his father, José Rubén, saw this as a teachable moment. He went to his computer, pulled up YouTube, and searched for videos that would show his son more about what life was like during that time.

"We watched videos where it is shown and everything," the father said as he recounted this scene for Amber Levinson, a Stanford researcher whose work informed a recent report from the Joan Ganz Cooney Center. Brandon and José Rubén's interests led them from one history video to another, and soon the two of them were watching a documentary about dinosaurs and other species.

What does watching Disney movies and a dinosaur documentary have to do with reading and literacy? So much more than you might think. Here was a moment in which Brandon was engaged in building his knowledge base, getting an introduction to concepts and ideas that not only gave him a little more understanding of the Ice Age, but also helped him put the Ice Age into context of other periods in history and start to gain a framework for thinking about how time passes and how change happens. He was hooked in enough to start to reflect upon and then store new information for recall sometime in the future when he may be asked to talk about, read about, or write about—*be literate about*—how life has changed on Planet Earth.

What's more, Brandon was also getting a lesson in media literacy and digital literacy too. Though his father may not have even realized it, he was modeling what it looks like to use digital information to gain a deeper sense of the world. He recognized the importance of Brandon's question and rewarded it by spending time helping him find answers. He showed what it looks like to search for information online and make distinctions between fiction (a movie) and non-fiction (a documentary).

When most people talk about the troubling state of children's reading in the United States, the untapped power of these kinds of learning moments are not likely on their minds. Instead they may think our country's problems are simply a function of whether children ever learned how to decode words on a page or read sentences with fluency. But the root of the problem may be in children's abilities to *comprehend* and make sense of the ideas that are built by those words and sentences. Recent vocabulary scores from the National Assessment of Educational Progress, for example, showed that American children are making few if any significant gains in understanding the meaning of complex words, with a wide gulf between white students and those of Hispanic students and African American students. So if there are ways to build that word learning and even more importantly build a deeper knowledge base that enables comprehension in today's children, don't we have a moral obligation to seize it?

JOINT MEDIA ENGAGEMENT AND KNOWLEDGE BUILDING

Given their potential, moments like those between Brandon and his father are now the subject of a growing body of scholarship. They have spawned a new term in the world of media research: "joint media engagement," sometimes shortened to JME. This kind of engagement can happen when any two or more people—parent and child, siblings, or peers—are looking at the same media at the same time, are involved in the content together, and are prompted by what they are seeing to interact with each other and bring more meaning to what they are watching or doing. The term was coined in 2010 by researchers at the LIFE Center, a collaborative lab, funded by the National Science Foundation, whose name is short for Learning in Informal and Formal Environments. Run by the University of Washington, Stanford University, SRI International, Northwestern University, and the University of California at Berkeley, the group has been pooling resources across neuroscience, cognitive science, education, and media research to examine what happens when people learn together with media. Research on JME includes traditional examples, such as parental "co-viewing" of *Sesame Street* and other TV shows, as well as just-emerging practices, like playing together with apps.

That kind of engagement is critical to helping children build a knowledge base, especially for struggling readers. Remember Dan Willingham, the cognitive scientist we introduced in chapter 2? Willingham had cited an experiment showing that children with mediocre reading skills but deep knowledge of baseball scored significantly higher than their peers on reading tests *when the subject matter was baseball*. Their interest in the content translated to a store of knowledge that enabled them to comprehend the text and whiz through the vocabulary that stumped other children.

Willingham's research builds upon theories that are often associated with E. D. Hirsch Jr., a professor emeritus at the University of Virginia, who has been vocal for decades about the importance of cultural literacy and background knowledge in helping children learn to read. For example, an introduction to the "Three Blind Mice" or the Statue of Liberty, Hirsch explains, can be helpful to children's future reading comprehension; there is a good chance they will come across a reference to that rhyme or statue in something they read in the future. In the 1990s, Hirsch wrote a series of books such as *What Your Kindergartner Needs to Know* and *What Your*

First Grader Needs to Know, which expounds on the need for all children to acquire some "common ground" in their knowledge of concepts, characters, and artifacts from the worlds of literature, art, history, geography, science, and more. He is best known for the 1988 book *Cultural Literacy: What Every American Needs to Know,* which made the *New York Times* bestseller list.

At the time of *Cultural Literacy*'s publication, Hirsch's ideas were highly controversial, and in many ways they still are. To conservative critics, the focus on acquiring background knowledge sounds too much like dictating curriculum and national standards. Liberal critics fault his choices of classic texts and important historical moments and warn readers that his books are the product of an old white man's point of view. But Hirsch's larger point jibes with what has become well understood in language learning and literacy: children need to gain some knowledge of a thing before they can fully comprehend texts with direct references or allusions to it. It is not fair to demand that children excel at reading comprehension tests (or recognize words from the Anglo-centric story of the Little Red Hen) when they have not been introduced to the concepts that might help them build that vocabulary. Children need exposure to the subject matter of the world.

That exposure can certainly come from books, as long as the books are rich in content; it can come from field trips (apple orchards, construction sites, aquariums); it can derive from observing and asking questions of people about what they are doing or what they know (cashiers, nurses, bus drivers); and it can come from all sorts of audiovisual media (TV shows about zoologists with pet lemurs, video games about the spread of infection, DVDs on the history of Martin Luther King Jr.).

That last category is the one that many e-literacy pioneers are now aggressively trying to tap into. Children of all backgrounds love audiovisual media, and children from immigrant households may have even more to gain because they are in the challenging and yet ultimately enviable position of acquiring more than one language at the same time. Their parents certainly see potential: according to the Cooney Center report *Aprendiendo en Casa*, which surveyed 682 Hispanic parents, "Most parents whose child used educational media regularly reported that their child learned academic skills from media, particularly in reading or vocabulary."

The survey also found that Spanish-only families generally spend more time in joint media engagement than English-only families. "There is value for both parents and children in media content that serves as a springboard for conversation and activities, as well as content that promotes joint media engagement," the authors write. "Such content is sorely needed across all platforms."

MAKING MEANING IN MAINE

Let us take you now to Milbridge, Maine, to see the power of joint media engagement when given a platform for success. Milbridge is a coastal town of 1,200 people southeast of Bangor with frigid waters, spires of narrow evergreen trees, and rocky shoreline. During the summer, the harvest is blueberries. Another source of work is Cherry Point Products, Inc., a nearby company that fishes, processes, freezes, and sells sea cucumbers and hagfish during the agricultural off-season.

It may sound like a remote place, but the challenges and opportunities within this town will probably sound familiar to anyone living in a part of the United States that has undergone rapid change in demographics. During the past fifteen years, Milbridge has undergone a dramatic demographic shift as migrant families from Mexico and other parts of Central America have been arriving to find jobs. The families piece together year-round work through a combination of blueberry harvesting, wreath making, and other seasonal labor. With little money for books and extracurriculars, and most parents still learning English, their children often struggle in school.

Recently several of these families have had the opportunity to take part in an unusual early childhood education program called Comienza en Casa | It Starts at Home. We first heard about Comienza en Casa in 2012, its founding year, when we interviewed one of its co-creators, a gregarious teacher and Maine resident named Bonnie Blagojevic. At the time, she was already known in early childhood circles for her ambitious approaches to blending storybooks and new technologies with hands-on activities. Blagojevic described a program in which a home visitor—who happened to be her daughter—arrived at homes with armfuls of learning materials and guided families in lively learning sessions that involved iPads, iBooks, podcasts, print books, toys, cardboard boxes, cooking recipes, and art supplies. It sounded like a blast. Better yet: almost every bit was offered in both English and Spanish.

We resolved to learn more. In May 2014, we sent Lindsey Tepe, a member of Lisa's team at New America, to Milbridge. She was guided by Ana Blagojevic, Bonnie's daughter, who designed the program as an educational initiative for the nonprofit organization for migrant families in Maine called Mano en Mano | Hand in Hand. Ana introduced Lindsey to teachers, parents, and children to help answer a flurry of questions: Were families genuinely interested in participating in the program? Were there any visible or measurable signs of success? And what exactly was the point of the iPad?

Nurturing a Scientist, On Screen and Off

Lindsey met the Vazquezes, a young family with an active, smiling, five-year-old with round cheeks, dark brown eyes, and an insatiable appetite for learning new things. Jayden was just a few months away from starting kindergarten. His mother, Juana, who spoke English and Spanish, said that before joining Comienza en Casa she had been unsure of what to do to help her son prepare for school. Fortunately the program had given her a bounty of ideas.

That afternoon Lindsey sat with Juana in her sunlit kitchen and watched how she nurtured one of her son's newfound interests: science. On their screened-in porch, several potted plants were set up for an experiment on how their proximity to sunlight would affect how fast they grew. A piece of paper was taped to Jayden's bedroom door that said "Scientist's Room."

"He's also really into rockets and space ships," Juana said. As Juana and Lindsey talked, Jayden used the iPad to pull up examples of a previous project, photos of a model spaceship he had built with his father. "Mom, can we save the rocket one, and record it?," Jayden asked, speaking in English for Lindsey's benefit. "Okay," Juana responded. During a prior visit with Ana, the family had started using an app called Shadow Puppet that enabled Jayden to narrate photographs and drawings. "Go to Shadow Puppet," she reminded him.

"So first, I'm going to pick a few photos," Jayden said aloud. "Pick a few photos—my rocket. Mom, what do we call it?" he asked as the app prompted him to name the video. He pressed the record button. "This is my rocket, you know about the rocket explodes up. It goes 100 miles up. I have all the materials to build it, so me and my dad built it." Then Jayden pressed "Save." Together, the photos he selected and his narration told a story that was now recorded for posterity.

"His vocabulary has gone up," Juana said. By using interactive photos and e-books, she explained, "he can click on the stuff and it tells you what it is. His vocabulary is much better than it was before."

Consider what unfolded as Jayden recorded his rocket story. Not only was he speaking fluently in his second language and translating concepts from what he knew in Spanish into English, he was using words about science and math. He had said the word *explode*. He had used terminology associated with measurement and distance: "It goes 100 miles up." No matter that in this example it was actually a toy that, according to the packaging, could only be propelled 1,100 feet, not 100 miles; those kinds of details are not understood by most five-year-olds. What mattered was Jayden getting practice in how to express himself and document what he had created or observed. Moreover, he was building the background knowledge to draw upon years later when he might come across paragraphs—in either English or Spanish—about space-craft, propulsion, and upward trajectories.

Of course, a touchscreen tablet is not required to entice children to make rockets, talk about explosions, or do arts and crafts. But here in

Milbridge, at least, it was evident the device played a stimulating role. "He really likes drawing on the iPad and stuff, and then after that he started to like doing it on paper," Juana said. "He didn't really know his letters at the beginning. I didn't know how to practice with him or show him, or what to really do." The materials curated by Comienza en Casa, she said, "gave me lots of ideas and activities I could do."

The tablet had become a handy device for organizing and personalizing material for the Vazquez family and other families in the Comienza en Casa program. A few months earlier, Blagojevic and her team had started creating iBooks to be used on each family's iPad with a combination of Spanish and English resources intentionally selected to meet the participating family's needs. Each iBook became a receptacle for monthly activity sheets for units of study that accompanied the Comienza en Casa visits. Blagojevic also loaded the iPads with Ready Rosie videos, podcasts, e-books, and games that related to the activities and specific themes. Not only were these materials now easily accessible, "families have really seemed to be enjoying them," Blagojevic said.

"Before we started the program," Juana admits, "we were reading a little bit, but not as often. Now we read every night, and he says 'Mom, it's time to read' and he's reading up to three books. Before, he would sit still, but he wasn't as interested."

Juana's ability to talk about her families' reading habits and how they have changed speaks volumes. Think back to the many examples in the last chapter, in which researchers were experimenting with text messages and other tools to encourage parents to talk with and read to their children. Here, in many ways, it was Jayden who was leading his mother to new levels of interaction. Her child's desires, sparked by learning prompted by the materials at his fingertips, were helping them both find new ways to build knowledge about the world

English and Spanish Connections for Parents

Later that day, Jayden and his parents traveled to the town's primary school to participate in one of Comienza en Casa's group meetings, at which parents and children share what they are learning. In the second half of the meeting, the kids were released to play and the adults broke into groups to look through ideas for the next unit of study. One of the groups was examining tadpole eggs that Ana had brought in to identify several characteristics of living things. She also had books on tadpoles. The books were only available in English, but part of the lesson focused on how parents could use Google Translate and other online resources to identify new vocabulary words and find answers to questions when they were unsure of the correct answer.

Bonnie and Ana had developed content-specific vocabulary lists for each unit. But this time the mothers developed vocabulary lists themselves based on what they were finding in their research and in the books on tadpoles. They listed the words in both English and Spanish (*gills, gel, eggs*) that could be emphasized throughout the unit. After leafing through picture books from the public library, they checked out books to support their family's exploration of living versus nonliving things.

Because the Comienza program is designed for parents and children together, it has led to some important discoveries about parents' needs and strengths as much as those of the kids. Not only were parents getting an introduction to English, they were also learning more words in their native language. "The vocabulary and content knowledge, even in [the] native language, families didn't know," Bonnie said. At the same time, the parents taking part in Comienza en Casa were clearly eager to learn. Their strong desire to give their children the best possible start, their openness to exploring new things, their ability to seek out new information, and their discoveries of the interplay and cultural connections between vocabulary in their first language and their second language: all of these were on view for their children to see, providing a model for their children of lifelong learning in a multicultural, multilingual world.

 Video Vignette: Comienza en Casa
bit.ly/tapclick4

TOOLS FOR BUILDING KNOWLEDGE

Like its hometown in Maine, the Comienza en Casa program is very small. About four or five families participate each year. But the general approach could easily be replicated in cities and towns around the country. In fact, many of the online and app-based resources curated by Ana and Bonnie Blagojevic are already available to millions of people every day. For example, Comienza makes heavy use of Ready Rosie, the video modeling company introduced in chapter 7. Because its videos are available in both English and Spanish, they became ideal vehicles for introducing Spanish-speaking families to activities to do at home.

Other apps and online tools could be harnessed for the same purpose. Take the Early Learning Environment, fondly known as Ele ("Ellie"), which is an interactive space designed by the Fred Rogers Center for Early Learning and Children's Media. Fred Rogers (aka Mister Rogers) was an early proponent of using media to help children. He saw getting involved as the answer to curtailing what might otherwise be media's negative effects. "I went into television because I hated it so," he once said during a CNN interview, "and I thought there's some way of using this fabulous instrument to nurture those who would watch and listen." Although Rogers passed away in 2003, his welcoming spirit is still alive in Ele. The home page presents a short welcoming video encouraging educators and parents to look around, browse through libraries of short videos that present fun activities for building word knowledge, and put together "playlists" of apps and games, online and off. Among the scores of examples are rhyming games to play while folding the laundry, science-building activities using food dye to make "colorful milk," and videos of Rogers and Eric Carle reading *The Very Hungry Caterpillar*.

Another research-based tool is Wonderopolis, a website and app from the National Center for Families' Learning, a national nonprofit focused on family literacy. Every day Wonderopolis publishes a "wonder," a question posed and an answer supplied in a brief video. Wonder #1331 ponders, "Why Are Your Feet So Ticklish?" (http://wonderopolis.org/wonder/why-are-your-feet-so-ticklish/) Wonder #706 asks, "Do Warthogs Really Have Warts?" (http://wonderopolis.org/wonder/do-warthogs-really-have-warts/). Through e-mail, Facebook, Twitter, or Pinterest, or simply by stopping by the website, tens of thousands of teachers and parents around the world are receiving these "wonders of the day" to show their kids. Kindergarten teachers have used them to kick off discussions during circle time. Science teachers assign them for homework. Anyone can nominate new wonders and vote for their favorites. At last check, the most popular wonder, with 841 votes, was Wonder #1048: "Is the Five Second Rule Really True?," a *PBS NewsHour* clip that ends with the disappointing news that, yes, bacteria will attach to that Dorito dropped on the cafeteria floor no matter how many seconds it has been there (http://wonderopolis.org/wonder/is-the-five-second-rule-really-true/).

And to encourage intergenerational learning and play, the Cooney Center recently created a guide for parents, written comic-book style, entitled *Family Time with Apps*, that encourages the creation of family media projects, new ways to connect with distant family members, and taking advantage of tools to explore of the outside world.

In short, the proliferation of interactive media and digital video has made it easier than ever to help children acquire that background knowledge that Hirsch, Willingham, and many other scholars have shown to be so important to literacy. Not only do these tools offer rich content, from the Ice Age to the Digital Age, they do it in a way that doesn't shut out parents who may not have perfect English reading skills themselves. No longer do parents have to read their children a book about plants or rockets to introduce them to activities involving plants or rockets. Even better, some of these media moments are being designed as launch pads for adults to engage children in conversation about what they are learning.

NOTES

Papi, at that time, what was it like?: He said this in Spanish.

"he recounted this scene": Levinson 2014

Brandon and José Rubén's interests: Lee and Barron 2015, 31.

Recent vocabulary scores: Nation's Report Card 2013.

the group has been pooling resources: Stevens and Penuel 2010.

In the 1990s: Hirsch Jr. and Holdren 1996, xvi. The full quote is worth reading and so we reprint it here: "Because individual children differ, and because localities across this big and diverse country also differ, kindergarten classrooms will offer different experiences. But classrooms do not, or should not, exist in isolation. In our public school system, classrooms are part of and should prepare our children for life in larger communities. Thus even as we want kindergarten teachers to bring out the best in our children as individual learners and the kindergarten classroom to reflect our particular local community, we also look to kindergarten to prepare our children to be part of a larger community, or rather, communities: the town, the state, the nation, the world. All communities require some common ground. What we have attempted to do in this book is give a concrete and specific sense of a common ground of learning for American kindergartners: not a comprehensive prescription for "everything every kindergartner needs to know," since such a prescription is undesirable, given individual and local differences, but a common ground for being an active, successful learner who is ready for the next big step, that is, first grade."

Most parents: Lee and Barron 2015, 5.

There is value for both parents and children: Ibid.

"I went into television because I hated it so": *Mr. Rogers' Neighborhood* 2000.

to encourage intergenerational learning: *Family Time* 2014.

13

An Expanding Universe of Reading Partners

With an ever-expanding playground of educational materials being created for digital distribution, it is tempting to see digital resources as a solution to disparities. We hear it all the time: If only *all* children had these resources. We just need to get them more e-books. More learning games. More educational apps.

But communities and school districts could purchase more and more of these resources and still fall short. Remember the library study in Philadelphia that used the occasion of a $20 million upgrade to probe whether buying new technologies and more books would help close literacy gaps? Let us take you to the two libraries at the heart of that soon-to-be-classic study on literacy. These libraries—Chestnut Hill and Lillian Marrero—were the site of ten years of study by Susan B. Neuman, Donna C. Celano, and their research assistants, all of whom sat quietly in these libraries for years taking careful notes on how parents and children used the books and computers within. In 2012, in a slim but powerful book called *Giving Our Children a Fighting Chance*, they recounted what they saw.

Lillian Marrero Library is located in the Philadelphia Badlands, an economically abandoned part of town where, Neuman and Celano write, "makeshift garbage dumps line the sidewalks." Many of the people who come to the library never finished high school and are struggling to find jobs. They use the books and computers to find Section 8 housing, to study for commercial trucking licenses, to lose themselves in poetry and dreams of a better life. Their children are often on their own in the preschool area, doing activities in "short bursts, picking up books and putting them down with little discrimination and involvement." Here's a glimpse of how the researchers observed the use of the computers in the children's section:

> We watch as a preschooler runs her cursor over a few icons, each of which shouts its name. Picking one called Green Eggs and Ham, she clicks on it and two options appear: "read to me" or "play the game." She starts the game, but can't follow the narrator's directions. Soon she clicks to another program, eventually becoming equally frustrated. She starts clicking away randomly.... In less than two minutes, she clicks, switches, clicks, switches about 20 times. As her frustration grows, she starts pounding the keys as if they are a piano—that is, until the computer screen freezes and shuts down.

Chestnut Hill Library is eight miles to the northwest, though it feels like it is a world away. "Teams of families stroll the sidewalks with their babies and children ride their bikes.... The sidewalks and streets are swept clear of debris, expensively wrought metal receptacles are emptied before they get full, and meticulously designed window boxes, sidewalk planters, and hanging baskets add a homey splash of color." The average household income in Chestnut Hill in 2012 was $110,000 a year. When you see children on computers in this library, here is what you see:

> Four-year old Scott and his mother are having a great time playing Millie's Math House.... His mother gives him directions, encouragement, and suggestions on how to play. She is very involved, laughing when something amusing happens on the screen and rubbing his back when he does something right. "See that one has seven jelly beans but you need five jelly beans for it to go in the number five slot. So what do you need

to do?" Scott clicks on the appropriate thing and his mother rubs his back, saying "Good job!" He stays with this activity for a while—about 10 minutes—while his mother continues to sit with him.

Children at this library are getting the benefit of parents and grandparents who "carefully mentor" how they choose books and steer them to content that will challenge them. The differences between these experiences had little to do with children's access to resources. In both libraries, due to the generosity of the William Penn Foundation, books and computers were plentiful. Instead, the differences in interactions were emanating from a much deeper inequality. With low education levels, the parents and grandparents at Lillian Marrero had probably not received opportunities to develop skills for exploring the information available through books, let alone ask a librarian to help guide their children to materials appropriately challenging to their age. Their computer literacy was low too. Neuman and Celano saw example after example of adults with only rudimentary computer skills struggling to fill out forms or work with new software; they would wait in line to use the computer stations but were allotted only thirty minutes at a time and received little help.

"What became clear," Neuman and Celano write, "is that while [an initiative to expand books and technology in the library] could greatly improve access to material resources, it could not make up for the intangible social and psychological resources—the parents and other adults who make the many pathways to reading and information-seeking meaningful and important to children."

Other studies have painted similar scenes of parents lacking the confidence, knowledge, or experience to help their children make sense of the information coming at them. In the study on e-books and iPads, described in chapter 9, parents were rarely observed asking questions of their children. None of the parents who participated in the study used information from the e-books to connect to something their child might already know. "Only half the parents asked open-ended questions," Katrina McNab wrote, "and only two parents discussed difficult or unfamiliar words." More than half the parents, McNab said, reported that their children "preferred to read e-books independently, with one child resisting the parents' attempts to engage the child in shared reading by walking off."

Co-reading with this kind of media is not always easy. In 2012, the Cooney Center studied the impact of highly interactive, multimedia experiences—enhanced e-books—on co-reading. The study compared three book formats: print books, basic e-books, and enhanced e-books. Researchers found that enhanced e-books offer observably different co-reading experiences than print and basic e-books. The highly enhanced e-books often distracted beginning readers from the story narrative and led to less positive interactions with the co-reading adult. In short, too many bells and whistles attached to otherwise engaging technologies were not helpful to building stronger reading skills. This mirrors results from the studies described in chapter 7 that found that parents were less likely to engage with children around a commercial e-book than a print-on-paper book.

But scholars have also discovered that the more an e-book was designed for *learning*, the more likely parents were to talk with their children, and even learn with their children, as they read together. Shared reading, joint media engagement, and serve-and-return conversation—all of this remains a critical component of literacy. "The provision of iPads is simply not enough," wrote McNab and her doctoral adviser Ruth Fielding-Barnes in a recent article documenting what scientists know so far about e-books, apps, and the role of shared reading with adults. Wherever they are, whoever they are, children who are learning to read will still need reading partners.

A central challenge of the twenty-first century may be to avoid becoming so dazzled by new technologies that we assume children do not need an adult by their side. Can we embrace new tools while still learning to spot situations in which the technology is getting in the way of those connections? And are there any human-powered but tech-assisted initiatives that might actually foster co-reading moments?

Yes. We have encountered pioneers out there who resolve to find new ways to bring one-on-one reading and interaction time to children in disadvantaged circumstances by leveraging the communication power in today's technologies. The national nonprofit called Innovations for Learning deserves a long look. For twelve years, it has been marrying personalized one-on-one tutoring with on-screen reading assistance. And it is quietly becoming part of first-grade classrooms in school districts across the country.

UNUSUAL TUTORS AT H. D. COOKE ELEMENTARY

It's 9:30 a.m. in a first-grade classroom at H. D. Cooke Elementary in Washington, D.C. The children are sitting in a semi-circle on the floor watching their teacher as she reads them a picture book.

A minute later, the group's reading time is interrupted by a ringing phone. Unfazed, one of the children stands up, walks over to a computer set up near the reading area, puts on a headset and says a quiet hello. "Is Jasmine* there?" asks the voice on the other end. "Yes, just a minute please," the child says, motioning to her a classmate in beaded pigtails already making her way to the computer station. Jasmine takes the headset from her friend, sits down to face the computer, and tells the caller that she has arrived.

It's time for some one-on-one tutoring, Skype style.

Except that in this Internet phone call, no face appears on screen. Jasmine hears only the encouraging voice of her off-site tutor while her computer displays a storybook with two or three sentences per page. After a few seconds of shy greetings—"How are you?" "Good." "How was your spring vacation?" "Good."—Jasmine begins the session, reading into her headset as her tutor listens. Jasmine can see her tutor's on-screen movements as her cursor darts across the page and then hovers over certain words.

---

*The names of children at H.D. Cooke Elementary have been changed.

The story on the screen is about two sisters on a trip to the dentist. Jasmine reads haltingly: "We are twins. . . . We are missing our front teeth. My sister and I like . . . look . . . the same." Jasmine pauses, then continues, "But we do not like the same—" Jasmine stops. Her tutor puts her cursor on the next word, *things*. Jasmine tries to sound it out: the, tuh. Finally it comes: "things." "This is hard," Jasmine says.

Then, through Jasmine's headset, comes the voice of her tutor: "You are doing great!"

Jasmine's eyes go back to the computer screen. The next ten minutes are about reading comprehension. The tutor flips back to some of the online book's first pages and asks Jasmine about the twin sisters she has just read about. "What do the sisters share?," the tutor asks, testing whether Jasmine was following the story. "What is alike about them?"

"I don't know," Jasmine says.

The tutor flips to a page and prompts again. Jasmine tries an answer, hesitating: "They like different foods?"

"That's what is different," the tutor says, gently correcting her. "What is alike about them?"

"Duh know," Jasmine says, her eyes wandering again.

"How do they look?," the tutor prompts.

"They are the same height."

Success! The tutor tells her she is right and they move on—the tutor prompting, Jasmine trying to focus, the cursor pointing to words to read on the page, Jasmine answering, the tutor asking another question and guiding her toward a response. Soon time is up, and Jasmine says a quiet good-bye.

Tutoring requires patience, as anyone who has volunteered in an elementary school knows well. Some students want to do anything but the task at hand. Now imagine tutoring through an Internet connection. The only teaching tricks available are the words on the screen and the sound of a disembodied voice. Yet for this program—called TutorMate and run by Innovations for Learning—the pros appear to outweigh the cons, at least if the program's growth is any indication. Since it started in 2003, the program has expanded into three hundred classrooms in fourteen school districts and continues to grow.

TutorMate tutors come from businesses big and small, but almost all of them are recruited from the metro area where the tutored children go to school. For example, several law offices, Boeing, and Booz Allen Hamilton provide tutors for the District of Columbia public schools. Employees from Janus Capital Group, Chase Bank, and Western Union volunteer in the Denver public schools. Quicken Loans, General Motors, and Chrysler volunteers help in the Detroit public schools. About 110 companies around the country have become involved. The advantage for the tutors is that they do not have to leave their offices in the middle of the day and travel back and forth to the schools. They simply reserve thirty minutes of their work week to login from their computers, make a phone call, and then spend that time with their assigned first grader. "Even with this flexibility, companies say: we still aren't sure we can commit," said Dan Weisberg, national director of the program. He travels the country and makes phone calls every day to answer questions and persuade companies to donate some of their employees' time.

Weisberg's persistence appears to be paying off: As of early 2015, more than 2,600 people had registered as tutors. Among them is Neil Bush, President George W. Bush's brother and the board chairman of the Points of Light Foundation and the Barbara Bush Houston Literacy Foundation. He has been working each week with a first grader in the Houston Independent School District and is helping to spread the word to other school districts. In December 2014 he tweeted a photo showing a little boy holding a laptop: "Had fun tutoring Hector today 30 min. Easy, guided, proven. @TutorMate Help a 1st grader read http://www.connect4literacy.org."

TutorMate Combined with TeacherMate

Making sure the tutors are in sync with the school takes training and coordination. Each school district has a "teacher ambassador" who is charged with connecting teachers to tutors, coping with technological hiccups, and keeping track of district policies. Tahra Tibbs, the ambassador for Innovations for Learning, floats between fifteen schools and thirty-five classrooms in the D.C. public schools. Within her first two years on the job, she had to relearn the DCPS system as schools were reclustered and new instructional superintendents were put in place. "We've had to be more visible, talking with principals more," Tibbs said.

Innovations for Learning has built a related program called TeacherMate that enables teachers to make reading and phonics-based assignments for individual students and keep track of their progress in a more systematic way than is possible with TutorMate. The nonprofit would prefer that schools sign up for both programs and use them in tandem so the tutoring sessions are aligned with what children are doing every day in their classrooms. At Cooke Elementary, TeacherMate is part of the routine, and the two first grade teachers—Caroline Doctor and Nicole Henderson—are even bigger fans of the TeacherMate program than the tutoring program. They teach children in small groups and split up their morning time so that sometimes one group of children can be on the computer using the software while one or two other children sit at a table for a more intensive session with their teachers. "It enables us to lead an interruption-free reading session," Henderson said, "because at the end of the day, that's what the kids need. That's the most important thing we do." Other school districts that use TutorMate and TeacherMate together include the Chicago public schools, Houston public schools, and the Duval County public schools and Broward County public schools in Florida.

Having tutors as reading partners can give teachers another connection to their students as well. After we observed the tutoring session of Jasmine (as well as another child, an energetic boy who spoke excitedly and whizzed through lessons with his tutor), Doctor received a message that afternoon from Jasmine's tutor worrying that Jasmine did not seem to be answering some of her questions and asking if there was something she should do differently. "I appreciated that the tutor wrote to me," Doctor said. With a class of more than twenty five students, teachers cannot always tune into when individual students may need an extra boost.

TutorMate lays bare some of the drawbacks and benefits of using online communication for learning. Because tutors are not in the school, they cannot possibly know the context of the children's mornings nor see the distractions in their classrooms. And because the tutors do not see the faces of their students, they may not be getting all of the subtle cues about when and if students are engaged. At the same time, the tutors have the opportunity to make a one-on-one connection with students without leaving their offices or driving across town. There are many barriers to volunteering, and two big ones are the hassles of transportation and the need to participate at a fixed time each week. TutorMate eliminates those barriers. Weisberg and some teachers have also noted that the focus on voice and text alone can ensure that tutors do not make assumptions about children based on their skin color or dress. Instead they can converse more freely as in a routine phone call.

A few months after the day we observed Jasmine with her tutor, we stopped by again to watch a poignant end-of-year meeting during which tutors and their tutees meet each other in person, often for the first time. The tutors arrive in the morning and await their "unveiling." They first huddle in the school's front office, exchanging tidbits of knowledge about their students and relating what it was like to call in to the school each week. As they enter their students' classrooms, the six-year-olds hush each other and wiggle with excitement.

One of the tutors steps forward. His name is Tyrone Umani, a tall young man wearing a white button-down shirt with his employer's AT&T logo. He's got a twinkle in his eye as he asks children to raise their hands if they had a TutorMate tutor this year. "Let me guess who my student is," he says, scanning the expectant faces. A boy leans forward and smirks, giving himself away. "You're José," he predicts, as José says hello. "You're the guy who beat me at tic-tac-toe every week."

Similar scenes played out that week across the District of Columbia, where eighty public school classrooms used the tutoring program that year. Yet as much as the children enjoyed the program and the two TeacherMate teachers saw it as a success, the program did not return to Cooke Elementary the next year. The school's leadership changed that summer, and the new principal was committed to a different reading system for her students. But nearly all the other D.C. principals found the program worth it: thirteen schools and thirty-two classrooms signed up to continue the program. The combination of the personalized software and the one-on-one experiences with the tutors was too good to pass up.

 Video Vignette: TutorMate
bit.ly/tapclick5

MEDIA MENTORS

Technology now allows for an expanded universe of reading partners. Coaches, tutors and reading guides can come into children's lives from almost anywhere in the world. Parents can search YouTube to find an abundance of videos and tutorials that can help their children comprehend new vocabulary or learn a foreign language. Apps like A Story before Bed capture the warmth of personal narration and make it available for anytime listening—a boon for parents in the military who may be away from their children for long periods of time. Google Helpouts, a new space for people seeking online assistance, has also been considered as a tool to help families. In Missouri in 2014, the home-visiting program Parents as Teachers partnered with the Google program to see how it might better serve parents with questions about their babies' development.

Even grandparents using FaceTime or Skype can enable one-on-one story time that would not have been possible ten years ago. Already scientists are seeing that video-chat conversations can help young children. A recent study led by Sarah Roseberry Lytle, a researcher at the University of Washington, showed that while toddlers could not learn new verbs from non-interactive video, they could learn those verbs over Skype.

In addition, the proliferation of new media has led to a need for some partners of another sort: people who can help parents and teachers make sense of the stream of material coming at them. Not only is literacy fostered with the presence of thoughtful human beings, whether first graders in Washington, D.C., or kindergartners in Tel Aviv, it also requires people with expertise in the marketplace of media, e- or otherwise, who can model the smart use of media with young children and know how to match it to a child's needs.

Tapping the Expertise of Children's Librarians

Librarians, for example, can play a huge role in modeling what it looks like to read print books and e-books with children and to help build discriminating tastes in quality books, e- or otherwise. Just because a book is in print, for example, doesn't mean that it's of higher quality than an e-book. Print books, wrote the librarians Maryanne Martens and Dorothy Stoltz, can just as easily feature "poor writing and mediocre illustrations that often function as promotional material for other branded merchandise." And just because a book is interactive doesn't mean that it is going to be more engaging than one in print.

Some literacy experts are what we and others have come to call *media mentors for children and families*. In the twenty-first century, as reading skills are increasingly critical and notions of literacy expand, we need these mentors more than ever. Institutions such as the TEC Center at Erikson Institute and the Fred Rogers Center for Early Learning and Children's Media, not to mention some schools of library science at universities, are starting to provide fellowships and training to help equip educators with this expertise. (The TEC Center, in particular, is a leader in providing professional development in this arena; don't miss the recent book edited by the center's founder, Chip Donohue: *Technology and Digital Media in the Early Years*.) And fortunately, in pockets across the United States, some innovative children's librarians are already starting to fill this role.

Cen Campbell, the founder of a blog called LittleELit, which focuses on children's e-books with a literary critic's eye, is one of the librarians leading the charge. Petite, gregarious, and unafraid to dye her hair bright pink, Campbell is often seen at literacy and education conferences dashing from one forum to another to raise the flag for children's librarians and remind early childhood teachers that libraries are a key resource for navigating digital media. "Evaluation and curation of children's media have always been essential elements in the children's librarian's job description," she says. Now those skills need to be applied to the app marketplace and brought to parents in an accessible way.

A number of projects around the country show this can be done. In the Arapahoe Library District just south of Denver, Colorado, librarians have renovated the children's sections of their branch libraries to spark both pretend play (children can climb on platforms and crawl through a makeshift treehouse) and adult-child interaction with digital media (tables are available for two or more people to sit together and explore touchscreens). In 2013, the libraries started offering story times titled "Tech with Tots" to give parents ideas on how to use e-books to promote sing-alongs and conversation with their children. We have seen these kinds of workshops pop up in California, Maryland, Pennsylvania, and Oregon in just the past two years. Today's "media mentors" are also taking their message to teachers and child care professionals. In 2014, Washington County in Oregon hosted a media workshop for child care providers who take care of multiple children in their homes. In 2015 the early childhood division of Fairfax County, Virginia, opened up weekly workshops to its educators on topics such as "The Connected Classroom," "Creative Outlets," and "Digital Storytime."

To get an even clearer picture of what media mentorship is starting to look like, meet Rachel C. Martin, an early childhood specialist in Fairfax County with a master's degree in early childhood who is now studying for a master's in library science. She designed the Fairfax courses so that she could give parents and teachers some tips on using media to its full potential as a literacy tool. A key aim is to show them how to be selective about what types of media they might choose. We got a hint of her growing abilities to discern quality in e-media when she offered to take a look at a free website called Unite For Literacy that had come across our radar screen. Within a few minutes of looking at the site, which provides simple e-books with audio narration in more than a dozen languages, Martin e-mailed back to say the site was "impressive in the quality and accuracy of the narration" and that she would mention it to providers as a new resource. Then she explained how the site could be even better: "I think it would be more powerful if they translated the text into multiple languages along with the narration. Having the narration is wonderful but pairing it with English text may be limiting. I would love to see bilingual text options. Then of course, adding text scaffolding to match the narration would just be excellent."

Media mentors like Martin can lessen frustration, help children find more engaging materials, prompt teachers and childcare providers to be more selective about materials, and give parents some encouragement to see themselves as part of their children's learning. They could be valuable partners for media developers as well. Readialand needs these mentors. Wouldn't coping with the avalanche of technology be easier and less stressful if those of us raising and working with children had a guide with this kind of expertise at our side?

NOTES

library study in Philadelphia: Neuman and Celano 2012b, 1.
We watch as a preschooler: Neuman and Celano 2012a, 64.
Teams of families stroll the sidewalks: Ibid., 9.
Four-year old Scott: Ibid., 67.
"What became clear": Ibid., 15.
Only half the parents asked: McNab 2013, 11.
too many bells and whistles: Takeuchi and Vaala 2014.
scholars have also discovered: Korat and Or, 2010.
The provision of iPads: McNab and Fielding-Barnsley 2013, 59.

all the other D.C. principals: Phone interview with Dan Weisberg on April 24, 2015.

A recent study: Roseberry, Hirsh-Pasek, and Golinkoff 2014.

Print books: See the June 2014 issue of *School Library Journal*, which includes a series of articles pitting e-books against print books, at http://www.slj.com/school-library-journal-print-issue-archive/school-library-journal-june-2014-issue-table-of-contents/.

Technology and Digital Media in the Early Years: Donohue 2014.

Evaluation and curation of children's media: Campbell 2014.

adding text scaffolding: Rachel C. Martin, e-mail correspondence, January 23, 2015.

Developing Focused Attention and Motivation

When Michael was in elementary school in the late 1960s, teachers valued one thing in particular: focus. His second grade teacher, Mrs. Caplan, would frequently raise her hand to the sky and say, "Children, pay attention!" Positive reinforcement was doled out for settling down and concentrating on the task at hand. "Michael may have a merit," she might declare, to a brief squeal of delight, but only once he had stopped talking to classmates, removed his attention from a friend's artfully smuggled comic book, and folded his hands neatly on top of the desk. Now the class was ready to receive the next lesson she had planned.

Though the two of us (Michael and Lisa) are from different generations, at professional conferences and in family gatherings we both hear familiar refrains harkening back to these (supposedly) good old days: "Kids today have such a short attention span, they just won't sit and read a book." "They really start to suffer this year," says a third grade teacher in East Harlem, "when the standardized tests expect some pretty advanced comprehension skills." "That's why I do read-alouds for twenty minutes a day in class," says another. "If it isn't a game or a video my kid won't finish it," says a parent participating in a research study on Internet search engines. Says a friend who complains about her own diminished focus: "Fast-paced media has taken over; kids need to be constantly entertained and reading feels like a chore." Finally, our favorite comment, one we both have heard countless times over the past five years: "Once the Harry Potter movies came out, the kids stopped reading the books."

How much of this conversation is based on friendly life laments, and how much is based on evidence of a media-dominated, unfocused style of learning that we all should be concerned about? Can kids learn how to navigate the fast-paced, media multi-tasking world to master an essential skill—reading—that for many generations has been seen as a rite of passage to good citizenship and a pathway to success?

We have introduced you to the ideas of Sherry Turkle, who has written extensively on how much new technologies challenge our ability to genuinely pay attention to each other, and Maryanne Wolf, who has wondered out loud how much the "reading brain" will change in the Digital Age. Nicholas Carr, the author of *The Shallows: What the Internet Is Doing to Our Brains* and "Is Google Making Us Stupid?," has worried that our depth of understanding has been compromised by the wealth of knowledge available from search engines and that children's skill to critically reflect, to formulate focused, unbiased, and substantive arguments is weakening. Other research scientists such as Don Leu at the University of Connecticut have a related worry: that the types of literacies needed for successful reading and information gathering are becoming more common among children from higher-income communities whose parents are themselves more likely to be trained for critical and focused attention to texts.

Undoubtedly, to become literate, children need two critical attributes: a motivation to read and learn, and the habits of mind that enable the focused work that comes with building a "reading brain." To instill these traits, parents and educators will need to sort out what is documented and truly worrisome and what are simply myths in our national consciousness. They may also need to learn some new tricks.

EXECUTIVE FUNCTIONING: THE HOT NEW SCIENCE OF EARLY LEARNING

Among the most prominent research areas fueling the current debate over attention and focus is a new emphasis on children's abilities to regulate their emotions and actions—known as "self-regulation" in child development circles—and to develop what neuroscientists refer to as "executive functioning skills." Executive functioning has become a critical concept for anyone trying to understand how the brain forms the ability in the early years to filter distractions and switch gears to make sense of all in the incoming noise. The "executive" part of the term derives from the fact that these are functions required by the brain to focus on multiple streams of information to complete a task, to revise plans and move forward, to execute. "Probably the best way to think about it is sort of like an air traffic control system in the brain," says Deborah Phillips, a psychology professor at Georgetown University. "Just like an air traffic control system has to manage lots of airplanes going on lots of runways and exquisite timing and so on, a child has to manage lots of information and distractions."

A few years ago, a book arrived to help parents and educators grasp the significance of skills like this. *Mind in the Making: The Seven Essential Life Skills Every Child Needs*, a bestselling book by Ellen Galinsky, the co-founder and president of Families and Work Institute, uses findings from hundreds of fascinating experiments to show what she calls "seven essential life skills" that lead a person to succeed. Nested in the first essential skill—focus and self-control—are four executive function aptitudes: focus, being able to pay attention; working memory, being able to keep information in mind in order to use it; cognitive flexibility, being able to adjust to shifting needs and demands; and impulse control, being able to resist temptation to do what is needed to achieve goals.

The book makes a strong case for helping children build a modern skill set that can transform both individual pathways to success and help

197

communities progress. Galinsky shares the research of top scholars throughout, including Adele Diamond of the University of British Columbia, who says, "If you look at what predicts how children will do later, more and more evidence is showing that executive functions actually predict success better than IQ tests." Other scholars such as Akira Miyake of University of Colorado are at the forefront of the movement to position executive level functioning as a critical life skill. He states, "Executive function involves managing thoughts, actions, and emotions to achieve goals."

Researchers are contemplating how to assess a child's executive functioning and self-regulation skills. But it's not like you can ask young kids, especially in infancy and toddlerhood, to answer questions about how they organize their thoughts. So what are the indicators that a child is developing these skills? Galinsky's book describes many examples including the famous marshmallow test designed by Walter Mischel of Columbia University that tempts children with the option of eating one marshmallow now or waiting several minutes so that they can eat two marshmallows later. The kids who can delay gratification, so the study found, will be the ones who are better at managing life now and when they are older. Other examples of tests that assess executive level function include games based on Simon Says, which require children to hold two or three thoughts in their heads at one time. Still others involve a wooden stick or peg used for a tapping game that requires intense focus. When the adult taps once, the child is supposed to tap twice, and vice versa.

Researchers are finding that some children do much better on these tests than others. In the days before the science of brain plasticity, one might have assumed that those test scores are a sign of innate ability or genetic traits that cannot be altered. Now, however, science shows quite the opposite. Research on interventions in schools and homes are demonstrating that under the right conditions children can learn self-regulation and improve their executive function. A classroom-based program called Tools of the Mind, for example, encourages children to engage in pretend play. By taking on the roles of different characters, the kids have to inhibit their first instincts of acting like themselves and instead hold in their minds ideas about how that character would act and speak.

"These skills are like muscles," Galinsky writes. "The more we work on them, the stronger they become. So there's always hope for our kids—and for us too!"

Galinsky recognized that not every parent has the time or ability to read a hefty parenting book (*Mind in the Making* weighs in at 352 pages of text). Meanwhile, she remained so captivated by the ongoing experiments from science labs that she and her team have continued to videotape experiments. After fifteen years of taping, the Mind in the Making team have amassed a library of nearly a hundred videos to accompany the book—and even, created an electronic version where video links have become embedded within the pages. Here was a new way to help bring this science to life for a wider audience. (Not to mention an inspiration in many ways for the inclusion of video in the book you're reading this very moment.)

Used both within the book and outside it, the *Mind in the Making* videos are now a cornerstone of a series of learning modules on the seven essential skills that Galinsky and her colleagues are bringing to dozens of communities around the country. The idea is to not just give lectures about executive functioning and other life skills, but to have parents and educators take virtual field trips to see research in action through the videos and experience new approaches for themselves.

The Earl Boyles Elementary School in East Portland, Oregon, is one of the sites where the learning modules are being rolled out. In one series about forty adults—ten teachers, thirty parents, and sometimes the school's principal—attended eight monthly sessions in the school library. The sessions start with brief messages about brain development by workshop facilitators who were trained in working with diverse families. (Facilitators conducted the course in both Spanish and English by using wireless headsets and taking turns as the interpreters for the two different languages.) Sometimes the adults were asked to jump into hands-on activities that build creativity and critical thinking. Videos of researchers doing experiments, such as the marshmallow video on self-control and delayed gratification, prompted discussion about what parents could do at home and teachers could do at school. Attendees received practical guidance on everything from professional development through multimedia training modules to tip sheets that help adults teach math and literacy skills in a brain-building fashion. In an article about the program published by the Children's Institute of Oregon, several teachers and parents recounted how it changed their thinking:

> Carrie Tercek, 34, a special education teacher, says both she and her husband, Chris Tercek, 37, who also took the class, play focus games such as Simon Says with their three-year-old more. They also ask questions about story characters when they read to her, which improves her perspective taking skills.
>
> Meri Cullins, 29, a restaurant server, says she and her husband are playing more board games with their three boys. The parents also ask their kids more questions, encourage role playing, point to objects that begin with certain letters and do other exercises to foster essential life skills. Her preschooler "is going to be SO ready for kindergarten next year," she says.

This crucial work by Galinsky—bringing research to practice and mobilizing communities—builds on over more than decades of scientific exploration of the roots of early learning and brain development. First popularized by two Carnegie Corporation-commissioned public reports, *Starting Points: The Task Force on Meeting the Needs of Young Children* (1994) and *Rethinking the Brain* (1997), which was released at the first White House Conference on Early Childhood Development, the research created a major response in policy and program circles in the late 1990s and is generally credited with having laid the foundation for new policies such as Early Head Start (a version of Head Start for mothers and babies). These were early family-based interventions to prevent what Carnegie Corporation president David Hamburg referred to as "rotten outcomes."

In the middle of all this foment of the 1990s, however, comes a cautionary tale: this new brain science, which was making headlines across broadcast TV and in magazines like *Newsweek* and *Time*, sparked overzealous interpretations. Some media companies saw a new role for themselves in delivering on-screen "stimulation" for cognitive growth. Toy shops and discount stores were overrun with a proliferation of brain stimulators such as *Baby Einstein* videos for one-year-olds and special Mozart CDs for pregnant mothers to play to their bellies. It also led to some overzealous advocacy on the critical importance of the first three years for all that follows. In 2000, the National Academy of Sciences brought clarity to the debate over the developmental sciences with the publication of the widely acclaimed *From Neurons to Neighborhoods* report, which set the field of early learning on more settled ground, in which early intervention and family supports were defined as relationship-based, pathway-building opportunities for children, but not determinative of all that would then follow.

The *Neurons to Neighborhood*'s study directors, Phillips of Georgetown and Jack Shonkoff of Harvard's Center for the Developing Child, have, in the ensuing decade, created a new approach to early learning and executive functioning that is gaining wide influence and adoption. Working with communications experts and cultural anthropologists at FrameWorks Institute, they have created an entirely new way to engage the public and policymakers about the importance of the early years.

This approach focuses in part on using a deft combination of rigorous research and communications science to spread ideas to parents, educators, and the public. Phillips's analogy of an "air traffic control system for the brain" is one example. It can be found in a free YouTube video (https://www.youtube.com/watch?v=efCq_vHUMqs) designed to explain the concept to policymakers, business people, educators, and the general public. (More multimedia resources can be accessed here: http://developingchild.harvard.edu/resources/multimedia/.)

Other pioneers are also doing their best to make the science inspirational and actionable for parents and caregivers. An initiative called Vroom, created and funded by the Bezos Family Foundation, starts with the simple but elegant premise, "Every parent has what it takes to be a brain builder." (Echoes perhaps of Dr. Spock's "Trust your instincts" mantra!) Offerings include tools for community-based organizations that help demystify the science of brain development; partnerships with consumer product companies that include "brain-building" prompts on their packaging, and a free mobile app. Parents who download the app are asked to input their child's age and first name so the app can tailor its advice. Information comes in chunks of two or three sentences, a "daily vroom" that is a simple activity designed to take everyday moments—bath time, meal time or anytime in between—into moments for the back-and-forth interactions that help build executive level functioning. A vroom for a one-year-old, for example, tells a parent he can talk aloud to his baby while she is reaching for something by saying, "You reached out your fingers and got your toy." Parents receive little messages like "Way to go brain builders!" and can earn badges for simple tasks. They can even set an alarm to remind them to complete their daily vroom. A pilot test completed at the end of 2014 generated positive initial findings about the impact of the program on parenting routines; the foundation is rolling out a more extensive program in several communities this year.

Another example comes from the University of Washington, at the I-LABS (short for Institute for Learning and Brain Science), which conducted much of the neuroscientific research which formed the basis for the Vroom initiative. They have produced free online modules to be used by adults training to become educators of children from birth through age five. A session on interactions begins with photographs of adults playing with babies. "We must become keen observers of interactions in everyday life," says the voice-over audio. "Infants and children learn a remarkable amount in every learning moment." Then the module takes us to four video clips, asking us to watch and write down all the aspects of the environment that contribute to interactions. One of the four clips shows a mother signing "Wheels on the Bus" while the baby looks at her and waves his arms, a father responding to his baby's pointing to the lights in the ceiling by labeling and pointing out all the lights above them, and a mother with a two-year-old taking apart the pieces of a train puzzle while each says words like "engine" and "caboose."

It's an open question as to whether these bite-sized chunks of information will be embraced by parents and educators. The "Good job!" messages and badges on Vroom seem a little childlike, and clicking through the I-LABS modules can feel like watching a low-resolution video in slow motion. Yet each makes an attempt to deliver practical information about helping children build executive function skills, focus, and self-control. Implicit in all of these tools is the message that it takes an accumulation of many everyday interactions to raise a child who has the skills for deep reading. It's those kinds of messages that may be the most powerful in helping to show children what it takes to persist and focus on a task.

And this means that we, the adults, need to be able to ignore distractions ourselves. In fact, when do we look at our smartphone to check a sports score or, yes, even retrieve an encouraging message about our children's development, and when do we keep the device out of sight and mind? The actions of parents and teachers help model for children what it takes to focus and pay attention. As adults finding our way in an always-on kind of world, we will need to find a way to provide children with focused and positive one-on-one interactions starting from their first days.

LEARNING FROM HARRY

Even with well-developed skills of focus and persistence, if children aren't motivated to read, becoming proficient will be an uphill battle. And so we turn to the poster child for motivating young readers: Harry Potter. The Harry Potter books have been a publishing success beyond anyone's wildest dreams. J. K. Rowling's story of a wizard boy, his magically endowed school friends, and their epic battle against the dark arts has captivated children (and grownups) around the world. Since the first book was published in 1999, 450 million books have been sold.

With the publication of the last book in the series, *Harry Potter and the Deathly Hallows*, many readers mourned. It was depressing to think of a world without marauder's maps, invisibility cloaks, and potion classes, a world without more Harry Potter. But the conclusion of the series did not mean that Harry would be forgotten. The stories from the books continued to make their way into popular culture, as Warner Brothers released eight movies over a decade that were painstakingly designed to mirror the books. Millions of households now own the DVDs.

Not everyone, however, has been thrilled with the fact that Potter lives on in digital media. Some parents who waited expectantly for their tots to reach reading age and start begging for the books have been disappointed to discover that their children seem content to just watch the movies. They ask the perennial question: Is the presence of the movies draining children of the desire to read the stories in print?

Data to confirm this lament are not so easy to come by. There is no body of empirical research on whether movie versions are choking or stoking children's desire to read the books. But a few studies have explored the intersection between mass media and children's reading, and they offer evidence of a complicated and mutually reinforcing connection between stories and characters in books and stories and characters on screen. They also reinforce the significance of understanding the multiple "literacies" children will need to start becoming critical thinkers about messages and authorship in media of all kinds.

Consider, for example, the following responses from multiple middle schoolers in northern Ohio who were part of research on how students choose books. (These happened to be special education students, though the study author found that having such a status seemed to play no role in how they made book choices.) Of the thirty-one students interviewed, eleven of them referenced movies or television shows related to books. Several of them described reading the books first:

I like to read the book and then watch the movie.

Usually I notice that the books are different than the movies and if I know what the book is before I see the movie, I can picture what it is going to be about.

I'd rather read the book because in my mind I get a totally different picture than the movie. I like my picture better.

Like on the Goosebumps books it's not always the same as in the [show].

Well, I like reading books first because if you start to read a book and you don't really think it's interesting, why go and rent the movie and watch it?

Another study, which observed the book selections of black children in elementary and middle school, also shows the media's influence on book reading. During a book fair at ten schools that were part of the study, books about sports and music stars were snapped up by children eager to learn more about people they had seen on TV. The kids would say: "'Oh! There's [name of singer]!' and within minutes a group of girls would be huddled together and intensely exploring the book." The study gave this advice to educators: books about figures that represent their interests and everyday culture will increase the likelihood that students will be engaged in reading.

And then there is the impact of something like Pottermore, the Web-based community created by Rowling in 2009 and under wraps for two years before it became known through secret messages and codes embedded in Google Maps. The messages eventually linked fans to a YouTube channel that featured a countdown to its pre-opening on July 31, 2011, to provide a sneak peek for die-hard fans before its public launch a few months later. When the site opened, the global crowd went wild, the site was jammed, and many fans couldn't get in. Some of them resorted to doing their own writing to pass the time. Here's a note from one of them: "I, like so many of you, spent my day trying to access Pottermore only to keep being disappointed by how much I had to keep waiting. After being inspired by a variety of funny tumblrs and twitters, I decide to write a short funny story to release my frustration and pass time until my clock strikes 12a PST." Posted below the note was a short story about Harry and his friends standing around a computer, trying to login to see what muggles were writing about them.

Getting into Pottermore in those early days required deep knowledge of the Harry Potter stories. Not just anyone could register for early admission. The only ones admitted were those who had collected clues from sites around the Web and answered questions about details from within the pages of the books. In an act of brilliant blending, J. K. Rowling had made sure that her readers had fully enjoyed the print version before they were admitted to fully enjoy the online space, including all the social networking, links to fan fiction sites, and new e-book chapters that would be eventually posted there. Today, Pottermore is filled with words and print, from the *Daily Prophet*, the wizarding world's sensationalist newspaper, to the elaborate background documents explaining the sinister origin of the concept of "pure bloods."

James Paul Gee, a professor of literacy studies at Arizona State University, has spent many years examining how digital games interact with reading. As seen in the case of fan fiction and Pottermore, he argues that video games can trigger sophisticated forms of reading at early ages, as gamers become highly motivated to seek out information and read messages in online forums about how to reach higher levels and acquire new characters. As described in an essay that Gee wrote with Michael a few years ago, "Many children, who are just learning to read, including those who are struggling at school, play video games like *Pokémon*, where they must learn to read the polysyllabic names and descriptions of hundreds of creatures. For example, in a description of the creature 'Shuckle,' they will see language like, '[Shuckle] stores berries in its shell. The berries eventually ferment to become delicious juices.' This language is more complex than what a first-grader will see in school for some time."

GETTING OVER THE SLUMP

Some children love to read and are self-motivated to pick up a book. Other kids require more encouragement. During the school year, that encouragement often comes from teachers. But during summer break, children are often on their own. According to the National Summer Learning Association, low-income students lose more than two months in reading achievement each summer, despite the fact that their middle-class peers make slight gains. That widens to three grade-level equivalents by the end of fifth grade.

The summer slide and the reading crisis are entwined. Which is why at the end of every school year, librarians and teachers contemplate how to get children jazzed for summer reading. They send children home with handouts about favorite books and talk up their favorite authors. They urge parents to take their children to the library to participate in reading contests. They bring story time to rec centers.

In 2012, Arizona launched a statewide literacy initiative and made a public commitment to improve reading levels in their state. As partners in the national Campaign for Grade-Level Reading, they too were determined to get over the summer slump. They formed a summer reading collaborative and within a year, one of their county library districts, Maricopa County, built an open-source online program called the Great Reading Adventure to enable students to earn online badges and track reading progress during the summer compared to other students. Users could also acquire badges and win gift certificates by attending story hour and other functions at their local library.

The Great Reading Adventure was an exciting development, but it was based on the expectation that students would be able to travel to libraries to check out books. Given the prevalence of hard-to-reach areas in Arizona, state literacy director Terri Clark knew some children would not have easy access. Fortunately, around the same time, Clark learned about a company called MyOn, which offers online books and creates a "personalized literacy platform" for schools to deliver to their students throughout the year and the summer months. She was intrigued: here was a way to offer a portable library of e-books, personalized for children's reading levels, that they could access from any Internet connection. Children would be able to log on through the MyOn website or app, enter username and password, and gain access to a collection of four thousand books geared to different reading levels, from pre-K through the twelfth grade. Read On Arizona partnered with MyOn for open access to their digital library for every child throughout the state, and the state library piloted the Great Reading Adventure in a majority of Arizona counties to make the summer reading experience seamless for students who wanted to use MyOn's books to earn badges and track their progress.

The program was launched in time for the start of summer 2014. By the time the children were back in school that fall, more than 406,000 virtual badges had been earned through the Great Reading Adventure, and through the MyOn library more than 14,000 books were opened and read, according to Clark. Children could track online how many minutes they were reading, and the average tally each day was around twenty minutes, which hit the mark that educators had been hoping for. Arizona extended access to the MyOn libraries through December, MyOn has since partnered with many public libraries in the state, and the Maricopa libraries are offering the Great Reading Adventure again in 2015.

In addition to knowing whether books are read and for how long, Clark is now able to gain a better sense of whether families in various districts are able to gain access to books. For some families in Arizona the closest library is two or three hours away, and it pained Clark to think of parents in those areas not having an easy way to check out new books for their kids. Data from the project showed, however, that people in rural areas were able to get online too, in some cases as often as those in urban areas, and that most were using smartphones and tablets to do so.

Sparking a desire to read is one of the holy grails of public education. It is a thrill to observe children taking real pleasure in reading. But not all children ever experience that pleasure. Researchers and education experts have pored over countless studies and spent decades trying to figure out the best ways to encourage reading. Now the impact of online badges and always-on digital libraries can be added to their list of promising new techniques to test.

If you are one of those people who has always loved reading and can get lost for hours in engrossing stories and beautiful writing, the thought of earning badges and tracking online minutes may leave you cold. But for children raised in an era of progress tracking and online markers of achievement, for kids who may not otherwise hear praise for their reading progress, new tools like badges and digital libraries may be just the push they need to get excited and eventually lose themselves in a good book.

NOTES

Nicholas Carr: Carr 2008; and Carr 2010.

Other research scientists such as Don Leu: "Achievement Gap" 2014.

Just like an air traffic control system: Phillips and Selazo 2012.

Mind in the Making: The seven skills needed for children to be able to "thrive in the future" are focus and self-control; perspective taking; communicating; making connections; critical thinking; taking on challenges; and self-directed engaged learning. Galinsky 2010, 5–11.

Nested in the first essential skill: Galinsky 2010.

Other scholars such as: Akira Miyake Miyake et al. 2000.

"These skills are like muscles": Galinsky 2010, 26.

In an article about the program: Graves 2014.

Starting Points: Starting Points 1994.

Rethinking the Brain: Shore 1997/2003.

These were early family-based interventions: Hamburg 1997.

From Neurons to Neighborhoods: Shonkoff and Phillips 2000.

More multimedia resources: *Talking Early* 2005.

Another example comes from the University of Washington: I-Labs Modules, https://trainingxchange.org/our-programs/i-labs.

poster child for motivating young readers: Based on information in a February 2, 2014, *Telegraph* article, "Harry Potter Should Have Married Hermione, Admits J. K. Rowling" by Sam Marsden at http://www.telegraph.co.uk/culture/harry-potter/10612719/Harry-Potter-should-have-married-Hermione-admits-JK-Rowling.html.

Several of them described: Swartz and Hendricks 2000.

books about figures that represent their interests and everyday culture: Williams 2008.

Pottermore: "Pottermore."

the global crowd went wild: Anonymous 2011.

how digital games interact with reading: Gee and Levine 2009.

students lose more than two months in reading achievement: Cooper et al. 1996.

That widens to three grade-level equivalents: National Summer Learning Association.

Read On Arizona partnered with MyOn for open access: Phone interview with Terri Clark on March 25, 2015. See also Clark's comments in this archived video of the "Anytime, Anywhere Summer Learning" event at New America in Washington, D.C., on June 10, 2014: http://www.newamerica.net/events/2014/anytime_anywhere_summer_learning.

Paper and Print? Yes.

In the second week of January 2015, the publisher Scholastic came out with a report that contained some surprises. The report was based on an annual survey of more than 2,500 parents and children around the United States. Several questions centered on e-books. In one, for example, the survey asked children and parents if they had ever read a book on an electronic device. In 2010, about 25 percent said yes. Two years later, that number jumped to 46 percent, and two years after that, the percentage climbed again to 61 percent. Among children ages six to eight, the increase was even sharper, jumping to 65 percent. Clearly, e-books are increasingly becoming part of the reading experience for kids and their parents.

But do they *prefer* e-books? That was where the surprises appeared. Scholastic asked how many children agreed with the statement, "I'll always want to read books printed on paper even though there are e-books available." With the increasing use of e-books and their embedded features such as audio and highlighted text, one might think children would become less and less likely to see a future in which they prefer to read on paper. But Scholastic's survey showed the opposite. The percentage of children saying they will always want to read printed books increased from 60 percent to 65 percent. (Parents' desires for printed books sharpened too.) Even when the survey posed the question differently, asking children who had experienced e-books which format they would prefer to read, kids still gave printed books a big thumbs-up. The preference was most pronounced among early elementary children, with two-thirds saying that printed books were their mode of choice.

The era of e-books is still in infancy, so it would be a mistake to interpret these numbers as a referendum on the format children or their parents will choose in the future. But they have stirred questions about whether a transition from paper to screens is as inevitable as e-book enthusiasts might think. In the publishing industry as a whole, analysts are parsing sales numbers and debating whether the growth rate of e-books has already hit its peak. This is leading to dilemmas for publishers, because the demand for printed books in general is still sinking and some commercial printers are folding or consolidating. The title of a 2014 report on the commercial printing industry is evidence of the pain felt by commercial printers: "Out of ink: Digital media alternatives and low demand will continue to threaten industry revenue."

Still, it would be wise to take kids' preferences seriously. There is something about paper and print that young children appear to appreciate. Is it the beauty of the colorful artwork and large, glossy photos in picture books? The feel of the paper under their fingers as they turn the pages? The fact that they can flip back and forth from page to page and experience the book as a concrete, tangible object? Child development experts have long favored giving children chances to touch real objects and explore tactilely. There is a reason that teachers use wooden blocks and math manipulatives like plastic unit blocks to help children grasp new concepts. Children seem to understand this intuitively. Those "Do not touch" signs in museums are not their friends. Little kids just cannot keep their hands off stuff.

Of course, printed books are also a form of technology—just of a much older sort. And it wasn't just the Chinese printing presses of the past millennium or the Gutenberg Press of 1450 that brought us the book. The physical format of the book arrived centuries earlier with a breakthrough called the *codex*, an innovation that involved stacking sheets of papyrus, vellum, or paper and binding them at one edge so that a person could flip from one page to another. Before the days of the codex, the only way to read was via a long scroll, which itself had rivaled the clay tablet. Here's how the editors of Wikipedia describe the impact of the codex innovation:

> The codex altogether transformed the shape of the book itself and offered a form that lasted for centuries. The spread of the codex is often associated with the rise of Christianity, which adopted the format for the Bible early on. First described by the 1st-century AD Roman poet Martial, who praised its convenient use, the codex achieved numerical parity with the scroll around AD 300, and had completely replaced it throughout the now Christianised Greco-Roman world by the 6th century.

We dare not predict the fate of the printed book in these pages. After all, we are clearly hedging our bets in producing the book you are reading right now in multiple formats, including print on paper, a ported electronic format for e-reader devices, and an enhanced e-book for devices that can display video. But in our reporting over the past several years, we have witnessed parents and teachers demanding both e-books and printed books. Just as television did not lead to the death of movies, nor radio, perhaps e-books will not be a print killer and will exist as yet another option for storytelling and information sharing. Instead of a transition that leads to a fadeout of print, we see a transition to a blended world.

MAKING LITERACY VISIBLE EVERYWHERE YOU LOOK

In our vision of Readialand, that place where community infrastructure promotes literacy and where reading and media are in happy partnership, we see an important role for the printed book. Why? It has to do with what child development experts call the "literacy environment." Research over the past several decades has shown that the physical environment children inhabit matters. Educators who understand this take pains to design spaces for young children that pay close attention to what children are seeing around them and whether they have opportunities for safe exploration and discovery. Objects and signs that indicate the presence of literacy are a significant part of those environments. One indicator is a simple count of how many books are in a child's home or classroom. Those numbers alone can expose big disparities for kids in low-income families compared to others. An often-cited statistic is that the ratio of books per child in middle-income neighborhoods is thirteen books to one child, while in low-income neighborhoods it is one book per three hundred children.

Literacy experts also look for "environmental print," the presence of printed words no matter where they appear, whether on streetscapes, on the fronts of buildings, or in child care centers. This search for signs of literacy was strongly influenced by the research of Susan Neuman, who discovered in her study of Philadelphia that children in impoverished areas had fewer opportunities to see words around them, and when they did, such as a dilapidated sign for a store called Discount Food, the sign was missing the letter *s*. Today, experts who inspect preschool classrooms keep an eye open for evidence that children are getting some exposure. Having signs and books at children's eye level is one indicator. Another is the presence of a play area where children can pretend to go to the store or post office. By placing paper, stamps, crayons or markers, and a few signs in the play area with the words *Exit* or *Sorry, we're closed*, teachers can help give children that exposure. This does not mean pushing four-year-olds to read those words—many experts would say it is not developmentally appropriate to expect children to read full words at that age. Instead it provides an opportunity for teachers to point out signs, read them aloud, and give children a model of what reading and writing looks like by, say, playing a clerk at a post office. These literacy-enriched environments are the subject of a growing number of studies showing a positive impact on children's growth in early reading skills.

Given this, it would be foolish to underestimate the simple presence of books made with paper. Yes, printed words can and do show up in screen-based media all over the place. Full chapters of this book have recounted the significance of onscreen print from the early days of closed captioning to the highlighted text of Starfall to the abundance of print in online video game manuals and spaces like Pottermore. But zoom out and consider what children see every day as they look around their homes or classrooms. Would you still consider a child's environment to be literacy enriched if every book or magazine was packed away into a hand-held screen? Do children realize that their parents are, in fact, reading the news or writing a letter when all of that activity happens on a screen the size of a deck of cards?

These questions became real for Lisa in the middle of writing this book, when she overheard a father talking to another father at a soccer practice. The father was complaining about the homework that was assigned to his elementary school–aged daughter. The teacher had asked her students to go through magazines at home and cut out pictures to create a collage. This dad was irked. "Magazines?," he groaned. "Who still has magazines? We get everything on our iPad."

Lisa wondered, Could it be that this child was living in a household with no magazines or catalogs strewn around the family room? From what she could tell, given the fathers' chatter about their careers that day sitting on the bleachers, this was not a low-income family. And yet she couldn't help but feel a sense of loss for the girl. What did literacy look like for her as she was growing up? Were books, magazines, and newspapers—now stored in devices—invisible? E-book websites and apps have been held up as a way to give children access to limitless libraries of material. In that way, yes, they open access. But could the reverse be simultaneously true? Could electronic materials also play a role in limiting access to physical literacy-rich environments, to ambient print?

It may be too early for answers to these questions, but there doesn't appear to be much research that even asks them yet. We predict, and are already seeing signs of, a hunger for more studies that explore the interplay between onscreen and off-screen print environments. The visible and physical literacy environment is changing in unpredictable ways that will surely have implications for the next generation of readers. Our understanding of literacy needs to broaden to include not only devices and books but also what is visible when we pull our heads out of our printed books and screens and look around.

As we searched for Digital Age pioneers in early literacy, we came across several leaders and initiatives that are by no means ready to give up on print. Reading Rockets, a comprehensive website run by WETA Public Broadcasting, provides teachers with access to podcasts, webcasts, and apps while also highlighting award-winning printed books each year. Literacy networks across the country are rooted in the work of national organizations that distribute printed books to children and families, such as Reading Is Fundamental, which partners with school libraries to distribute free books for children to keep; Raising a Reader, which hands out book bags of books to preschool-age children; and Reach Out and Read, which distributes books to families through pediatricians' offices. Millions of books are distributed through these organizations each year.

These organizations and many others are not ignoring the explosion in e-media. Instead they are making strategic decisions about how to use interactive technologies and partner with media companies to continue to build children's interest in reading. They are taking advantage of new technologies (information networks, digital scanners, YouTube, and more) to make sure these older technologies (printing presses, paper, and the codex-like book) can continue to be part of the landscape of literacy. We see them as important allies in a transition to a world of blended print-and-digital resources. In this final leg of our journey, we give you a glimpse of how they are deftly maneuvering in this borderland.

THE STORY OF FIRST BOOK

Thank you for giving us that wonderful book. If it was not for you, I wouldn't even know about the long necked sea lizard. I would travel every country day and night to get that book!
—Second grade student who is a fan of the literacy organization
First Book

In 1992, First Book was created by the social justice lawyer Kyle Zimmer to confront a fundamental problem in many pockets of the education system: access to decent, low-cost literacy materials. She was stunned to discover that many important initiatives that serve children—after-school programs, Head Start sites, Boys & Girls Clubs, migrant worker camps, soup kitchens—lacked books.

Her response was First Book, a system for disseminating books that would otherwise be discarded by publishers because they were not being purchased. The idea was to aggregate all those books in one place and create a way to distribute them, for free or at very low cost, to the children who needed them. Zimmer developed a system for screening and identifying organizations that wished they could give children more access to books. First Book has now distributed more than 125 million books, and the First Book network totals more than 160,000 programs, which Zimmer calls "the base of the economic pyramid." After-school programs and preschools are part of their distribution network, which has doubled over the past two years. These programs are now able to access content through the First Book National Book Bank, which is a clearinghouse for free age-appropriate books (members get a monthly e-mail to notify them of new books as they become available), and the First Book Marketplace, an online access point for more than six thousand popular and award-winning books at 50–90 percent off retail, including shipping. Its offerings are sustained through a hybrid business model that includes revenues generated from buying books at heavily discounted rates and reselling them, philanthropic donations and other fee-based services.

First Book has also been a pioneer in identifying new ways to attune the marketplace to the needs of culturally and linguistically diverse students and families they serve. Before connecting with First Book, 73 percent of the classrooms and programs in its network had few, if any, books featuring Latino culture and heritage, for example. Roxanna Barillas, director of

Hispanic engagement for First Book, has been trying to change that. She recently related this story:

> Alfonso, at age 4 had never willingly visited the library at his early-learning center. But one morning Alfonso's teacher had something new to show her class—a brand-new collection of children's books about Latino culture and history. Later that day, instead of going to the playground during his free play period, Alfonso headed straight to the library, excitedly pointing out a book about the Mexican folktale *La Llorona* to his friends."

In the United States, the traditional market for book buyers, Barillas explains, "has been the top 10 percent of the socioeconomic strata." These are the families with enough disposable income to buy an ever-expanding home library of books for their kids, and historically, these families are typically white and middle class. "For decades," Barillas said, "publishing insiders have argued that like it or not, this is what the market wants. Books about 'other' kinds of children, 'other' kinds of families and communities, they say, simply don't sell. But they're wrong. Diverse books can and do sell. We've just been looking at the wrong market."

In 2013, through the Clinton Global Initiative, First Book committed to pioneer a market-driven solution to the lack of diversity in children's books. Over a two-year period, with support from major corporations such as Target and Disney, they are selecting and distributing books that highlight not only racial and ethnic diversity, but also the experiences of people with disabilities and the stories of people with different religious beliefs, socioeconomic backgrounds, and sexual orientations.

On its website, the organization sums up its ripple effects on the field of literacy: "Each of our books has had a two-fold impact: first, they elevate the efforts of heroic teachers and volunteers allowing them to build more robust curriculum and literacy learning models; and second, every book goes to a child who would otherwise lack access, giving them tools to explore the world and dramatically expand their opportunities."

Two internal studies of the First Book model confirmed that First Book books greatly expand children's interest in reading. The creation of a national system and the momentum of its success have now pushed First Book to create a new "Digital Marketplace" that will debut in 2015. Jane Robinson, chief operating officer, says the marketplace, which will offer research-based e-books, apps, and games, will have the ambitious goal of "confronting the growing digital divide by revolutionizing access to digital content and educational media."

MIXING MEDIA, INCLUDING PRINT ON PAPER

Once you look for them, examples of the interplay between technology and printed books emerge in abundance. Some can be classified as classic "marketing" approaches—using media messages to prompt children to read more books. For example, JumpStart, a nonprofit that places college volunteers in preschool classrooms to read with children, conducts Read for the Record, a nationwide reading challenge, every year. Hundreds of thousands of people across the United States pledge to read the same book on the same day. Last year's book was Rosemary Wells's *Bunny Cakes*. To spread the word, JumpStart enlisted the help of *The Meredith Vieira Show* and Josh Duhamel, the actor and fashion model, who went hopping around Southern California in a pink bunny suit cajoling passersby to read the book or act out the scene when Ruby scolds her brother Max. (Watch the YouTube video at https://www.youtube.com/watch?v=t9QhrXBq3I8 and be ready to laugh out loud.)

Some efforts are coming straight from publishers and developers. Move over, movie trailers. Now there are book trailers, which are emerging as significant ways for teens and adults to hear about new books. And unusual app-makers such as Osmo are inventing ways for children to play with an array of physical objects, such as letter tiles, that can be detected by an iPad equipped with a special camera to transfer learning from the screen to the table and back again. Other examples emerge from teachers, classrooms, and libraries. In Milbridge, Maine, Suzen Polk-Hoffses, the kindergarten teacher who works with Comienza en Casa sometimes uses the iPad's video camera in shared reading activities. Two children pair up to read short books to each other. One child videotapes the other reading the book and then they watch it together, reinforcing the meaning of the book and getting a second chance to improve their fluency. Once, when students were pairing up to read together, a student placed the iPad on a stack of pencil boxes so that he and his friend could both be on screen, reading together at the same time. "The smiles that were on their faces as they read to each other was wonderful to see," Polk-Hoffses said.

Schools and libraries are experimenting with interactive crowdsourcing. Last summer, for example, the Alexandria City Public Library created an online summer reading competition that encouraged children to not only log the books they read, but also write and publish reviews of those books, creating an online conversation about what children liked or didn't like about the stories they were reading. And some educators are using barcodes and scanners to link paper to screen. Sheree Schulson, a second- and third-grade teacher in Florida, encourages teachers to experiment with QR codes, those black-and-white bar codes on posters and business cards that can be scanned by a mobile device to immediately bring up a website. On eSchoolNews last year, she suggested this approach:

> After your students read a book, have them create an audio or visual book review. Upload their work to your website and create a QR code out of it. (There are many easy-to-use QR code generators online that can be found through a quick Google search.) Then, print out and place the QR code on the back cover of the book so that future readers can scan it with their smart phone or tablet. After listening to or reading the review, students can decide whether they want to read the book.

Not to be forgotten are the technologies that enable children to make their own books and write their own stories. This can take many forms.

Some teachers compile children's digital photography into pages that can be printed on a classroom printer, bound with yarn, and then captioned by the kids themselves. Other teachers scan and digitize children's artwork or journal entries so that they can be inserted into photo books printed by commercial outfits like Tiny Prints or Shutterfly. In the later elementary school grades, teachers work with students to create e-books of longer stories to share with the world and also download in printed form.

Each one of these examples gives children an opportunity not only to read words on a page but become an author and start to grasp the questions of motivation, message, and audience that come with authorship. They are also getting practice in critical thinking and some of the central tenets of media literacy. These experiences give children important practice in reading and writing skills while also setting a foundation for a much richer understanding of literacy than the act of reading words on a page.

NOTES

The report was based on an annual survey: *Kids & Family* 2015, 64.

The percentage of children: Ibid., 68.

a 2014 report on the commercial printing industry: "Out of Ink" 2014.

The codex altogether transformed: "Codex."

An often-cited statistic: Neuman and Dickinson 2006, 31.6; Neuman and Celano 2012, 25.

Susan Neuman: Miller and Warschauer 2013. In particular, see pages 13–17, which discuss several areas ripe for more research on e-reading in children.

We predict, and are already seeing signs: For example, a recent report for Reading Is Fundamental states: "To date, we have delivered more than 410 million new, free books to underserved children across the country." See page 5 of *Books Have the Power to Change Lives*, the Reading Is Fundamental 2013 annual report, at http://www.rif.org/documents/us/RIF-2013-Annual-Report.pdf.

Millions of books are distributed: "Innovation in Publishing."

First Book was created: For more on the origins of First Book and Zimmer's personal story, see the "First Book Story" on www.firstbook.org.

Its offerings are sustained: Barillas 2014.

Alfonso, at age 4: Ibid.

"For decades," Barillas said: "First Book's Impact."

Each of our books has had a two-fold impact: Personal correspondence, February 6, 2015, with Jane Robinson, Chief Operating Officer, First Book.

Two internal studies: Personal communication, June 11, 2014, with Jane Robinson, Chief Operating Officer, First Book.

Now there are book trailers: Milliot 2014a.

On eSchoolNews last year: Schulson 2014.

PART 4

Homesteading for the Next Generation

16

What Educators, Parents, Developers, and Policymakers Can Do

Settling the Wild West is now up to us: educators, parents, developers, business leaders, and policymakers, and everyone in between. We are at a crossroads. The untamed nature of the app marketplace showed one path. The intentional and creative work by our pioneers showed another. That latter path made clear that reading and media do not have to be, and in fact, are not, in opposition. Tapping and clicking can, and should, be connected to literacy opportunities for all children and their families, especially those who need support the most. Readialand can be realized—if we seize this moment to adjust our approaches in our homes and classrooms, develop research-based products and initiatives, and reform public policies to put greater attention on early learning for fostering both traditional and twenty-first-century literacies.

TAKING STOCK: WE ARE STUCK

More than thirty years after the landmark study *A Nation at Risk*, and the subsequent hundreds of billions of dollars spent trying to ramp up children's mastery of basic skills through national programs and policies such as Head

Start, Title I, and No Child Left Behind, American school performance is stuck in wet cement. In the United States today, the majority of low-income children and a shocking one-third of their more affluent peers are behind according to, perhaps, the best key predictor of future achievement: fourth grade reading. In 2012, only 14 percent of African American and 17 percent of Hispanic children were deemed proficient readers as judged by the National Assessment of Educational Progress scores in fourth grade.

Researchers have found a nearly 80 percent correlation between being two years behind in reading at the fourth grade mark and dropping out of high school later. But instead of meeting these pressing needs with modern approaches and new technologies, we have squandered billions of dollars pursuing programs of limited effectiveness, often ignoring settled research evidence, lagging in reforming our teacher preparation programs, neglecting resources in public media and public libraries, and moving too slowly to scale proven effective programs or to incorporate potential new breakthroughs. And, at least so far, we have ignored the central modernizing force of the twenty-first century: the technologies that have transformed most elements of life today except schools.

In a recent report from the Pew Research Center, tech scholars were asked to describe the world of 2025. They predicted that people would be working in "an ambient information environment where accessing the Internet will be effortless and most people will tap into it so easily it will flow through their lives 'like electricity.'" Also forecast: "mobile, wearable, and embedded computing will be tied together . . . allowing people . . . to tap into artificial intelligence-enhanced cloud-based information storage and sharing. The positive and negative trends [will] extend and expand in the next decade, revolutionizing most human interaction, especially affecting health, education, work, politics, economics, and entertainment."

We aren't even close to being prepared to confront the implications of these mass communications breakthroughs and how they could exacerbate divides in our country. The United States does not yet have the requisite staff training, community-based infrastructure, or family-centered program models to respond to the wave of technology now in place, let alone the new world predicted by experts.

Given the stubborn reading gaps we have described as a kind of "quiet crisis" that has drained our national bank of human capital, we need a fresh start. We must harness new technologies to assist, while simultaneously getting serious about the humans who will lead: Educators. Parents. Mentors who can ensure all children and families have the opportunity to participate in literacy learning. We can do a much better job of raising a generation of readers in a world of screens. Now the question is, How?

In the pages to follow, we suggest new ways to think about literacy and technology, raise children in a ubiquitous media culture, and teach in our classrooms and communities. Many of these ideas were inspired by the pioneers you read about in part 3. You will see that these ideas borrow from the old (using lessons from decades of research on the importance of parents' and teachers' capabilities) and draw from the new (utilizing effective technologies more deftly than ever before).

Our approach is based on an understanding of the inextricable ties between learning and key developmental influences at the family, community, and policy levels. Merging recommendations from years of work at the Cooney Center on families, learning, and technology, and from an approach to building a Digital Age architecture for early education proposed by New America, we offer ideas for everyone. Imagine what bounty of opportunity could be available for the next generation if our country's educators, parents, developers, and policy leaders were all working toward this goal.

CALLING ON AMERICA'S LEADERS

Here are four interrelated actions that must come from America's leaders in government, philanthropy, business, and education to get serious about addressing the literacy crisis: build a coherent pathway for the early years of learning, advance digital equity in our infrastructure, create connected teachers, schools and communities, and engage families by recognizing the assets in their cultures and approaches to raising their children.

The Early Years: Build a Coherent Pathway

Starting early is the first step to raising strong readers and promoting life-long literacy. Many people think this means ensuring that all children have access to preschool or pre-K in the year or two before kindergarten. And yes, those years are critical. But we have to recognize that children need opportunities for deeper learning before and after preschool too. Developmental science defines early childhood as birth through age eight (often referred to as zero to eight), with eight being that age when children should have mastered cognitive and social skills that enable them to think about concepts in the abstract, hold multiple ideas in their head at once, and read fluently enough to gain new knowledge at much greater speed. By this age, children need to transition from "learning to read" to "reading to learn."

But as it stands, many aspects of the American system do little to help and may be making things worse. When children are infants and toddlers, low-income families are often careening from one low-quality child care center to another. Mothers and fathers have no choice but to go back to work right away because only three states in the country (California, New Jersey, and Rhode Island) have paid parental leave laws. When children are three and four, parents have to navigate confusing channels between child care programs and more learning-focused pre-K programs. The transition from the pre-K year to the more academic kindergarten year then follows, which can be an especially difficult time for families, with children distraught and confused by drastically different expectations for behavior from one year to another and by misaligned curricula that lead to redundant lessons that leave children bored. Last, during those years between kindergarten (which may run on a shorter schedule than the rest of the elementary school) and the first through third grades, parents often feel out of touch with educators about their children's academic progress and social-emotional needs.

If all of this sounds daunting, imagine what it feels like for immigrant parents who are still learning English. Creating a coherent pathway for early learning will require an acknowledgment of the needs of dual-language learners and their families at each of these steps. English-only policies, for example, will need to be overturned across the education system to enable global literacy and bilingualism.

Many existing programs for infants, toddlers, preschoolers, and elementary school children will need to work together to form a coherent whole. As described in a recent New America paper, "Each year of their lives, children and their families should have the benefit of ascending a sturdy, well-lit staircase of development and learning rather than navigating disconnected and uneven platforms where they can easily fall through the cracks."

Fixing all of this will take hard work, but it could reap huge dividends for children's literacy learning. It starts by reframing the early years of children's lives as "learning" years that should be supported not only through effective social policies but also through the public education system. When school districts see themselves as part of the early learning continuum, they are more prone to work collaboratively with essential family strengthening initiatives such high-quality home-visiting programs, child care, and Head Start programs. Once policymakers recognize that public funding for education should start with these 0–8 years, they can create funding streams that enable families to experience a more efficient and seamless system, one based on clear outcomes and one in which parents don't have to confront the bureaucratic red tape of enrolling in multiple programs every year.

Better alignment is also necessary for the teachers and other adults who work in programs across this spectrum. The report *Transforming the Workforce for Children Birth through Age Eight: A Unifying Foundation* from the Institute of Medicine and National Academy of Sciences provides a strong model for aligning the currently disjointed system of teacher preparation, workforce training, and professional development programs that our teachers must navigate. Higher education institutions, community colleges, and accreditation systems will need to modernize their approaches so that teachers see themselves as "in it together" to help children develop the wide range of literacy skills they need by the end of third grade.

Advance Digital Age Equity: Families First

Digital innovation and literacy learning cannot coexist if the technical infrastructure and community support elements are not in place. The United States lacks both the "hardware" (technology "pipes" such as broadband availability and server capacity) and "software" (the professional and parent development, content knowledge, and applications needed to integrate new tools for discovery). For example, we rank in the bottom half of countries in broadband availability in schools and in low-income homes; most early learning programs have inadequate Internet connections; and families with income at or near the poverty line still have spotty access.

Given how critical the Internet has become in everyday life, policymakers may assume that everyone has a computer and is online. Indeed, national surveys show that the majority of American families have access to the Internet and the vast majority of adults have smartphones. But that does not mean it is always easy for teachers or students to get connected. Recent reports show that in some cases, the Internet—whether through wired or mobile connections—is only available in a limited number of classrooms. A *Ready to Learn* study funded by the US Department of Education found that only 29 percent of pre-K programs had Internet connections that teachers could use to give children a chance to access multimedia materials.

To address this lack of connectivity, the Federal Communications Commission (FCC) is taking steps to update the E-rate program that subsidizes Internet access for public schools and libraries, refocusing funds to prioritize broadband deployment. But this commitment does not apply to most of the nation's preschool, Head Start, and child care centers.

Despite our weak national infrastructure, we have seen examples of "digital equity" experimentation for younger children throughout this book, from the insights provided by Comienza en Casa in rural Maine, to the deftly trained home visitors in the PALs program in Houston, to the inspiring Too Small to Fail and Univision media campaigns. New mass communication tools can help promote substantial opportunities for underperforming students.

But we need to do even more. Consider the role of public media, which are facing significant financial scrutiny in a multichannel, commercially driven environment. Several PBS stations in the past century, for example, had a key role to play in enabling closed captioning, and the emphasis on inclusivity and supporting families of all kinds, especially those in need, continues to come through in public media projects around the country. Four decades of independent research on iconic programming such as *Sesame Street* and rigorous recent research by the Center for Children and Technology and SRI International demonstrates that public television programs, when embedded in high-quality preschool classrooms, can improve preschoolers' skills, especially among those in low-income families.

Unfortunately, such inspiration and innovation is lacking at scale in all too many low-income communities. There are patches of great ideas in libraries, public media, home-visiting programs, school-based early reading programs, and science-based and professional development programs at organizations such the Erikson Institute and the Ounce of Prevention Fund. But these organizations are swimming against a tide that has been strengthened by commercial forces. As our scan of the digital marketplace has documented, the act of creating thousands of digital apps and other tech "fixes" isn't yet reaching those most in need with the research-based tools that promote success. Addressing this market failure is ultimately a matter of equity: if we don't invest in both free or low-cost Internet access and a revitalized public media capacity in the future, we will likely see achievement gaps widen, not close.

Create Connected Teachers, Schools, and Communities

If we had a more coherent system of early learning programs that was supported by a publicly financed technology infrastructure, we would have a real shot at addressing fundamental gaps in literacy learning. But those efforts alone would fall short if we ignored a pressing need to scale quality programs, the many school and community efforts that are showing great promise.

Our book has included an examination of programs across the 0–8 age spectrum that are using technology to reach parents and teachers, an approach that shows more depth and promise than the thinness we saw in our app store analysis in chapter 6. We have discovered pioneering projects that help the adults in children's lives, especially those in disadvantaged families, learn how to promote literacy and use media for language development and eventual reading skills. Examples highlighted include using on-demand video for parenting education and home visits; deploying social media as new resources to parents and teachers; sending daily texts and Web-based messages to prompt storytelling, school–home links, and conversation; Skype-like tutoring in elementary schools; and employing media mentors in pre-K and library programs.

A recent analysis of technology and learning by the Aspen Institute Task Force on Learning and the Internet concluded that "the digital revolution has turned passive viewers into active users." And this personalized learning could be a boon for children. To illustrate, an edition of the widely respected journal *The Future of Children* devoted to literacy included this observation:

> Innovative technology applications show promise for supporting the development of advanced reading skills that students need to master discipline-specific knowledge areas and that may be particularly challenging for students from low socioeconomic backgrounds and non-English-speaking homes. Self-paced tutorials have led to gains in self-questioning, error detection, inference, summarization, and concept-mapping skills and strategies to enhance readers' use of reading strategies and comprehension of texts.

These examples, and a recognition of what good teaching with new tools entails, highlight the need to invest in the adults working with children if we wish to create sustainable solutions to America's early literacy crisis. It is not enough to prepare teachers for the Digital Age by simply instructing them on how to use a device, app, or learning platform. In a recent survey by the LEAD Commission, a bipartisan group designed to support the US Department of Education and Federal Communications Commission, 82 percent of teachers said they are not receiving the necessary training to use technology to its fullest potential in the classroom. Even more critical is providing prospective and current teachers a solid grounding in the latest developmental science and ensuring they are mentored through practical experiences in real settings with young children, using new tools appropriately.

Robust professional development was a key recommendation by the Digital Age Teacher Preparation Council convened in 2011 by the Cooney Center in conjunction with the Stanford Educational Leadership Institute. That council's landmark report, *Take a Giant Step: A Blueprint for Teaching Young Children in a Digital Age*, laid out key goals to achieve by 2020. These included various ways to integrate technology tools in teaching and learning efforts tied to curriculum, assessment, and instruction, via new forms of public media investment and by including educators' knowledge of technology uses in determining standards for high quality programs.

Since the release of that report, it has become clear that educators also need to be equipped to answer questions from parents. Families today are buzzing with questions about which apps to download, whether a child should be allowed to watch a particular video, and whether they should spend hundreds of dollars on touchscreen tablets. Media literacy specialists, early literacy teachers, children's librarians and others will need to develop skills to become what we have described as "media mentors" so they can train individuals to help families, including young children, use new tools to become creators while also being selective and thinking critically about what games they play or which shows they watch.

Engage Parents: Mine Cultural Capital

Because learning with digital technologies begins at home for families from all socioeconomic and cultural backgrounds, could we improve early learning if we were more adept in mobilizing what researchers refer to as "untapped cultural capital"? We believe so. In *Learning at Home,* a recent national survey of 1,577 parents with children ages two to ten, Cooney Center researchers asked parents to report on their children's home-based media use for educational purposes. Eight in ten parents reported that their children engaged with educational media at least weekly, and nearly six in ten said that their children had "learned a lot" from educational media, ranging from subject domain knowledge to general skills. Significant numbers of parents reported that their children engaged in interactive activities that are important catalysts for ongoing learning experiences, as noted in Figure 16.1.

Most parents surveyed said that their children's engagement in media was reflected in actions such as question asking, requests to do projects, conversations, and imaginative play. The survey findings also noted some trends worth considering for policymakers interested in tapping into the potential of the multitude of families who are often overlooked. The findings

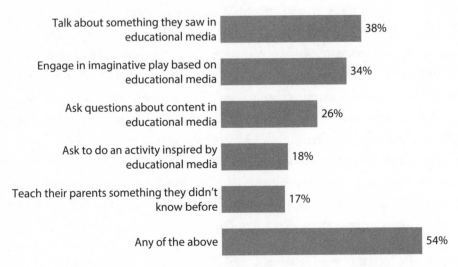

Figure 16.1 Actions Taken as a Result of Educational Media.

Among parents of two- to ten-year-olds who use educational media weekly, percentage who say their child takes a particular action as a result of something they saw or did with educational media. Source: Cooney Center, 2014.

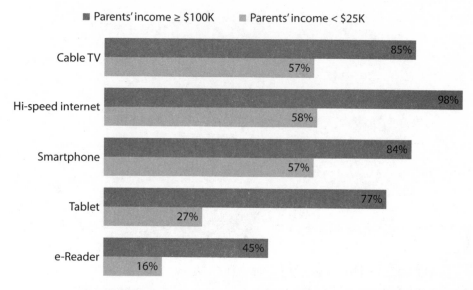

Figure 16.2 Mobile, Cable, and Online Access, by Income.

Among two- to ten-year-olds, percentage with each item in the home. Source: Cooney Center, 2014.

show that families need culturally responsive, equitable opportunities to learn. Lower-income families lacked access to many media platforms, as seen in Figure 16.2.

This trend is true even though low-income families are using educational media more frequently than higher income ones are. The percentages of parents report that their children use educational media daily, by income, are shown in Figure 16.3.

In a corollary report, *Aprendiendo en Casa,* the Cooney Center examined a subsample of nearly seven hundred Hispanic families and also found that the majority see their children's engagement in media reflected in question asking, requests to do projects, conversations, and imaginative play. Many report that children are learning English and early academic skills from their educational media use. Additionally, some parents report that their children have taught them something based on what they have learned from media.

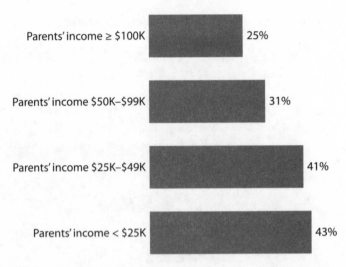

Figure 16.3 Daily Users of Educational Media, by Platform and Income.

Percentage of two- to ten-year-olds who use educational media on a daily basis, by parent income.
Source: *Cooney Center, 2014.*

However, access differs by language, with Spanish-only families experiencing far less access to digital technologies than other families. Hispanic families most commonly access educational content through television rather than the computer, video games, or mobile devices. This points to the need to continue to create strong educational television content for this audience, while developing more mobile content (in Spanish and English) that serves their needs.

Media access also has implications for *parents'* learning. Parents' regular use of digital tools to find information is closely tied to access to a high-speed Internet connection at home. Parents who often used digital technology for learning had children who used educational media more often, highlighting an important association between parents' and children's media use. This suggests that an intergenerational approach can be especially useful for media design and deployment to culturally diverse families. Parents value media content that serves as a springboard for conversation and activities, as well as content that promotes joint media engagement. Such content is sorely needed, according to this research, across all platforms.

WHAT EDUCATORS CAN DO

Those of you on the front lines of education need the support that would be forthcoming with the policy changes outlined above. You can also start today, in your classrooms and communities, by doing the following:

- *Adopt a tap-click-read mind-set* toward your students' literacy learning: *Tap* into learning networks and tap open new media opportunities for them. *Click* into resources yourself while recognizing that the clicks of children are actions emanating from their curiosities; help steer their desire for interactivity toward materials that help them learn. And hold dear the act of *reading* and the importance of helping your students become literate in multiple ways.

- *Remember the skills + knowledge approach.* For children in preschool and up, this could mean teaching letters and sounds to help them practice the "decoding" of written words *while also* immersing them in stories and back-and-forth dialogue about the multilayered worlds of science, art, history, literature, different cultures, and more.

- *Seek opportunities for joint engagement with media* (including print books, of course), either among children or with adults and children working and learning together.

- *Do not turn literacy software into isolated "technology time."* Instead, integrate media and other technologies into curricula and lesson plans.

- *Partner with librarians and media specialists.* Take stock of the e-book resources and availability of literacy specialists at your school library and local public library. Librarians are educators too.

- *Differentiate e-book deployment* depending on skill level; pay attention to whether children are choosing "Read it to me" versus "I'll read it myself" and explore why.

- *Test-drive digital games* and other forms of media to see whether, if well-deployed, they might allow students to see how complex language and other symbol systems are relevant to their own lives.

- *Borrow from and take advantage of public media* for classroom use. *Sesame Street* and *The Electric Company*, for example, have music videos and games that, say, illustrate the importance of learning letters and sounds as well as the various ways in which "silent E" transforms a "plan into a plane" or "slop into a slope." Embedded media of this type deployed in well-designed reading intervention programs have lasting positive effects on struggling students' capabilities.
- *Recognize the huge untapped assets of cultural traditions and second language competencies.* Immerse children with opportunities to build bilingual literacy as a pathway to success.
- *Advocate for better resources and environments* for literacy learning. Push for a Readialand in your city, school district, and neighborhood by bringing equity issues to the attention of your administrators, school board, and state leaders.

WHAT PARENTS CAN DO

Individually parents can bring literacy learning to their youngsters by being open to some new approaches. Collectively parents can have a real impact by voicing demands for the tools, resources, and coherent system of education and mentorship that children need. They can:

- *Adopt a tap-click-read mind-set* toward your child's use of media for literacy learning. Just like educators, you can *tap* into learning networks, *click* along with your children as they learn to be actively engaged in texts; and emphasize the need to *read* and analyze texts, images, and media.
- *Remember the Three Cs* (borrowed from Lisa's previous book, *Screen Time*). To choose and use media wisely, consider the *content*, the *context*, and the individual *child*.
- *Seek out media mentors* in local public libraries, early learning centers, and schools to help guide your family's use of media as a learning tool.

- *Read, watch, and play* with your children to jointly engage with them around media, or engage them in conversation about what they have read, watched, or played with on their own.
- *Be a model for how to use media as a learning source.* Demonstrate and describe to your children why you are using certain media in certain ways at certain times. ("Let's Skype with Grandma so she can see your painting." "I'm going to use Google Maps to find the nearest library.")
- *Advocate for attention to a Fourth C: Community.* Push your leaders for better conditions for early learning and literacy across your school, county, and state.

WHAT DEVELOPERS CAN DO

The creators of media and technology have the ability to shape young children's minds and become part of daily life in households and schools around the country. But with that power comes responsibility. Developers can:

- *Be transparent.* Provide information about your product so that educators and parents know who is behind it, whether it has been tested for effectiveness, and how it will help children of particular age ranges or developmental stages.
- *Recognize that literacy is more than flashcard repetition of the ABCs.* Help parents and educators see how to use media to augment and invigorate lessons, spark new conversations, and tap into children's curiosity.
- *Create media that includes characters and storylines that reflect the diversity of today's families.* Make products that enable children to find books (e- or paper) with characters who look like them. Produce media for families that speaks their language and recognizes their culture.
- *Work with educators and researchers.* For too long, the publishers and producers have been in one world, and the educators and researchers have been in another. Use literacy experts in product design and invite academic researchers to study the use of your products.

TWELVE ACTIONS POLICYMAKERS SHOULD TAKE NOW

We've outlined above the four large-scale actions that will help fix our systems and propel improvement for all kids. Here are twelve concrete steps to take this week, this month, this year:

1. Invest in early learning programs to support families and make high-quality learning environments the norm from birth through elementary school.

2. Finance culturally responsive, large-scale programming through public media providers. These media providers need to return to their original mission: to devise robust community programming that successfully taps into the assets of low-income families and families that speak a language other than English.

3. Build better technology access through public-private partnerships to provide low-income families with low-cost educational content and broadband access. Develop dual-generation or family-centered models for the use of digital technologies in lifelong learning (that is, career training) for parents at the same time that those technologies support learning for children.

4. Help to create access to easily searchable, parent- and educator-friendly "one-click" rating systems and curation tools that take into account research standards and children's developmental stages; make more widely available to lower-income and non-English-speaking parents.

5. Tap into hidden assets such as libraries, community organizations (for example, Boys & Girls Clubs, the Y, and churches), and museums that offer treasure troves of materials that early educators may not even know exist.

6. Create a place in every community where children can gain confidence in their literacy and interactive technology skills and where parents will feel welcome to learn some new skills too.

7. Modernize existing teacher training programs and introduce new digital teaching techniques in preschools and the primary grades.

8. Build a digital teacher corps and media mentorship pipeline that combines educators' talents across settings (for example, schools, libraries).

9. Stimulate more independent and peer-reviewed research and investigation about what works and what doesn't. Encourage connections among researchers, educators, and creators of children's media.

10. Hold local, state, and national meetings to listen, crowdsource, and propose new investments in human-led, tech-assisted approaches to children's literacy learning.

11. Revise the National Education Technology Plan to expand technology diffusion in under-resourced schools and ensure inclusion of early learning (0–8) in the plan.

12. Ensure that school leaders communicate to parents about shifts to digital learning platforms and do so at a pace that enables parents to get up to speed on changes in how their children learn, read, write, and do their homework.

CONCLUSION

Today's young children will soon grow into the middle schoolers of the next decade, the high school graduates of 2030, and the citizens and workforce of the future. By paying attention to the way they use technologies and media to learn vital skills like reading—and by ensuring educators, mentors, designers and parents are prepared to help them—every community in the United States can promote successful learning environments. But we won't get there, and we will more likely exacerbate existing gaps, unless national policy priorities are laser focused on making equitable learning opportunities for all children and families available through better technology access and supports.

As we hope this book makes clear, only a new approach to help support the vital work of effective teachers and engaged parents will help break through a long festering quiet crisis around early literacy. As we chart a course to a place where reading and media converge and all children get a decent start, capable, responsive adults will still matter most. The consequences of poor reading skills and disengagement from literacy have never been greater. Our leaders, parents, and educators who recognize the importance of literacy truly can build the communities that children need to thrive. Those are the places we cannot wait to continue to visit and learn from. See you in Readialand.

NOTES

In 2012, only 14 percent: *2013 Reading Assessment*, 5.

In a recent report from the Pew Research Center: Anderson and Rainie 2014, 5.

The United States does not yet have: Guernsey 2014; and Katz and Levine 2015.

Our approach is based: Jordan and Romer 2014.

But as it stands: The *EdCentral* blog at New America publishes articles and analysis on these issues every week. Another source of historical information and recommendations for rethinking the early years and elementary school is a forthcoming book, *First Things First*, by Ruby Takanishi, former president of the Foundation for Child Development.

Each year of their lives: Bornfreund et al. 2014.

The report *Transforming the Workforce*: Institute of Medicine and National Research Council 2015.

national surveys show: Eighty-five percent of parents have a computer at home with high-speed Internet access, according to data from page 34 of *Parenting in the Age of Digital Technology: A National Survey*, 2013, by Ellen Wartella et al. (Evanston, IL: Northwestern University, June), at http://vjrconsulting.com/storage/PARENTING_IN_THE_AGE_OF_DIGITAL_TECHNOLOGY.pdf; see also Smith 2013.

A report from the US Department of Education's Ready to Learn study: Pasnik and Llorente 2011, 4.

the Federal Communications Commission (FCC) is taking steps: "Summary of the E-Rate."

Four decades of independent research: Fisch and Truglio 2001.

rigorous recent research: Penuel et al. 2009.

A recent analysis of technology and learning: *Learner at the Center* 2014, 3.

Innovative technology applications: Biancorsa and Griffiths 2012.

82 percent of teachers said: *Paving a Path* 2013.

These included various ways: Barron et al. 2011.

"untapped cultural capital": Katz 2014.

Lower-income families lacked access: Rideout 2014.

Figure 16.3: Ibid.

Aprendiendo en Casa: Lee and Barron 2015.

some parents report: Ibid.

Such content is sorely needed: Ibid.

Test-drive digital games: Levine and Gee 2011; Gee 2008.

Embedded media of this type: Chambers, et al. 2011; Slavin, Madden, and Chambers 2006.

Modernize existing teacher training programs: Guernsey 2014; Barron et al. 2011.

Build a digital teacher corps: Gee and Levine 2009.

Resources

The following is an alphabetical list of tools, projects, and programs described in the pages of this book. See TapClickRead.org for updates.

- Accelerated Reader from Renaissance Learning
  https://hosted77.renlearn.com/139920/
- Balefire Labs
  http://www.balefirelabs.com/apps/
- Behavioral Insights and Parenting Lab at the Harris School of Public Policy at the University of Chicago
  http://web.harrisschool.uchicago.edu/centers/chppp/bip/training
- Born Reading
  http://www.born-reading.com/
- Children's Technology Review
  http://childrenstech.com/
- Comienza en Casa
  http://www.manomaine.org/programs/mep/comienzaencasa
- Common Sense Media (Ratings for parents and teachers)
  https://www.commonsensemedia.org/
  https://www.graphite.org/

- Community Action Project of Tulsa
  https://captulsa.org/wp/
- Digital Storytime
  http://digital-storytime.com/
- Every Child Ready to Read
  http://www.everychildreadytoread.org/
- First Book—First Book National Book Bank, First Book Marketplace
  http://www.firstbook.org/
  http://www.firstbook.org/first-book-story/innovation-in-publishing/national-book-bank
  http://www.firstbook.org/first-book-story/innovation-in-publishing/marketplace
- Global Literacy Project
  http://globallit.org/
- The Great Reading Adventure
  http://greatreadingadventure.com/
- I-LABS (Institute for Learning and Brain Sciences) free online modules
  http://ilabs.washington.edu/outreach-modules
- Innovations for Learning /TutorMate/TeacherMate
  http://www.innovationsforlearning.org/
  http://www.innovationsforlearning.org/tutormate/
  http://www.innovationsforlearning.org/teachermate
- Joan Ganz Cooney Center
  http://www.joanganzcooneycenter.org/
- Jumpstart conducts Read for the Record
  http://www.jstart.org/campaigns/read-for-the-record
- LIFE Center (Learning in Informal and Formal Environments)
  http://life-slc.org/
- Maternal, Infant, and Early Childhood Home Visiting (MIECHV)
  http://mchb.hrsa.gov/programs/homevisiting/
- Mind in the Making videos
  https://www.youtube.com/user/MITMChannel

- Moms with Apps
    https://momswithapps.com/
- myON
    https://www.myon.com/
- New America's EdCentral blog
    http://www.edcentral.org/
- Nurse–Family Partnership
    http://www.nursefamilypartnership.org/
- Parent University
    http://parentuniversity.co/
- Parents' Choice Foundation
    http://www.parents-choice.org/
- PBS Parents Play & Learn app
    http://pbskids.org/apps/pbs-parents-play-learn.html
- Pequeños y Valisosos (Young and Valuable)
    http://noticias.univision.com/educacion/pequenos-y-valiosos/
    http://www.univisioncontigo.com/en/education/early-childhood/
- Play and Learning Strategies (PALS)
    http://www.childrenslearninginstitute.org/our-programs/program-overview/PALS/
- Providence Talks
    http://www.providencetalks.org/
- Raising a Reader
    http://www.raisingareader.org/site/PageServer?pagename=rar_homepage
- Reach Out and Read
    http://www.reachoutandread.org/
- Reading Is Fundamental
    http://readingisfundamental.org/
- Reading Rainbow
    https://www.readingrainbow.com/

- Reading Rockets
  http://www.readingrockets.org/
- Ready Rosie
  http://readyrosie.com/
- Sesame Street
  http://www.sesamestreet.org/
- A Story before Bed
  http://www.astorybeforebed.com/
- Success for All Foundation
  http://www.successforall.org/
- Teachers with Apps
  http://www.teacherswithapps.com/
- Thirty Million Words
  http://thirtymillionwords.org/
- Too Small to Fail
  http://toosmall.org/
- Unite for Literacy
  http://uniteforliteracy.com/
- Video Interaction Project
  http://www.med.nyu.edu/pediatrics/developmental/research/belle-project/belle-video-interaction-project
  http://childrenofbellevue.org/video-interaction-project/
- Vroom
  http://www.joinvroom.org/
- Wonderopolis
  http://wonderopolis.org/
- Word Play in Pittsburgh
  http://remakelearning.org/blog/2013/08/29/in-pittsburgh-young-children-learn-while-they-wait/

About the Authors

Lisa Guernsey is director of the Early Education Initiative and the Learning Technologies Project in the Education Policy Program at New America. She leads teams of writers and analysts to tell stories, examine policies, and generate ideas for new approaches to help disadvantaged students succeed. Prior to her work at New America, Lisa worked as a staff writer at *The New York Times* and *The Chronicle of Higher Education*. She has also contributed to several national publications, including *The Atlantic, The Washington Post, Newsweek, Time, Slate, and USA TODAY*, and she is the author of *Screen Time: How Electronic Media—From Baby Videos to Educational Software—Affects Your Young Child* (Basic Books, 2012). She won a 2012 gold Eddie magazine award for a *School Library Journal* article on e-books and has served on several national advisory committees on early education, including the Institute of Medicine's Committee on the Science of Children Birth To Age 8. She holds a master's degree in English/American studies and a bachelor's degree in English from the University of Virginia. Lisa lives in Alexandria, Virginia, with her two daughters.

Michael H. Levine is the founding executive director of the Joan Ganz Cooney Center at Sesame Workshop. The Center conducts research, builds multi-sector alliances, and catalyzes industry and policy reforms needed to advance high-quality media experiences for vulnerable children. Levine serves on the senior team at Sesame Workshop where he focuses on educational initiatives and philanthropic partnerships for the global nonprofit.

Prior to joining the Center, Levine was Vice President for Asia Society, managing interactive media and educational initiatives to promote knowledge and understanding of other world regions and cultures. Michael previously oversaw Carnegie Corporation of New York's groundbreaking work in early childhood development and educational media, and was a senior advisor to the New York City Schools Chancellor, where he directed dropout prevention and afterschool programs. Levine serves on several boards including the Forum for Youth Investment, We Are Family Foundation, Classroom, Inc., Journeys in Film, Woot Math, and DigiLearn. Michael is a Pahara-Aspen Education Reform Fellow and a frequent adviser to the White House and the US Department of Education. He writes for professional and public affairs journals, including a regular column for *Huffington Post,* and is a frequent keynote speaker at education and technology conferences around the world. Levine and his wife Joni have three children and live in Teaneck, New Jersey.

Acknowledgments

This book was a team effort from start to finish. A cast of colleagues at our institutions contributed in significant ways from the earliest days of planning meetings to hours and hours of interviews and site visits to the last bleary-eyed nights of final editing. We are especially indebted to Sarah Vaala, Anna Ly, and Lindsey Tepe, as well as Lori Takeuchi, Amber Levinson, Michelle Miller, Catherine Jhee, Olivia Ginn, Alan Tong, and Shayna Cook, who helped at critical times with strategic thinking, research, editing, blogging, and outreach. We are also very grateful for our partnership with HiredPen, a communications firm run by the forward-thinking and talented Barbara Ray and Sarah Jackson. Barbara, Sarah, and several of their writers, including Kathleen Costanza, Maureen Kelleher, and Heidi Moore, conducted interviews and reported for our pre–book launch blog, originally called *Seeding Reading*. Barbara spent many long hours traveling and directing our video shoots, and her storytelling expertise shone through at every turn. HiredPen's video crew, led by Nat Soti of Zero-One Productions, did a masterful job shooting video and weaving together the beautiful video vignettes that are sprinkled throughout the book.

Jeff Schoenberg of the Pritzker Children's Initiative saw the potential and promise of the ideas in this book many years before we had written the first sentence. We are incredibly thankful for Jeff's stewardship and smart critiques, and for the generous funding from J. B. and M. K. Pritzker and the Pritzker Children's Initiative that made this book possible. We will be forever indebted to Ralph Smith of the Campaign for Grade-Level Reading and the Annie E. Casey Foundation, whose brainstorming sessions in early 2012 helped us see the significance of these issues. Funding from The Campaign for Grade-Level Reading and the Tides Foundation led to *Pioneering Literacy in the Digital Wild West,* the paper that sparked this book. We are also indebted to Jackie and Mike Bezos, Megan Wyatt of the Bezos Family Foundation, and Liz Simons, Deanna Gomby, and Holly Kreider of the Heising-Simons Foundation for their essential support of our teams' ongoing research on families' use of media.

We give special thanks to Marjorie McAneny, our editor at Wiley/ Jossey-Bass, for her dedication to this project and for her smart insights in editing, and to our early manuscript editor, Sabrina Detlef, who did a masterful and careful edit of our first draft. Thanks too to Peter Gaughan who manages content development and assembly at Wiley/Jossey Bass for his wonderful strategic eye and critical comments, to Cathy Mallon for her fabulous project management skills, and to our most able copyeditor Pam Suwinsky. It is no easy job to edit and help sell a book with so many players and moving parts; we were so lucky to have them.

Dozens of people around the country gave of their time and energy toward this project by leading us to the right stories to tell or providing comments and critiques on early drafts. Special thanks go to Marilyn Jager Adams, Terri Clark, Yolie Flores, Ellen Galinsky, Roberta Golinkoff, Kathy Hirsh-Pasek, Lisa Kane, Susan Neuman, Conor Williams, and Kyle Zimmer, as well as the team at the Campaign for Grade-Level Reading: Lisa Kane, Yolie Flores, Susanne Sparks, Jessica Young, Kelly Trop, Lacy McAlister, and Daniel Bernick. For helping to set up the video shoots, which can require days of coordination, we thank Ana and Bonnie Blagojevic at Comienza en Casa at Mano en Mano in Milbridge, Maine; Ursula Johnson and Susan Landry at the Children's Learning Institute at the University of Texas; Ariel

Kalil and Jill Gandhi at the Harris School of Public Policy at the University of Chicago; Dan Weisberg and Tahra Tibbs at Innovations for Learning; Stephen Massey and Patti Miller at Too Small to Fail; and Paola Hernandez, Iveliesse Malave, and Bob Llamas at Univision. We also want to acknowledge thoughtful contributions from the advisory group on tech and literacy that we assembled through the Campaign for Grade-Level Reading: Terri Clark, Margaret Doughty, Mike Eggleston, Robert Gordon, Sandra Gutierrez, Ann Hanson, Joe Manko, Patti Miller, Tony Raden, Daryl Rothman, and Sheila Umberger.

We come from two different places, and both of our institutions strive to uncover and promote new ideas that will advance the well-being and development of all children, especially those from low-income families. That broader work at New America and the Joan Ganz Cooney Center at Sesame Workshop has informed the ideas in this book and we are incredibly thankful for the philanthropic support behind it. At New America, the Education Policy Program's Early Education Initiative relies on generous support from the Alliance for Early Success, the David and Lucile Packard Foundation, the Evelyn and Walter Haas Jr. Fund, the Foundation for Child Development, the Heising-Simons Foundation, the Joyce Foundation, the Pritzker Children's Initiative, the W. Clement and Jessie V. Stone Foundation, and the W. K. Kellogg Foundation. At the Cooney Center we receive generous support for our research and core operations from Pete Peterson and Joan Ganz Cooney, Sesame Workshop, the Bill & Melinda Gates Foundation, the Bezos Family Foundation, the Heising-Simons Foundation, Ford Foundation, Carnegie Corporation, the Grable Foundation, and the National Science Foundation.

Last, we say a big thank you to family and friends who inspired us and buoyed us through the years of this book-writing journey. Lisa thanks her mother and father, Betty Guernsey and Roger Guernsey, for their love and continual support; her friends Laura Dove, Sabrina Detlef, Allison O'Grady, and Luisa Tio for keeping her afloat when the going got rough; Kevin Carey, her director at New America, who gave her wide berth for research, writing, and exploration; Laura Bornfreund and her early ed colleagues at New America for making the Early Education Initiative shine when she was stuck in her book-writing cave; and her daughters Janelle and Gillian for their boundless energy, open minds, and agility with new technologies that inspire her to think in new ways and imagine what literacy could look like for future generations.

Michael thanks all of his colleagues who have encouraged him to write about digital media and learning, with special thanks to his colleagues and mentors Joan Ganz Cooney, Lloyd Morrisett, Gary Knell, Jeff Dunn, Lewis Bernstein, David Hamburg, and Vivien Stewart. He is also deeply indebted to his wonderful parents Marion and Irving Levine for their inspiration, encouragement, and keen commitment to educational change, his life partner Joni Blinderman for her unflagging support, passion for social justice, and all-around loveliness, and his children Sam, Zach, and Sarah for teaching him just about everything that is important to know about technology and parenting.

Bibliography

"Achievement Gap Exists in Online Reading Skills." 2014. *UConn Today* blog, September 29. http://today.uconn.edu/blog/2014/09/achievement-gap-exists-in-online-reading-skills/.

Adams, Marilyn Jager. 2011. *Technology for Developing Children's Language and Literacy: Bringing Speech-Recognition to the Classroom.* New York: Joan Ganz Cooney Center at Sesame Workshop. http://www.joanganzcooneycenter.org/wp-content/uploads/2011/09/jgcc_tech_for_language_and_literacy.pdf.

Alexander, Karl L., Linda Steffel Olson, and Doris R. Entwisle. 2007. "Lasting Consequences of the Summer Learning Gap." *American Sociological Review* 72 (April): 167–80. http://www.nayre.org/Summer%20Learning%20Gap.pdf.

Alper, Meryl. 2014. "Can You Caption How to Get, How to Get to Sesame Street?" Joan Ganz Cooney Center blog, November 17. http://www.joanganzcooneycenter.org/2014/11/17/can-you-caption-how-to-get-how-to-get-to-sesame-street/.

Alper, Meryl and Rebecca Herr-Stephenson. 2013. "Transmedia Play: Literacy across Media." *Journal of Media Literacy Education* 5, no. 2: 366–69. http://digitalcommons.uri.edu/jmle/vol5/iss2/2/.

Anderson, Daniel R., Aletha C. Huston, Kelly L. Schmitt, Deborah Linebarger, and John C. Wright. 2001. *Early Childhood Television Viewing and Adolescent Behavior: The Recontact Study.* Monographs of the Society for Research in Child Development 66, no. 1. http://www.ncbi.nlm.nih.gov/pubmed/11326591.

Anderson, Janna and Lee Rainie. 2014. *Digital Life in 2025*. Washington, DC: Pew Research Center, March 11. http://www.pewinternet.org/2014/03/11/digital-life-in-2025/.

Anonymous. 2011. "Harry Potter and the Pottermore Crisis." *Fan Fiction*, July 31. http://www.fanfiction.net/s/7236949/1/Harry-Potter-and-the-Pottermore-Crisis.

"Apple Reinvents the Phone with iPhone." 2007. Apple press info, January 9. http://www.apple.com/pr/library/2007/01/09Apple-Reinvents-the-Phone-with-iPhone.html.

Barillas, Roxana. 2014. "Five Reasons Why Everybody Benefits from More Diverse Children's Books." *Huffington Post Education* blog, June 25 (updated August 25). http://www.huffingtonpost.com/roxana-barillas/5-reasons-why-everybody-b_b_5529656.html?1403710142/.

Barr, Rachel, Alexis Lauricella, Elizabeth Zack, and Sandra L. Calvert. 2010. "Infant and Early Childhood Exposure to Adult-Directed and Child-Directed Television Programming: Relations with Cognitive Skills at Age Four." *Merrill-Palmer Quarterly* 56, no. 1 (January): 21–48. http://digitalcommons.wayne.edu/mpq/vol56/iss1/3/.

Barron, Brigid, Gabrielle Cayton-Hodges, Laura Bofferding, Carol Copple, Linda Darling-Hammond, and Michael H. Levine. 2011. *Take a Giant Step: A Blueprint for Teaching Young Children in a Digital Age*. New York: Joan Ganz Cooney Center at Sesame Workshop. http://www.joanganzcooneycenter.org/wp-content/uploads/2012/01/jgcc_takeagiantstep1.pdf.

The Behavioural Insights Team. Website. http://www.behaviouralinsights.co.uk/.

Berkule, Samantha B., Carolyn Brockmeyer Cates, Bernard P. Dreyer, Harris S. Huberman, Jenny Arevalo, Nina Burtchen, Adriana Weisleder, and Alan L. Mendelsohn. 2014. "Reducing Maternal Depressive Symptoms through Promotion of Parenting in Pediatric Primary Care." *Clinical Pediatrics* 53, no. 5: 460–69.

Biancorsa, Gina and Gina G. Griffiths. 2012. "Technology Tools to Support Reading in the Digital Age." *Future of Children* 22, no. 2 (Fall): 139–60. http://futureofchildren.org/publications/journals/article/index.xml?journalid=78&articleid=577&sectionid=3990.

Bigelow, Kathryn M. and Edward K. Morris. 2001. "John B. Watson's Advice on Child Rearing: Some Historical Context." *Behavioral Development Bulletin* 1 (Fall): 26–30. http://www.baojournal.com/BDB%20WEBSITE/archive/BDB-2001–01–01–026–030.pdf.

Birkerts, Sven. 1994. *The Gutenberg Elegies: The Fate of Reading in an Electronic Age*. Boston: Faber and Faber. http://us.macmillan.com/thegutenbergelegies/svenbirkerts.

Bornfreund, Laura, Clare McCann, Conor P. Williams, and Lisa Guernsey. 2014. *Beyond Subprime Learning: Accelerating Progress in Early Education*. Washington, DC: New America, July. http://www.newamerica.net/sites/newamerica.net/files/policydocs/ Beyond_Subprime_Learning_by_Bornfreund-et-al_New_America_Jul2014.pdf.

Brooks, M. K. and M. Moon. 2013. "Children's Learning from Mobile Devices. The Case of Big Bird's Words." Unpublished presentation, Sesame Workshop.

Buckleitner, Warren. 2013. "The Art and the Science of the Children's eBook." http: //dustormagic.com/wp-content/uploads/2013/03/ebookarticle.pdf.

Bus, Adriana G., Zsofia K. Takacs, and Cornelia A. T. Kegel. 2015. "Affordances and Limitations of Electronic Storybooks for Young Children's Emergent Literacy." *Developmental Review* 35: 79–97. http://www.sciencedirect .com/science/article/pii/S0273229714000501.

Campaign for Grade-Level Reading. n.d. "Summer Learning Loss." http://gradelevel reading.net/our-work/summer-learning-loss.

———. 2013. "The 30 Million Word Gap: The Role of Parent-Child Verbal Interaction in Language and Literacy Development." http://gradelevelreading.net/wp-content/uploads/2013/05/GLR-Issue-brief-on-oral-language-research.pdf.

Campbell, Cen. 2014. "Children's Librarians as Digital Media Mentors." Blog for the Fred Rogers Center for Early Learning and Children's Media, posted on April 21. http://www.fredrogerscenter.org/blog/childrens-librarians-as-digital-media-mentors.

Carey, Bjorn. 2013. "Language Gap between Rich and Poor Children Begins in Infancy, Stanford Psychologists Find." *Stanford News*, September 25. http://news.stanford.edu/ news/2013/september/toddler-language-gap-091213.html.

Carnegie Corporation. 1994. *Starting Points: Meeting the Needs of Our Youngest Children*. New York. Link to abridged report at http://carnegie.org/fileadmin/ Media/Publications/PDF/Starting%20Points%20Meeting%20the%20Needs%20of%20 Our%20Youngest%20Children.pdf.

Carr, Nicholas. 2008. "Is Google Making Us Stupid? What the Internet Is Doing to Our Brains." *Atlantic*, July/August. http://www.theatlantic.com/magazine/archive/ 2008/07/is-google-making-us-stupid/306868/.

Carr, Nicholas. 2010. *The Shallows: What the Internet Is Doing to Our Brains*. New York: Norton. http://books.wwnorton.com/books/978–0–393–07222–8/.

Center for Applied Special Technology (CAST). "About UDL: What Is Universal Design for Learning?" http://www.cast.org/udl/.

Center on the Developing Child at Harvard. "Serve & Return Interaction Shapes Brain Circuitry." Video. http://developingchild.harvard.edu/resources/multimedia/videos/three_core_concepts/serve_and_return/.

Chambers, B., P. C. Abrami, R. E. Slavin, and N. A. Madden. 2011. "A *Three-Tier Model* of Reading Instruction Supported by Technology." *International Journal of Innovation and Learning* 9, no. 3: 286–97.

Chiong, Cynthia and Carly Shuler. 2010. *Learning: Is There an App for That?* New York: Joan Ganz Cooney Center at Sesame Workshop. http://www.joanganzcooneycenter.org/publication/learning-is-there-an-app-for-that/.

Chiong, Cynthia, Jinny Ree, Lori Takeuchi, and Ingrid Erikson. 2012. *Print Books vs. E-Books: Comparing Parent-Child Co-Reading on Print, Basic, and Enhanced e-Book Platforms.* New York: Joan Ganz Cooney Center at Sesame Workshop. http://www.joanganzcooneycenter.org/wp-content/uploads/2012/07/jgcc_ebooks_quickreport.pdf.

Christakis, Dimitri A., Frederick J. Zimmerman, David L. DiGiuseppe, and Carolyn A. McCarty. 2004. "Early Television Exposure and Subsequent Attentional Problems in Children." *PEDIATRICS* 113, no. 4 (April): 708–13. http://pediatrics.aappublications.org/content/113/4/708.

"Codex." Wikipedia. http://en.wikipedia.org/wiki/Codex.

Cooney, Joan Ganz. 1966. *The Potential Uses of Television in Preschool Education.* New York: Children's Television Workshop. http://www.joanganzcooneycenter.org/wp-content/uploads/2014/01/JGC_1966_report.pdf.

Cooper, Harris, Barbara Nye, Kelly Charlton, James Lindsay, Scott Greathouse. 1996. "The Effects of Summer Vacation on Achievement Test Scores: A Narrative and Meta-Analytic Review." *Review of Educational Research* 66, no. 3 (Fall): 227-268. http://rer.sagepub.com/content/66/3/227.abstract.

Costanza, Kathleen. 2014. "App Reviews to Help Choose Ed Tech This Holiday Season." *New America EdCentral* blog, December 18. http://www.edcentral.org/holidayapp-reviews/.

Costello, Sam. 2014. "How Many Apps Are There in the iPhone App Store?" *About Tech*, October 16. http://ipod.about.com/od/iphonesoftwareterms/qt/apps-in-app-store.htm.

Daugherty, Lindsay, Rafiq Dossani, Erin-Elizabeth Johnson, and Cameron Wright. 2014. "Getting on the Same Page: Identifying Goals for Technology Use in Early

Childhood Education." RAND Corporation. http://www.rand.org/pubs/research_reports/RR673z1.html.

de Jong, Maria T. and Adriana G. Bus. 2002. "Quality of Book-Reading Matters for Emergent Readers: An Experiment with the Same Book in a Regular or Electronic Format." *Journal of Educational Psychology* 94, no. 1 (March) 145–55. dx.doi.org/10.1037/0022–0663.94.1.145.

DeLoache, Judy S. et al., 2010. "Do Babies Learn from Baby Media?" *Psychological Science* 21, no. 11: 1570–74. http://www.centenary.edu/attachments/psychology/journal/archive/feb2011journalclub.pdf.

DeNavas-Walt, Carmen and Bernadette D. Proctor. 2014. "Income and Poverty in the United States: 2013: Current Population Reports," US Census, September. http://census.gov/content/dam/Census/library/publications/2014/demo/p60–249.pdf.

Dickinson, David K. and Allyssa McCabe. 2001. "Bringing It All Together: The Multiple Origins, Skills, and Environmental Supports of Early Literacy." *Learning Disabilities Research and Practice* 16, no. 4: 186–202. http://www.academia.edu/2820222/Bringing_it_all_together_The_multiple_origins_skills_and_environmental_supports_of_early_literacy.

Donohue, Chip, ed. 2014. *Technology and Digital Media in the Early Years: Tools for Teaching and Learning*. New York: Routledge. http://teccenter.erikson.edu/tech-in-the-early-years/.

EveryoneOn. "About Us." http://everyoneon.org/about/.

Family Time with Apps: A Guide to Using Apps with Your Kids. 2014. New York: Joan Ganz Cooney Center at Sesame Workshop. http://www.joanganzcooneycenter.org/publication/family-time-with-apps/.

Federal Communications Commission. "Summary of the E-Rate Modernization Order." http://www.fcc.gov/page/summary-e-rate-modernization-order.

Federal Trade Commission. 2012. "Mobile Apps for Kids: Disclosures Still Not Making the Grade." http://www.ftc.gov/sites/default/files/documents/reports/mobile-apps-kids-disclosures-still-not-making-grade/121210mobilekidsappreport.pdf.

Fenstermacher, Susan K., et al. 2010. "Interactional Quality Depicted in Infant and Toddler Videos: Where Are the Interactions?" *Infant and Child Development* 19, no. 6 (November/December): 594–612. http://onlinelibrary.wiley.com/doi/10.1002/icd.714/abstract.

Fernald, Anne, Virginia A. Marchman, and Adriana Weisleder. 2013. "SES Differences in Language Processing Skill and Vocabulary Are Evident at 18 Months." *Developmental Science* 16, no. 2 (March): 234–48. http://onlinelibrary.wiley.com/doi/10.1111/desc.12019/abstract.

"Fingerreader: A Wearable Interface for Reading On-the-Go." Fluid Interfaces Group at MIT Media Lab. http://fluid.media.mit.edu/projects/fingerreader.

"First Book's Impact." First Book. http://www.firstbook.org/first-book-story/our-impact.

Fisch, Shalom M. and Rosemarie T. Truglio, eds. 2001. *"G" Is for Growing: Thirty Years of Research on Children and "Sesame Street."* Mahwah, NJ: Lawrence Erlbaum. http://eric.ed.gov/?id=ED450939.

Fresh Air. 2012. "In Constant Digital Contact, We Feel 'Alone Together.'" NPR interview of Sherry Turkle, October 17. http://www.npr.org/2012/10/18/163098594/in-constant-digital-contact-we-feel-alone-together.

Frye, Sheila K. 2014. *The Implications of Interactive eBooks on Comprehension*. PhD diss. New Brunswick, NJ: Rutgers University. https://rucore.libraries.rutgers.edu/rutgers-lib/42343/.

Gaddy, Gary D. 1986. "Television's Impact on High School Achievement." *Public Opinion Quarterly* 50, no. 3 (Autumn): 340–59. http://www.jstor.org/stable/2748723.

Galinsky, Ellen. 2010. *Mind in the Making: The Seven Essential Life Skills Every Child Needs*. New York: Harper Collins. http://www.harpercollins.com/9780061987908/mind-in-the-making.

———. 2012. "Executive Function Skills Predict Children's Success in Life and in School." *Huffington Post Education* blog, June 21. http://www.huffingtonpost.com/ellen-galinsky/executive-function-skills_1_b_1613422.html.

Gee, James Paul. 2008. *Getting Over The Slump: Innovation Strategies to Promote Children's Learning*. New York: Joan Ganz Cooney Center at Sesame Workshop. http://www.joanganzcooneycenter.org/publication/policy-brief-getting-over-the-slump-innovation-strategies-to-promote-childrens-learning/.

Gee, James Paul and Michael Levine. 2009. "TV Guidance: Educators Should Embrace—Not Castigate—Video Games and TV." *Democracy* 12 (Spring). http://www.democracyjournal.org/12/6673.php?page=all.

Golinkoff, Roberta Michnik and Kathy Hirsh-Pasek. 1999. *How Babies Talk*. New York: Dutton.

Goodwin, Bryan. 2011. "Research Says . . . One-to-One Laptop Programs Are No Silver Bullet." *Teaching Screenagers* 68, no. 5 (February): 78–79. http://www.ascd .org/publications/educational_leadership/feb11/vol68/num05/One-to-One_Laptop _Programs_Are_No_Silver_Bullet.aspx.

Graves, Bill. 2014. "Learning Together: Early Boyles Parents, Staff Gain New Perspectives through Mind in the Making." Newsletter from the Children's Institute, Summer. http://www.childinst.org/images/stories/ci_publications/CI_Learning-Together_2014 .pdf.

Guernsey, Lisa. 2012. *Screen Time: How Electronic Media—From Baby Videos to Educational Software—Affects Your Young Child.* New York: Basic Books.

———. 2013. "Toddlers, Electronic Media, and Language Development: What Researchers Know So Far." *Zero to Three* 33, no. 4: 11–17.

———. 2014. *Envisioning a Digital Age Architecture for Early Education.* Washington, DC: New America. http://www.newamerica.net/sites/newamerica.net/files/ policydocs/DigitalArchitecture-20140326.pdf.

Guernsey, Lisa, Michael Levine, Cynthia Chiong, and Maggie Severns. 2012. *Pioneering Literacy in the Digital Wild West: Empowering Parents and Educators.* Washington, DC: Campaign for Grade-Level Reading. http://gradelevelreading.net/wp-content/uploads/2012/12/GLR_TechnologyGuide_final.pdf.

Gutnick, Aviva Lucas, Michael Robb, Lori Takeuchi, and Jennifer Kotler. 2011. *Always Connected: The New Digital Media Habits of Young Children.* New York: Joan Ganz Cooney Center at Sesame Workshop. http://www.google.com/url?q=http %3A%2F%2Fwww.joanganzcooneycenter.org%2Fwp-content%2Fuploads%2F2011%2 F03%2Fjgcc_alwaysconnected.pdf&sa=D&sntz=1&usg=AFQjCNFNFZvYefdtqWEFj N9g3–2EDyxCng.

Hamburg, David. 1997. *Perspective on Carnegie Corporation's Program, 1983–1997.* New York: Carnegie Corporation. http://files.eric.ed.gov/fulltext/ED413042.pdf.

Hart, Betty and Todd R. Risley. 1995. *Meaningful Differences in the Everyday Experience of Young American Children.* Baltimore, MD: Brookes Publishing. http://products .brookespublishing.com/Meaningful-Differences-in-the-Everyday-Experience-of-Young-American-Children-P14.aspx.

Hernandez, Don. 2011. "Double Jeopardy: How Third-Grade Reading Skills and Poverty Influence High-School Graduation." Annie E. Casey Foundation. http://www.aecf .org/m/resourcedoc/AECF-DoubleJeopardy-2012-Full.pdf.

Herr-Stephenson, Becky, Meryl Alper, and Erin Reilly. 2013. *T Is for Transmedia: Learning through Transmedia Play*. New York: Joan Ganz Cooney Center at Sesame Workshop. http://www.joanganzcooneycenter.org/wp-content/uploads/2013/03/t_is_for_trans media.pdf.

Hirsch Jr., E. D. and John Holdren, eds. 1996. *What Your Kindergartner Needs to Know: Preparing Your Child for a Lifetime of Learning*. New York: Bantam Doubleday Dell. http://www.randomhouse.com/book/80421/what-your-kindergartner-needs-to-know -revised-and-updated-by-ed-hirsch-jr.

Hirsh-Pasek, Kathy, Jennifer M. Zosh, Roberta Michnick Golinkoff, James H. Gray, Michael B. Robb, and Jordy Kaufman. 2015. "Putting Education in 'Educational' Apps: Lessons from the Science of Learning." *Psychological Science in the Public Interest* 16, no. 1: 3–34.

Hobbs, Renee and David Cooper Moore. 2013. *Discovering Media Literacy: Teaching Digital Media and Popular Culture in Elementary School*. Thousand Oaks, CA: Corwin. http://www.sagepub.com/books/Book236882?productType=Books&prodTypes= books&publisher=%22Corwin%22&sortBy=defaultPubDate%20desc&fs=1.

"Innovation in Publishing." First Book. http://www.firstbook.org/first-book-story/innova tion-in-publishing.

Institute of Medicine (IOM) and National Research Council (NRC). 2015. *Transform- ing the Workforce for Children Birth through Age 8: A Unifying Foundation*. Wash- ington, DC: The National Academies Press. https://www.iom.edu/Reports/2015/ Birth-To-Eight.aspx.

Jenkins, Henry, Ravi Purushotma, Margaret Weigel, Katie Clinton, and Alice J. Robi- son. 2009. *Confronting the Challenges of Participatory Culture: Media Education for the 21st Century*. Cambridge, MA: MIT Press. https://mitpress.mit.edu/sites/default/ files/titles/free_download/9780262513623_Confronting_the_Challenges.pdf.

Jordan, Amy B. and Daniel Romer, eds. 2014. *Media and the Well-Being of Chil- dren and Adolescents*. New York: Oxford University Press. http://ukcatalogue.oup .com/product/9780199987467.do.

Katz, Vikki S. 2014. *Kids in the Middle: How Children of Immigrants Negotiate Commu- nity Interactions for Their Families*. New Brunswick, NJ: Rutgers University Press. http://rutgerspress.rutgers.edu/product/Kids-in-the-Middle,5208.aspx.

Katz, Vikki S. and Michael H. Levine. 2015. *Connecting to Learn: Promoting Digital Equity for America's Hispanic Families*. New York: Joan Ganz Cooney Center at Sesame Workshop.

http://www.joanganzcooneycenter.org/wp-content/uploads/2015/02/jgcc_connecting tolearn.pdf.

The Kids & Family Reading Report. 2015. 5th ed. Scholastic. http://www.scholastic.com/ readingreport/Scholastic-KidsAndFamilyReadingReport-5thEdition.pdf?v=100.

Kirkorian, Heather, Koeun Choi, Tiffany A. Pempek, and Elizabeth Schroeder. 2014. "Toddlers' Learning from Interactive vs. Non-Interactive Video on Touchscreens." Poster for the International Society on Infant Studies 2014 conference.

Korat, Ofra and Tal Or. 2010. "How Technology Influences Parent–Child Interaction: The Case of e-Book Reading." *First Language* 30, no. 2 (May): 139–54. http://fla .sagepub.com/content/30/2/139.abstract.

Kotler, Jennifer A., Jennifer M. Schiffman, and Katherine G. Hanson. 2012. "The Influence of Media Characters on Children's Food Choices." *Journal of Health Communication: International Perspectives* 17, no. 8: 886–98. http://www.tandfonline.com/ doi/abs/10.1080/10810730.2011.650822#.VMuXSWR4qSc.

Krcmar, Marina, Bernard Grela, and Kirsten Lin. 2007. "Can Toddlers Learn Vocabulary from Television? An Experimental Approach." *Media Psychology* 10, no. 1: 41–63. http://www.tandfonline.com/doi/abs/10.1080/15213260701300931#preview.

Kuhl, Patricia K., Feng-Ming Tsao, and Huei-Mei Liu. 2003. "Foreign Language Experience in Infancy: Effects of Short-Term Exposure and Social Interaction on Phonetic Learning." *Proceedings of the National Academy of Sciences* 100, no. 15 (July 22): 9096–101. http://ilabs.washington.edu/kuhl/pdf/Kuhl_etal_PNAS_2003.pdf.

Landry, Susan H., Karen E. Smith, and Paul R. Swank. 2006. "Responsive Parenting: Establishing Early Foundations for Social, Communication, and Independent Problem-Solving Skills." *Developmental Psychology* 42, no. 4: 627–42.

Landry, Susan H., Karen E. Smith, Paul R. Swank, Tricia Zucker, April D. Crawford, and Emily F. Solari. 2012. "The Effects of a Responsive Parenting Intervention on Parent-Child Interactions during Shared Book Reading," *Developmental Psychology* 48, no. 4 (July): 969–86. http://www.psy.miami.edu/faculty/dmessinger/c_c/rsrcs/ rdgs/intervention/landrysmithswank2006.dp.pdf.

Lapierre, Matthew A., Jessica Taylor Piotrowski, and Deborah L. Linebarger. 2012. "Background Television in the Homes of U.S. Children." *PEDIATRICS* 130, no. 5 (November): 1–8. http://pediatrics.aappublications.org/content/early/2012/09/26/ peds.2011-2581.full.pdf+html.

Learner at the Center of a Networked World. 2014. Washington, DC: Aspen Institute Task Force on Learning and the Internet. http://csreports.aspeninstitute.org/documents/AspenReportFinalPagesRev.pdf.

Lee, June and Brigid Barron. 2015. *Aprendiendo en Casa: Media as a Resource for Learning among Hispanic-Latino Families.* New York: Joan Ganz Cooney Center at Sesame Street. http://www.joanganzcooneycenter.org/wp-content/uploads/2015/02/jgcc_aprendiendoencasa.pdf.

Lerner, Claire and Rachel Barr. 2014. "Screen Sense: Setting the Record Straight: Research-Based Guidelines for Screen Use for Children under 3 Years Old." Washington, DC: ZERO TO THREE. http://www.zerotothree.org/parenting-resources/screen-sense/screen-sense_wp_final3.pdf

Lesaux, Nonie K. 2013. *PreK–3rd: Getting Literacy Instruction Right.* PreK–3rd Policy to Action Brief 9. New York: Foundation for Child Development, May. https://drive.google.com/?tab=Xo&authuser=0#folders/0B3Gd-dOuICTaSU1zdHlLelg5N3c.

Leu, Donald J., Charles K. Kinzer, Julie L. Coiro, and Dana W. Cammack. 2004. "Toward a Theory of New Literacies Emerging from the Internet and Other Information and Communication Technologies." In *Theoretical Models and Processes of Reading*, 5th ed. Robert B. Ruddell and Norman Unrau, eds. International Reading Association, April. http://www.readingonline.org/newliteracies/leu/.

Levenstein, Phyllis, Susan Levenstein, James A. Shiminski, and Judith E. Stolzberg. 1998. "Long-Term Impact of a Verbal Interaction Program for At-Risk Toddlers: An Exploratory Study of High School Outcomes in a Replication of the Mother–Child Home Program." *Journal of Applied Developmental Psychology* 19, no. 2: 267–85. www.aventinomedicalgroup.com/documents/LevensteinetalJADP1998.pdf.

Levine, Michael H. and James Paul Gee. 2011. "The Digital Teachers Corps: Closing America's Literacy Gap." Progressive Policy Institute, September. http://progressivepolicy.org/wp-content/uploads/2011/09/09.2011-Levine_Gee-The_Digital_Teachers_Corps.pdf.

Levinson, Amber M. 2014. *Tapping In: Understanding how Hispanic-Latino families engage and learn with broadcast and digital media* (doctoral dissertation). Retrieved from Stanford Digital Repository, http://purl.stanford.edu/bb550sh8053.

Linebarger, Deborah L. 2001. "Learning to Read from Television: The Effects of Using Captions and Narration." *Journal of Educational Psychology,* 93, no. 2: 288–98.

Linebarger, Deborah L., R. Barr, M. A. Lapierre, and J. T. Piotrowski. 2014. "Associations between Parenting, Media Use, Cumulative Risk, and Children's Executive

Functioning." *Journal of Developmental & Behavioral Pediatrics* 35, no. 6 (July–August): 367–77. http://www.ncbi.nlm.nih.gov/pubmed/25007059.

Linebarger, Deborah L., Katie Mcmenamin, and Deborah K. Wainwright. 2009. "Summative Evaluation of SUPER WHY! Outcomes, Dose, and Appeal." University of Pennsylvania: Children's Media Lab. http://www-tc.pbskids.org/read/files/SuperWHY_Research_View.pdf.

Linebarger, Deborah L., J. T. Piotrowski, and C. R. Greenwood. 2010. "On-Screen Print: The Role of Captions as a Supplemental Literacy Tool." *Journal of Research in Reading* 33, no. 2 (May): 148–67.

Linebarger, Deborah L. and Dale Walker. 2005. "Infants' and Toddlers' Television Viewing and Language Outcomes." *American Behavioral Scientist* 48, no. 5 (January): 624–45. http://abs.sagepub.com/content/48/5/624.abstract.

Ma, Weiyi, Roberta Michnick Golinkoff, Derek Houston, and Kathy Hirsh-Pasek. 2011. "Word Learning in Infant- and Adult-Directed Speech," *Language Learning and Development* 7: 209–25. http://www.iupui.edu/~babytalk/pdfs/Word_Learning_in_Infant_and_Adult_Directed_Speech_MaW_Language_Learning_and_Development_9–11.pdf.

Maier, Thomas. 2003. *Dr. Spock: An American Life*. New York: Basic Books.

Mansilla, Veronica Boix and Anthony Jackson. 2011. *Educating for Global Competence: Preparing Our Youth to Engage the World*. New York: Asia Society. http://asiasociety.org/files/book-globalcompetence.pdf.

McDaniel, Marla and Christopher Lowenstein. 2013. *Depression in Low-Income Mothers of Young Children: Are They Getting the Treatment They Need?* Washington DC: Urban Institute, April. http://www.urban.org/UploadedPDF/412804-Depression-in-Low-Income-Mothers-of-Young-Children.pdf.

McNab, Katrina. 2013. "Bridging the Digital Divide with iPads: Effects on Early Literacy." Paper presented at the International Society for Technology in Education conference in San Antonio, Texas, June. http://www.isteconference.org/uploads/ISTE2013/HANDOUTS/KEY_80377343/McNab_ISTE_Conference_Paper_RP.pdf.

McNab, Katrina and Ruth Fielding-Barnsley. 2013. "Digital Texts, iPads, and Families: An Examination of Families' Shared Reading Behaviours." *International Journal of Learning: Annual Review* 20: 53–62. http://ijlar.cgpublisher.com/product/pub.287/prod.13.

Media Access Group at WGBH. "The Educational Uses of Closed Captioning." *MAG Guide* 7. http://main.wgbh.org/wgbh/pages/mag/resources/guides/mag_guide_vol7.html.

Mendelsohn, Alan H., Harris Huberman, Samantha Berkule, Carolyn A. Brockmeyer, Lesley M. Morrow, and Bernard P. Dreyer. 2011. "Primary Care Strategies for Promoting Parent-Child Interactions and School Readiness in At-Risk Families." *Archives of Pediatric and Adolescent Medicine* 165, no. 1: 33–41.

Michael Cohen Group. 2008. "Text on Screen: A Research Review." March. http://mcgrc .com/wp-content/uploads/2012/06/Text-on-Screen1.pdf.

Miller, Elizabeth B. and Mark Warschauer. 2013. "Young Children and E-Reading: Research to Date and Questions for the Future." *Learning, Media, and Technology*. Routledge.

Milliot, Jim. 2014a. "Children's Books: A Shifting Market." *Publishers Weekly*, February 24. http://www.publishersweekly.com/pw/by-topic/childrens/childrens-industry-news/ article/61167-children-s-books-a-shifting-market.html.

———. 2014b. "Print, Digital Book Sales Settle Down." *Publishers Weekly*, April 25. http://www.publishersweekly.com/pw/by-topic/industry-news/publisher-news/article /62031-print-digital-settle-down.html.

Miyake, Akira, Naomi P. Friedman, Michael J. Emerson, Alexander H. Witzki, Amy Howerter, and Tor D. Wager. 2000. "The Unity and Diversity of Executive Functions and Their Contributions to Complex 'Frontal Lobe' Tasks: A Latent Variable Analysis." *Cognitive Psychology* 41: 49–100. http://wagerlab.colorado.edu/files/ papers/Miyake_2000_Cogn%20Psychol.pdf.

Moore, Heidi. 2014. "Parent Voices: Doubts, Then Excitement on Texts to Promote Literacy." July 11, 2014. *EdCentral*. http://www.edcentral.org/parents-reactions-using- texting-promote-literacy/.

"Mr. Rogers' Neighborhood. . ." 2000. CNN Interview, aired December 31. http: //transcripts.cnn.com/TRANSCRIPTS/0012/31/impc.00.html.

Multimedia from the Center on the Developing Child. Harvard University. http: //developingchild.harvard.edu/resources/multimedia/.

National Assessment of Educational Progress. 2014. "The NAEP Glossary of Terms." Institute of Education Sciences. http://nces.ed.gov/nationsreportcard/glossary.aspx?nav= y#proficient.

National Association of Young Children. "Learning to Read and Write: Developmentally Appropriate Practices for Young Children." 1998. Washington, DC. http://www.naeyc.org/files/naeyc/file/positions/PSREAD98.pdf.

National Association for the Education of Young Children and the Fred Rogers Center for Early Learning and Children's Media at Saint Vincent College. 2012 "Technology and

Interactive Media as Tools in Early Childhood Programs Serving Children from Birth through Age 8." http://www.naeyc.org/content/technology-and-young-children

National Council of Teachers of English. "NCTE Framework for 21st Century Curriculum Assessment." NCTE Positions and Guidelines, February, 2013. http://www.ncte.org/library/NCTEFiles/Resources/Positions/Framework_21stCent_Curr_Assessment.pdf.

National Institute for Literacy. 2009. *Early Beginnings: Early Literacy Knowledge and Instruction.* http://www.nichd.nih.gov/publications/pubs/documents/NELPEarlyBeginnings09.pdf.

National Summer Learning Association. "Know the Facts." http://www.summerlearning.org/?page=know_the_facts.

The Nation's Report Card. 2012. "Reading Age 9 Results." From the 2012 National Assessment of Educational Progress (NAEP) long-term trend assessments in reading. http://www.nationsreportcard.gov/ltt_2012/age9r.aspx.

———. 2013. "Vocabulary." From the National Assessment for Educational Progress (NAEP). http://www.nationsreportcard.gov/reading_2013/vocabulary/# .

Neuman, Susan B. and Donna C. Celano. 2012a. *Giving Our Children a Fighting Chance: Poverty, Literacy, and the Development of Information Capital.* New York: Teachers College Press. http://store.tcpress.com/0807753580.shtml.

———. 2012b. "Worlds Apart: One City, Two Libraries, and Ten Years of Watching Inequality Grow." *American Educator* Fall: 13–23. http://www.aft.org//sites/default/files/periodicals/Neuman_0.pdf.

Neuman, Susan B. and David K. Dickinson, eds. 2006. *Handbook of Early Literacy Research*, Vol. 2. New York: Guilford Press. http://www.guilford.com/books/Handbook-of-Early-Literacy-Research-Volume-2/Dickinson-Neuman/9781593855772.

"New Report on Educational Media for Babies, Toddlers, and Preschoolers." 2005. Henry J. Kaiser Family Foundation, November 30. http://kff.org/other/issue-brief/new-report-on-educational-media-for-babies/.

"Out of Ink: Digital Media Alternatives and Low Demand Will Continue to Threaten Industry Revenue." 2014. Printing Market Research Report, *IBISWorld*, December. http://www.ibisworld.com/industry/default.aspx?indid=433.

Parish-Morris, Julia, Neha Mahajan, Kathy Hirsh-Pasek, Roberta Michnick Golinkoff, and Molly Fuller Collins. 2013. "Once upon a Time: Parent-Child Dialogue and Story-book Reading in the Electronic Era." *Mind, Brain, and Education* 7, no. 3 (September): 200–211. http://onlinelibrary.wiley.com/doi/10.1111/mbe.12028/abstract.

Pasnik, Shelley and Carlin Llorente. 2011. "Year One Context Studies: Executive Summary, Report to the *Ready to Learn Initiative*." Education Development Center, September. http://cct.edc.org/sites/cct.edc.org/files/publications/Y1_RTL_Context_Studies_Report_012012–2.pdf.

Paving a Path Forward for Digital Learning in the United States. 2013. Washington, DC: Leading Education by Advancing Digital (LEAD) Commission, September. http://www.leadcommission.org/sites/default/files/LEAD%20Commission%20Blueprint.pdf.

Penuel, William, et al. 2009. *Preschool Teachers Can Use a Media-Rich Curriculum to Prepare Low-Income Children for School Success: Results of a Randomized Controlled Trial.* New York: Education Development Center, Inc. and SRI International. http://rtl.cct.edc.org/pdf/RTLEvalReport.pdf.

Phillips, Deborah, and Philip Selazo. 2012. "Executive Function Across the Lifespan." *Frontiers of Innovation Webinar Series.* Center on the Developing Child at Harvard. http://developingchild.harvard.edu/activities/frontiers_of_innovation/webinar_series/.

"Pottermore." Wikipedia. http://en.wikipedia.org/wiki/Pottermore.

Pressey, Briana. 2013. "Comparative Analysis of National Teacher Surveys." New York: Joan Ganz Cooney Center at Sesame Workshop. http://www.joanganzcooneycenter.org/wp-content/uploads/2013/10/jgcc_teacher_survey_analysis_final.pdf.

Puma, Michael, et al. 2012. "Third Grade Follow-up to the Head Start Impact Study: Final Report." US Department of Health and Human Services, Office of Research and Policy Evaluation, Report 2012–45, October. http://www.acf.hhs.gov/sites/default/files/opre/head_start_report.pdf.

Radesky, Jenny S., et al. 2014. "Patterns of Mobile Device Use by Caregivers and Children during Meals in Fast Food Restaurants." *PEDIATRICS* 133, no. 4 (April 1): e843–e849. http://pediatrics.aappublications.org/content/early/2014/03/05/peds.2013–3703.full.pdf+html.

Ray, Barbara. 2014. "A Q-and-A with Alexis Lauricella on Parenting Texts and Early Literacy." July 11. *EdCentral.* http://www.edcentral.org/q-alexis-lauricella-parenting-texts-language-development/.

Recht, Donna R. and Lauren Leslie. 1988. "Effect of Prior Knowledge on Good and Poor Readers' Memory of Text." *Journal of Educational Psychology* 80, no. 1: 16–20.

Reiser, Robert A., Martin A. Tessmer, and Pamela C. Phelps. 1984. "Adult-Child Interaction in Children's Learning from Sesame Street." *Educational Communication and Technology Journal* 32: 217–23. http://link.springer.com/article/10.1007/BF02768893.

Richert, Rebekah A., Michael B. Robb, Jodi G. Fender, and Ellen Wartella. 2010. "Word Learning from Baby Videos." *Archives of Pediatric and Adolescent Medicine* 164, no. 5: 432–37. http://cmhd.northwestern.edu/wp-content/uploads/2011/06/Richert.Robb_.Fender.Wartella.2010.-WordLearning.pdf.

Rideout, Victoria. 2011. *Zero to Eight: Children's Media Use in America*. Washington, DC: Common Sense Media, Fall. http://www.commonsensemedia.org/research/zero-to-eight-childrens-media-use-in-america.

———. 2013. *Zero to Eight: Children's Media Use in America*. Washington, DC: Common Sense Media, Fall. https://www.commonsensemedia.org/research/zero-to-eight-childrens-media-use-in-america-2013.

———. 2014. *Learning at Home: Families' Educational Media Use in America*. New York: Joan Ganz Cooney Center at Sesame Workshop. http://www.joanganz cooneycenter.org/wp-content/uploads/2014/01/jgcc_learningathome.pdf.

Robson, Gary D. 2004. *The Closed Captioning Handbook*. New York: Elsevier Press. http://robson.org/gary/CCH_chapter4.pdf.

Rogow, Faith. 2014. "Media Literacy in Early Childhood Education: Inquiry-Based Technology Integration." In Chip Dohohue, ed., *Technology and Digital Media in the Early Years: Tools for Teaching and Learning*. Washington, DC: National Association for the Education of Young Children. http://www.routledge.com/books/details/9780415725828/.

Roseberry, Sarah, Kathy Hirsh-Pasek, and Roberta M. Golinkoff. 2014. "Skype Me! Socially Contingent Interactions Help Toddlers Learn Language." *Child Development* 85, no. 3 (May/June): 956–70. http://onlinelibrary.wiley.com/doi/10.1111/cdev.12166/abstract.

Royne, Marla B. and Marian Levy. 2011. "Marketing for Public Health: We Need an App for That." *Journal of Consumer Affairs* 45, no. 1 (Spring): 1–6. http://onlinelibrary.wiley.com/doi/10.1111/j.1745–6606.2010.01189.x/abstract?deniedAccessCustomised Message=&userIsAuthenticated=false.

Salomon, Gavriel. 1973. "Effects of Encouraging Israeli Mothers to Co-observe *Sesame Street* with Their Five-Year-Olds." *Child Development* 48, no. 3: 1146–51. http://eric.ed.gov/?id=ED086174.

Schmidt, Marie Evans, Michael Rich, Sheryl L. Rifas-Shiman, Emily Oken, and Elsie M. Taveras. 2009. "Television Viewing in Infancy and Child Cognition at 3 Years of Age in a US Cohort." *PEDIATRICS* 123, no. 3 (March): e370–e375. http://pediatrics .aappublications.org/content/123/3/e370.abstract.

Schulson, Sheree. 2014. "Five Stimulating Web Apps That Will Engage K–5 Students." *eSchool News*, August 25. http://www.eschoolnews.com/2014/08/25/apps-k5-students-052/3/.

Segal-Drori, Ora, Ofra Korat, Adina Shamir, and Pnina S. Klein. 2010. "Reading Electronic and Printed Books with and without Adult Instruction: Effects on Emergent Reading." *Reading and Writing* 23, no. 8 (September): 913–30. http://link.springer .com/article/10.1007%2Fs11145–009–9182-x.

Shamir, Adina and Ofra Korat. 2006. "How to Select CD-ROM Storybooks for Young Children: The Teacher's Role." *Reading Teacher* 59, no. 6: 532–43. http://online library.wiley.com/doi/10.1598/RT.59.6.3/abstract.

Shapiro, Jordan. 2013. "Can an iPad App Help Solve the Literacy Problem?" *Forbes* blog, August 1. http://www.forbes.com/sites/jordanshapiro/2013/08/01/an-app-that-is-good -at-teaching-kids-how-to-read/.

Shonkoff, Jack P. and Deborah A. Phillips, eds. 2000. *From Neurons to Neighborhoods: The Science of Early Childhood Development*. Washington, DC: National Academy Press. http://www.nap.edu/openbook.php?record_id=9824.

Shore, Rima. 1997. *Rethinking the Brain: New Insights into Early Development*. New York: Families and Work Institute, rev. 2003. http://books.google.com/books/about/ Rethinking_the_Brain.html?id=k2xHAAAAMAAJ.

Shuler, Carly, Zachary Levine, and Jinny Ree. 2012. *iLearnII: An Analysis of the Education Category of Apple's App Store*. New York: Joan Ganz Cooney Center at Sesame Workshop. http://www.joanganzcooneycenter.org/wp-content/uploads/ 2012/01/ilearnii.pdf.

Shulman, Lee S. 1987. "Knowledge and Teaching: Foundations of the New Reform." *Harvard Educational Review* 57, no. 1: 1–22. http://people.ucsc.edu/~ktellez/shulman.pdf.

Singer, Jerome L. and Dorothy G. Singer. 1998. "*Barney & Friends* as Entertainment and Education: Evaluating the Effectiveness of a Television Series for Preschool Children." In *Research Paradigms, Television and Social Behavior,* edited by J. K. Asamen and G. Berry, 305–7. Thousand Oaks, CA: Sage. http://www.uk.sagepub.com/ books/Book6799/toc.

"Sir Arthur's Quotations." Arthur C. Clarke Foundation website. http://www.clarke foundation.org/sample-page/sir-arthurs-quotations/.

Slavin, Robert E., Nancy A. Madden and Bette Chambers. 2006. "Evidence-Based Reform in Education: Success for All, Embedded Multimedia, and the Teaching-Learning Orchestra" Unpublished paper. Towson, MD: Success for All Foundation. http://www.successforall.org/SuccessForAll/media/PDFs/EBR-and-TLO.pdf

Smeets, Daisy J. H. and Adriana G. Bus. 2012. "Interactive Electronic Storybooks for Kindergarteners to Promote Vocabulary Growth." *Journal of Experimental Child Psychology* 112, no. 1 (May): 36–55. http://www.ncbi.nlm.nih.gov/pubmed/22265347.

Smith, Aaron. 2013. "Smartphone Ownership 2013." Report brief, Pew Research Center, June 5. http://www.pewinternet.org/2013/06/05/smartphone-ownership-2013/.

Stevens, R. and W. R. Penuel. 2010. "Studying and Fostering Learning through Joint Media Engagement." Paper presented at the Principal Investigators Meeting of the National Science Foundation's Science of Learning Centers, Arlington, VA.

Strasburger, Victor C. and Marjorie J. Hogan. 2013. "Children, Adolescents, and the Media." *PEDIATRICS* 132, no. 5 (November): 958–61

"Study Shows Learn with Homer Reading App Could Close Literacy Gap." 2014. *PRWeb*, October 14. http://www.prweb.com/releases/2014/10/prweb12244516.htm.

"Survey of Parents Finds Apps Beneficial for Children." 2014. *PRNewsWire*, November 11. http://www.prnewswire.com/news-releases/survey-of-parents-finds-apps-beneficial-for-children-282265691.html

Suskind, Dana L. et al. 2015. "A Parent-Directed Language Intervention for Children of Low Socioeconomic Status: A Randomized Controlled Pilot Study." *Journal of Child Language* (June): 1–41.

Swartz, Mary Katherine and Cindy Gillespie Hendricks. 2000. "Factors That Influence the Book Selection Process of Students with Special Needs." *Journal of Adolescent & Adult Literacy* 43, no. 7 (April): 608–18. http://eric.ed.gov/?id=EJ604660.

Takeuchi, Lori M. and Sarah Vaala. 2014. *Level Up Learning: A National Survey on Teaching with Digital Games*. New York: Joan Ganz Cooney Center at Sesame Workshop. http://www.joanganzcooneycenter.org/wp-content/uploads/2014/10/jgcc_levelup learning_final.pdf.

Talking Early Child Development and Exploring the Consequences of Frame Choices. 2005. Washington, DC: FrameWorks Institute, July. http://www.frameworksinstitute .org/assets/files/ECD/ecd_message_memo.pdf.

Tare, Medha, Cynthia Chiong, Patricia Ganea, and Judy DeLoache. 2010. "Less Is More: How Manipulative Features Affect Children's Learning from Picture Books." *Journal of Applied Developmental Psychology* 31, no. 5 (September): 395–400. doi: 10.1016/j.appdev.2010.06.005. http://www.ncbi.nlm.nih.gov/pmc/articles/PMC29 52631/.

Thoman, Elizabeth and Tessa Jolls. 2005. *Literacy for the Twenty-First Century: An Overview & Orientation Guide to Media Literacy Education.* Malibu, CA: Center for Media Literacy. http://www.medialit.org/sites/default/files/mlk/01_MLKorienta tion.pdf.

To Read or Not To Read: A Question of National Consequence. 2007. Washington, DC: National Endowment for the Arts. http://arts.gov/sites/default/files/ToRead.pdf.

Tomopoulos, Suzy, Benard P. Dreyer, Samantha Berkule, Arthur H. Fierman, Carolyn Brockmeyer, and Alan L. Mendelsohn. 2010. "Infant Media Exposure and Toddler Development." *Archives of Pediatrics & Adolescent Medicine* (now *JAMA Pediatrics*) 164, no. 12 (December): 1105–11. http://archpedi.jamanetwork.com/article .aspx?articleid=384030.

2013 Reading Assessment Report Card: Summary Data Tables with Additional Detail for Average Scores and Achievement Levels for States and Jurisdictions. National Center for Education Statistics. http://www.nationsreportcard.gov/reading_ math_2013/files/Results_Appendix_Reading.pdf.

"Univision Out-Delivered One or More of the English-Language Broadcast Networks (ABC, CBS, NBC or FOX) on Five Out of Seven Nights Last Week among Adults 18–34." 2014. Univision press release, October 7. http://corporate.univision.com/2014/10/univision- out-delivered-one-or-more-of-the-english-language-broadcast-networks-abc-cbs-nbc -or-fox-on-five-out-of-seven-nights-last-week-among-adults-18–34–2/.

US Department of Education. 1998. "Checkpoints for Progress in Reading and Writing for Families and Communities." February. http://www2.ed.gov/pubs/Check Families/index.html.

———. 2013. Office of Non-Public Education. E-Rate Program, August 21. http://www2 .ed.gov/about/offices/list/oii/nonpublic/erate.html.

"Utah UPSTART Program Evaluation Program Impacts on Early Literacy: Third Year Results Cohort 3 Technical Report." 2013. Evaluation and Training Institute, May. http: //www.schools.utah.gov/legislativematerials/2013/UPSTART_External_Evaluation_on _Year_3.aspx.

Vaala, Sarah and Lori Takeuchi. 2012. *QuickReport: Parent Co-Reading Survey*. New York: Joan Ganz Cooney Center at Sesame Workshop. http://www.joanganzcooney center.org/wp-content/uploads/2012/11/jgcc_ereader_parentsurvey_quickreport.pdf.

Vaala, Sarah E., et al. 2010. "Content Analysis of Language-Promoting Teaching Strategies Used in Infant-Directed Media." *Infant and Child Development* 19, no. 6 (November/December): 628–48. http://onlinelibrary.wiley.com/doi/10.1002/icd.715/abstract.

Vandewater, Elizabeth A. 2011. "Infant Word Learning from Commercially Available Video in the U.S." *Journal of Children and Media* 5, no. 3: 248–66. http://www.tandfonline .com/doi/abs/10.1080/17482798.2011.584375#preview.

Vasquez, Vivian Maria and Carol Branigan Felderman. 2013. *Technology and Critical Literacy in Early Childhood*. New York: Routledge. http://www.routledge.com/books/ details/9780415539517/.

Walker, Christina. 2014. "Head Start Participants, Programs, Families and Staff in 2013." CLASP, August. http://www.clasp.org/resources-and-publications/publication-1/HS preschool-PIR-2013-Fact-Sheet.pdf.

Wartella, Ellen and Nancy Jennings. 2000. "Children and Computers: New Technology—Old Concerns." *Future of Children* 10, no. 2 (Fall/Winter).

Wartella, Ellen and M. Robb. 2008. "Historical and Recurring Concerns about Children's Use of the Mass Media." In *Handbook on Children and the Media*, edited by S. Calvert and B. Wilson. Malden, MA: Blackwell.

Whitebook, Marcy, Deborah Phillips, and Carollee Howes. 2014. *Worthy Work, STILL Unlivable Wages: The Early Childhood Workforce 25 Years after the National Child Care Staffing Study*. Berkeley, CA: Center for the Study of Child Care Employment. http://www.irle.berkeley.edu/cscce/wp-content/uploads/2014/11/Executive-Summary -Final.pdf.

Whitehurst, Grover and Christopher J. Lonigan, 1998. "Child Development and Emergent Literacy." *Child Development* 69, no. 3 (May): 848–72.

Williams, Lunetta M. 2008. "Book Selections of Economically Disadvantaged Black Elementary Students." *Journal of Educational Research* 102, no. 1 (September): 51–64. http://eric.ed.gov/?id=EJ809604.

Willingham, Daniel. 2009. "Teaching Content *Is* Teaching Reading." YouTube video, January 9. https://www.youtube.com/watch?v=RiP-ijdxqEc.

Willingham, Daniel. 2015. *Raising Kids Who Read: What Parents and Teachers Can Do*. San Francisco: Jossey-Bass.

Wolf, Maryanne. 2007. *Proust and the Squid: The Story and Science of the Reading Brain*. New York: Harper Collins. http://www.harpercollins.com/9780060933845/proust-and-the-squid.

Wright, John C., et al. 2001. "The Relations of Early Television Viewing to School Readiness and Vocabulary of Children from Low-Income Families: The Early Window Project." *Child Development* 72, no. 5: 1347–66. http://www.andrews.edu/~rbailey/Chapter%2014/5548963.pdf.

York, Benjamin N. and Susanna Loeb. 2014. "One Step at a Time: The Effects of an Early Literacy Text Messaging Program for Parents of Preschoolers." National Bureau of Economic Research, Working Paper no. 20659, November. http://www.nber.org/papers/w20659.

Yoshikawa, Hirokazu, et al. 2013. "Investing in Our Future: The Evidence Base on Preschool Education." The Society for Research in Child Development and the Foundation for Child Development. http://www.srcd.org/sites/default/files/documents/washington/mb_2013_10_16_investing_in_children.pdf.

Zickuhr, Kathryn. 2010. *Generations 2010*. Washington, DC: Pew Research Center. http://www.pewinternet.org/files/old-media//Files/Reports/2010/PIP_Generations_and_Tech10.pdf.

Zickuhr, Kathryn and Lee Rainie. 2014. *E-Reading Rises as Device Ownership Jumps*. Washington, DC: Pew Research Center, January 16. http://www.pewinternet.org/2014/01/16/e-reading-rises-as-device-ownership-jumps/.

Zimmerman, Frederick J. and Dimitri A. Christakis. 2007. "Associations between Content Types of Early Media Exposure and Subsequent Attentional Problems." *PEDIATRICS* 120, no. 5 (November): 986–92. http://pediatrics.aappublications.org/content/120/5/986.

Index